SHEFFIELD HALLAM UNIVERSITY
LEARNING CENTRE
PSALTER LANE CAMPUS,
SHEFFIELD, S11 8UZ

D0321104

Thinking in Images

✓ 2007

8 FEB 2008

SHEFFIELD HALLAM UNIVERSITY
LEARNING CENTRE
WITHDRAWN FROM STOCK

Thinking in Images

Film Theory, Feminist Philosophy and Marlene Dietrich

Catherine Constable

 Publishing

SHEFFIELD HALLAM UNIVERSITY
WL
791.43652
CO 042
PSALTER LANE LEARNING CENTRE

For my parents, Mary and David Constable,

And my husband, David Wood,

With love.

First published in 2005 by the
BRITISH FILM INSTITUTE
21 Stephen Street, London W1T 1LN

The British Film Institute's purpose is to champion moving image culture in all its richness and diversity across the UK, for the benefit of as wide an audience as possible, and to create and encourage debate.

Copyright © Catherine Constable 2005

Cover image: *Shanghai Express* (Josef von Sternberg, 1932, Paramount Publix Corporation)
Cover design: couch
Set by Fakenham Photosetting Ltd, Fakenham, Norfolk
Printed in the UK by St Edmundsbury Press, Bury St Edmunds, Suffolk

British Cataloguing-in-Publication Data
A catalogue record for this book is available from the British Library

ISBN 1–84457–101–7 (pbk)
ISBN 1–84457–100–9 (hbk)

Contents

Acknowledgments

This book builds on the research undertaken for my PhD dissertation. I would like to thank my supervisor, Christine Battersby, for her rigorous and stimulating tuition in feminist philosophy, particularly the work of Luce Irigaray, and my fellow students, Helen Chapman and Margrit Shildrick, for their positive feedback and support. The generous hospitality of Anna and Chris Trye was a great help during the early years of the PhD, while the typing skills of Lori Robinson were essential to its completion. My parents, Mary and David Constable, will not easily forget the last weeks of writing up and their unstinting support, providing chocolate desserts and printing pages, even in the early hours of the morning, was greatly appreciated.

Early versions of Chapters 1 and 2 of this book appeared in the journal, *Women's Philosophy Review*, whose editors provided some very useful feedback. My colleagues at Sheffield Hallam University have been most helpful, particularly Steve Neale, whose advice was indispensable for rethinking the PhD as a book. Valerie Orpen's painstaking researches on my behalf at the BFI library provided essential material and Adrian Armstrong's meticulous proof reading helped polish the final product. I must also thank my husband, David Wood, for enabling me to finish the book by shouldering my share of the household tasks and taking over the kitchen – a situation I hope will long continue!

A number of people have played a significant part in both the PhD and the book. I would like to thank Richard Dyer for teaching me the techniques of detailed textual analysis and for his boundless enthusiasm for both projects, which inspired me to continue. Jane Robinson's careful proof reading, bibliographic skills and calming advice have also been indispensable. I am greatly indebted to Rachel Jones: her participation in many, lengthy and occasionally circular discussions on key concepts, such as the eternal return, and her detailed and thoughtful feedback on numerous drafts, have been absolutely crucial to the development of both projects. Indeed, I could not imagine undertaking them without her. It has not been possible to name everyone who supported me throughout this time – so to all those who have enabled me to think again – thank you.

Introduction

Film theory is in crisis. This frequently made assertion can be seen as a reflection of a general concern about the status and value of theory and theorising. Lyotard's famous attack on grand narratives raises serious questions about how theory is to be defined and what it is to become in the twenty-first century. Within Film Studies, the ways in which the crisis is defined and the corresponding solutions that are offered are varied and diverse. Responses range from the apocalyptic vision of the end of all theory to the precipitation of different forms of theorising. This book will explore the latter option by offering a new methodology for relating theory and film texts that utilises the resources of feminist philosophy, specifically the work of Michèle Le Doeuff, Luce Irigaray and Sarah Kofman.

The future of theory in Film Studies became a topic of heated debate with the publication of *Post-Theory* in 1996. The book's title has become more notorious than its content. The term 'post-theory' has been co-opted to indicate the death of all theory and theorising, sustaining the position that Tessa Perkins characterises as 'theorycide'.[1] The trajectory of *Post-Theory* is much more specific in that David Bordwell and Noel Carroll are concerned to attack a dominant tradition in Anglo-American Film Studies, specifically 'that aggregate of doctrines derived from Lacanian psychoanalysis, structuralist semiotics, Post-structuralist literary theory and variants of Althusserian Marxism'.[2] Their critique draws on analytic philosophy, setting up a scientific model for future theorising, which will be discussed in Chapter 1.

Feminist psychoanalytic film theory has come under attack from the post-theorists and others for taking up and perpetuating theoretical paradigms that are said to be inherently flawed. Alison Butler's damning summary of the feminist use of Freudian and Lacanian psychoanalysis is a typical response. 'For feminist film scholars studying a cultural form so massively dominated by men, the construction of a theoretical paradigm in which the absence of female subjectivity is a first principle has been more or less a disaster.'[3]

Such accounts of the allegedly inevitable failure of specific theoretical models are used to justify some rather drastic solutions to the problem. One such solution has been the suggestion that all theory should be abandoned because it is overly complex and ultimately unproductive, a response that Perkins characterises as 'theoryphobia'.[4] However, I would argue that complexity is not an indication of lack of efficacy and the claim that all theory should be simple if it is to be useful is itself a problematic assumption. The more considered solution is a move away from 'film theory *per se*' in favour of empirical work such as cinema history.[5] However, the construction of this move as an abandonment of the theoretical is unconvincing as it clearly involves the substitution of one set of theoretical frameworks for another.

Both these proposed solutions are underpinned by the assumption that theory can simply be left behind. As such, they are reliant on a common conception of theory as that which is entirely separate from day-to-day reality. Thus, the theoretical is conceived as a realm of abstraction that hovers above everyday life and is ultimately not necessary to it. I do not share this view. Indeed, I would argue that there is no such thing as 'theory *per se*' because all theories have practical implications, constructing the world and the place of the people in it in different ways. The process of abstraction that is part of the theoretical should not be conceived as an obliteration of the everyday but rather as the crystallisation of specific moments that come to count as key exemplars. Thus, creating theories is a process, which both utilises and feeds back into the everyday, reconstructing or reinforcing social conceptions of gender, sexuality and culture. To rewrite Le Doeuff: 'whether we like it or not, we are *within* [theory], surrounded by masculine–feminine divisions that [theory] has helped to articulate and refine.'[6]

In arguing that theory has social implications, I am also suggesting that it is intrinsically political. This clearly conflicts with the recent drive to rid theory of political 'bias' most vociferously championed by Carroll.[7] Carroll's anti-political stance arises out of his insistence that film theory should aim to become a model of scientific neutrality but his arguments resonate with the general message of post-feminism promulgated by the Western media at the present time. While the arrival of the post-feminist era has been greeted with appropriate scepticism within the humanities, those departments where feminist theory has been less secure, such as philosophy, have made use of the current climate to sideline feminist research. I would suggest that this move is particularly unfortunate given the general crisis about the status and value of theory because it restricts access to a vital source of ideas at a time when it is most needed. Feminist philosophy has repeatedly challenged traditional conceptions of the nature of theory, offering diverse accounts of the future of theorising. This book will demonstrate that Le Doeuff, Irigaray and Kofman can provide the means to find some answers to the questions that are being raised about the forms film theory should take in the future.

One of the key questions is how theory and film images are to be satisfactorily interrelated. This is a matter of some urgency given the 'theoryphobia' lobby which views the application of theory to film texts as an utterly unnecessary imposition. This book sets out a new methodology for linking philosophical and filmic images, which takes up and develops Le Doeuff's key thesis that imagery plays a crucial role in the process of theorising. Le Doeuff's work challenges a long tradition within Western philosophy, beginning with Plato, in which images are viewed as either textual decorations that do not add to the overall argument, or examples that serve to translate complex ideas into a more accessible form. In contrast to these constructions of the image as a more or less useful form of decoration, Le Doeuff argues that imagery is integral to philosophy, serving as the means through which concepts are created and expressed. Furthermore, the imagery is said to provide a link between theory and social practices in that philosophers are said to take up images circulating in other socio-cultural discourses, such as literature, art and film. Le Doeuff's work can thus be seen to have two important consequences: it positions the image at the heart of theorising and denies philosophy a privileged, meta-discursive status, presenting it as another form of socio-cultural discourse.

Le Doeuff's focus on imagery means that she treats philosophical works as texts that require interpretation. This method of reading philosophical texts is used throughout this book in order to create and sustain a proper rapport between the philosophy and film texts, rendering them all equally subject to detailed textual analysis. While theorists within Film Studies have taken up philosophy in a variety of ways, both the analytic and continental lobbies have tended to treat it with a certain reverence, giving it the status of a meta-discourse that validates their different approaches. In contrast, this book will offer detailed readings of philosophical texts, focusing on Nietzsche's use of gendered imagery in key works, such as *The Birth of Tragedy*, before examining the work of three commentators: Jacques Derrida, Sarah Kofman and Jean Baudrillard. This focus on the take-up and expansion of Nietzsche's images of woman in his accounts of beauty, art and truth will be linked to detailed textual analyses of the highly glamorised representation of woman in selected films from the Dietrich/Sternberg cycle.

I have chosen to focus on Nietzsche and his successors because their constructions of femininity differ considerably from those promulgated by the psychoanalytic models that have gained such ascendancy within Film Studies. Nietzsche capitalises on woman's link to appearance and beauty, allocating her a series of significant and varied roles, including truth, fiction and the acceptance and enjoyment of life as illusion. By tracing the take-up and alteration of this imagery in Derrida's and Baudrillard's work, I will draw attention to the gendered iconography that underpins their key concepts, such as *différance*, defined as the endless proliferation of meaning, and seduction. As Mary-Ann Doane comments ' – it is quite striking that the woman comes to represent all these things, as though . . . [they] could somehow not be *thought* except in and through the figure of the woman.'[8] The focus on gender is a way of demonstrating each theorist's perpetuation of particular constructions of femininity. My approach differs from Doane's in that I aim to draw attention to the range of positive constructions of the figure of woman offered by Nietzsche and his successors.

Drawing attention to the construction of gender in the Derridean and Baudrillardian texts enables me to undercut the assumption that their respective presentations of meaning proliferation and fakeness are gender free. I am not interested in adopting a post-modern position, which valorises fictionality or fakeness *per se*. My theoretical position is one of pragmatic perspectivalism that arises through my readings of Nietzsche via Kofman. I am interested in showing how the link between femininity and appearance can be rethought in order to capitalise on the radical potential of woman's presentation as the icon of illusion, fiction and fakeness. This involves thinking through the ways in which perspectivalism links fictionality with the creation of new values and the reconstruction of truth, which will be addressed in Chapter 4.

The theories will be related to three key films from the Dietrich/Sternberg cycle: *The Scarlet Empress*, *The Devil Is a Woman* and *Shanghai Express*. I have chosen to focus on the cycle because it constitutes a significant body of work that does not fit into the models of woman as object that have gained ascendance in feminist film theory. This book can therefore be seen to follow on from the welcome reappraisal of the cycle during the late 1970s and 1980s, which drew attention to the ways in which these films actually engage with the issues of objectification and femininity as spectacle.[9] Robin Wood suggests that Dietrich's star persona can be formulated in terms of a question, namely: 'How does a woman assert herself in a world where all the rules are made by men?'[10] Each of the chosen films shows Dietrich playing a character who succeeds in a man's world, and I would add that she does so by using the resources of femininity, thus gaining success on her own terms. It is here that the Dietrich/Sternberg cycle can be seen to offer something very different from current representations of the female hero, who succeeds only by conforming to the values and standards of masculinity. The female hero can be seen as one logical outcome of the discourses of feminisms of equality, which have unfortunately resulted in the valorisation of masculinity.

In contrast, I want to focus on the representation of femininity, showing how the films engage with Nietzschean, Derridean and Baudrillardian constructions of woman, and tracing the ways in which they restate, reconstruct and subvert them. Le Doeuff argues that the images used within philosophy have a doubled aspect, serving both to secure and to disrupt the theoretical systems in which they appear. In this way, philosophical imagery is said to act as a future resource in that it remains ambiguous, subject to further interpretation, thus holding open the possibility of other theorisations. I will show that the filmic images offered by the Dietrich/Sternberg cycle also constitute a theoretical resource in that they hold open other ways of theorising femininity, offering positive spins on the figures of the torturess, woman as caprice and the seductress. The films can therefore be seen to be instrumental in the creation of new concepts, providing feminist theory with much-needed, positive reconstructions of femininity.

In what follows the first chapter will address a number of the proposed solutions for the current crisis in film theory. I will examine three very different models for future theorising: Bordwell's and Carroll's accounts of theory as science, Slavoj Žižek's argument for theory as Lacanian–Hegelian dialectic and Bill Nichols' analysis of theory as rhetoric. I shall argue in favour of the last and will go on to compare key aspects of Nichols' model of pragmatic perspectivalism to Le Doeuff's and Irigaray's theoretical methodologies in

Chapter 2. While the first chapter explores the solutions to the crisis which are circulating within Film Studies, the second utilises the resources of feminist philosophy in order to outline another alternative.

Chapter 2 explores Le Doeuff's conception of theory as intrinsically provisional and precarious, linking her work with that of Irigaray. Both feminist theorists can be seen to offer similar theoretical methodologies, which involve tracing the repetition of particular images and accompanying structures of thought within philosophical texts. I will outline Le Doeuff's definition of chiasmic logic and will go on to trace the ways in which it recurs in aspects of Nietzsche's and Derrida's work in Chapter 4, as well as in the films discussed in Chapters 5 and 7. Combining Le Doeuff and Irigaray draws attention to their complementary strategies: tracing the re-emergence of familiar images and structures, which form well-worn imaginary pathways; while also being alert to the possibility of different readings that would sustain alternative theorisations – the roads not yet taken.

Chapter 3 offers a key instance of Le Doeuff's and Irigaray's methodologies in action. This will involve looking at theoretical work on masochism and the way in which it has been taken up by Gaylyn Studlar to form an aesthetic model for the Dietrich/Sternberg cycle. I will examine her attempt to move beyond the construction of woman as object, arguing that she is ultimately unsuccessful. This argument will involve tracing some key changes that occurred during the development of the theory of masochism: from the work of Sacher-Masoch through Deleuze to Studlar, noting how each offers slightly different roles for the figure of the torturess. The chapter will offer a detailed reading of *The Scarlet Empress* in order to demonstrate the ways in which the film challenges the limitations of the theoretical models, thus opening up the possibility of alternative theorisations.

Chapter 4 focuses on Nietzsche, tracing the very different constructions of woman in the debates on art and truth that are offered in key works, specifically *The Birth of Tragedy*, *The Gay Science* and *The Will to Power*. I will explore the ways in which the notes that constitute the final text replicate familiar imaginary pathways, tracing their re-emergence in Derrida's later commentary. In contrast, I will argue that the first and second texts constitute key theoretical resources because Nietzsche uses the figures of Helen, Maya and Baubô to link woman's role as a symbol of appearance to the concept of affirmation. This will form the basis of my reading of Kofman's commentary, which builds on her analysis of Baubô as a camera obscura. I trace the theoretical implications of the encounter between Baubô and Demeter, reading it as a perspectival shift and thereby augmenting the model of theory that is developed in Chapter 2.

The last chapters offer a series of productive encounters between specific theoretical models and film texts. Chapter 5 explores the limits of Mary-Ann Doane's take-up of Nietzsche and Derrida in relation to film, arguing that her model shuts down the potentiality of the images. I will demonstrate the ways in which the presentation of Concha

Perez in *The Devil Is a Woman* goes beyond the Derridean construction of woman as the absence of depth, truth or meaning. This will involve drawing attention to the theoretical implications of the text's unusual construction of the female protagonist as a conjunction of two very different figures: the *femme fatale* and woman as caprice.

Chapter 6 adds the seductress to the range of figures of woman as affirmation explored in Chapter 4. This requires a considerable reworking of Baudrillard's *Seduction*, expanding on key moments in which he suggests that the seductress presents the play of appearances as a site of truth. This model will be augmented further by a detailed textual analysis of *Shanghai Express*, which will focus on characterisation and performance style. I will argue that Shanghai Lily can be seen to construct herself as illusion and that the ways in which she plays up her decadent role form a critique of bourgeois values and ultimately enable her to express her own perspective.

In the final chapter, I will use the figure of the seductress as a lens through which to view other presentations of woman as a glamorous illusion. I am concerned to demonstrate that this figure can be used to map the diverse ways in which woman functions as a play of appearances within films other than the Dietrich/Sternberg cycle. However, the seductress does not form a textual template, stamping out her likeness on each film. I will offer readings of *Gilda*, *Eyes Wide Shut* and *Moulin Rouge*, tracing the ways in which each inflects the figure differently. I have chosen to end with these films because they explicitly deal with the theme of woman as illusion and also provide a means of considering other female stars: Rita Hayworth and Nicole Kidman. The two contemporary films serve as a means of demonstrating the usefulness of the figure of the seductress within the current cinematic context.

This use of the seductress as a theoretical concept that is repeatedly remade and reviewed through the key images that instantiate her is intended to act as an example of the kind of provisional, perspectival theorising that I advocate throughout this book. The theoretical concept is provisional and precarious because it can be seen to arise out of specific configurations of philosophical and filmic images. It is a concept that is of vital importance at this present moment, allowing the charting of positive representations and reconstructions of femininity, at a time when the ascendance of feminisms of equality has resulted in the promotion of masculinity as the privileged ideal for women. This book also offers a general methodology for linking philosophical and filmic images, which I hope will be useful to others. This methodology can be seen to facilitate a wide range of projects, sustaining one possible future for film theory as a series of productive encounters between philosophy, film theory and film texts.

Notes

1. T. Perkins, 'Who (and What) Is It for?', in C. Gledhill and L. Williams (eds), *Reinventing Film Studies* (London: Arnold, 2000), p. 83.
2. D. Bordwell and N. Carroll (eds), *Post-Theory: Reconstructing Film Studies* (Madison and London: University of Wisconsin Press, 1996), p. xiii.
3. A. Butler, 'Feminist Theory and Women's Films at the Turn of the Century', *Screen* vol. 14 no. 1, Spring 2000, p. 74.
4. Perkins, 'Who (and What) Is It for?', p. 83.
5. A. Kuhn (ed.), 'Millenial editorial', *Screen* vol. 41 no. 1, Spring, 2000, p. 2.
6. M. Le Doeuff, *The Philosophical Imaginary*, C. Gordon (trans.) (London: Athlone Press, 1989), p. 101. The original quote has no italics and uses the word 'philosophy' rather than 'theory'.
7. N. Carroll, 'Prospects for Film Theory: A Personal Assessment', in Bordwell and Carroll (eds), *Post-Theory*, pp. 44–6.
8. M-A. Doane, *Femmes Fatales, Feminism, Film Theory, Psychoanalysis* (London: Routledge, 1991), p. 62. Doane is referring specifically to Derrida but her comment holds good for Nietzsche and his successors.
9. See for example: R. Wood, 'Venus de Marlene', *Film Comment* vol. 14, March/April 1978, pp. 60–1, 63 and F. Jacobowitz, 'Power and the Masquerade: *The Devil Is a Woman*', *CineAction!*, no. 8, Spring 1987, p. 33.
10. Wood, 'Venus de Marlene', p. 61.

1 | Theories Proper and Improper

I suggested in the introduction that the current crisis in film theory has provoked a range of responses: from the premature announcement of the death of theory to the promotion of new forms of theorising. This chapter will focus on four theorists who have argued that the future of film theory is reliant on the take-up of particular modes of theorising. I am not offering a comprehensive description of the current debates within film theory because this has been done elsewhere. Instead, I will concentrate on three key emergent theoretical paradigms, addressing important areas of difference and elucidating the wider philosophical underpinnings of each system. The first section will examine David Bordwell's and Noel Carroll's positions in *Post-Theory*, which I will argue, utilise a scientific paradigm of the theoretical. The second section will focus on Slavoj Žižek's 2001 work, *The Fright of Real Tears*, in which he responds to Bordwell and Carroll by clarifying his Lacanian–Hegelian model of theory as dialectic. The last section will address Bill Nichols' conception of theory as rhetoric, and I will argue that Bordwell's and Carroll's concept of 'middle-range theorising' is more consistent with this last paradigm.

My analysis of the paradigms will also involve an examination of the presentation of the political within each theoretical system. Tessa Perkins notes that the current crisis in film theory has raised questions about both the future of theory and the place of politics in the subject. She comments 'some wish ... to abandon both and others are determined that the former should cleanse itself of all contamination by the latter, fantasising, perhaps, that a pseudo-scientific objectivity will emerge from the funeral pyre.'[1] This fantasy of apolitical objectivity is very clear in Carroll's work. However, the metaphor of purification applies both to the post-theorists and to Žižek, in that all three offer accounts of what should constitute theory 'proper'. In choosing to end with Nichols' paradigm of rhetoric, that which traditional philosophy deemed thoroughly improper, I am indicating the overall direction of this book. I will argue that it is the improper modes of theorising promulgated by Nichols, Michèle Le Doeuff and Luce Irigaray that can provide solutions to the current crisis in film theory.

1 Theory as Science

The introduction to *Post-Theory* presents Bordwell's and Carroll's arguments for future forms of theorising as fundamentally similar.[2] This view has been reflected in later references to their approach as a united appeal for the recognition of the historical situatedness of theoretical projects.[3] I want to disentangle the two theorists in order to examine the very different ways in which each approaches the possibility of political theorising. Bordwell argues that middle-level research has already been conducted by a number of political theorists, providing a list that includes Vito Russo's *Celluloid Closet* and Richard Dyer's *Now You See It*.[4] However, I will demonstrate that this pro-political stance is jeopardised by the scientific paradigm which underpins Bordwell's critique of 'grand theory'.[5] In contrast, Carroll is utterly consistent in his deployment of scientism to rid theory of political 'bias'. My reading of Bordwell and Carroll will also make use of Bordwell's earlier work *Making Meaning*, which underpins a number of their central arguments. This will bring out the issue of the relation between theory and interpretation addressed in Chapter 2.

Bordwell's article in *Post-Theory*, 'Contemporary Film Studies and the Vicissitudes of Grand Theory', is an attack on both subject position theory and culturalism. Bordwell argues that subject position theory, which deploys Barthes and Lacan as well as Derrida and Foucault, is organised around the key question: 'What are the social and psychic functions of cinema?'[6] Thus film theory can be seen to have drawn on continental philosophy to provide its basic frameworks for conceptualising both society and subjectivity. Furthermore, these two areas of concern mark the continuity between subject position theory and Cultural Studies. Bordwell contends that the diversity of projects within Cultural Studies disguises a common premise in which social institutions and practices are defined as cultural constructs.[7] Both schools are also said to focus on subject formation in that accounts of Lacanian misrecognition can be paralleled with those of Althusserian interpellation.[8] Finally, both schools are said to privilege linguistic paradigms and to have a common theoretical basis in structuralism.[9]

These 'doctrinal' continuities are used to contend that both schools borrow from continental philosophy in order to construct top-down, totalising theoretical systems. This characterisation of 'grand theory' as an 'abstract theoreticism' that is devoid of sociohistorical detail has now become standard and I will argue that this is not a helpful way to view the history of the take-up of continental philosophy within Film Studies in the final section of this chapter. For now, I want to focus on Bordwell's critique of the methodological practices deployed by subject position and cultural theorists, because it is here that the scientific paradigm he is using becomes most obvious. Bordwell offers a distinctive critique of 'grand theory' and I will demonstrate that in effect he criticises it for not being grand enough.

Bordwell's critique of the methodological practices of 'grand theory' is fourfold. He argues that the deployment of continental philosophy results in 'doctrine-driven' models of theory, criticism and historical research in which films function as examples.[10] Furthermore, he suggests that the appeal to French theorists is symptomatic of a desire for academic respectability in Film Studies.[11] This leads to the second objection, namely the eclectic accumulation of diverse aspects of incompatible theories which results in an incoherent *bricolage* that passes for argument.[12] The means of argument are the third feature of the critique. Bordwell contends that 'grand theory' relies on a loose model of 'associational reasoning' which deploys analogies and 'interpretive leaps'.[13] Finally, the overemphasis on interpretation is said to result in a proliferation of film readings that do not actually entail the theory they purport to instantiate. This point clearly draws on the main argument from *Making Meaning* in that textual interpretation is defined as 'a set of craft-like reasoning routines which do not depend on any abstract theory'.[14]

Bordwell's critique characterises French philosophy as 'celebrity- and fashion-driven'.[15] These connotations of superficiality gain resonance when contrasted with the description of the new mode of middle-level theorising as 'in-depth research'.[16] The take-up of French philosophy is thus encoded as a mistake. Film theorists have simply been starstruck by French *boulevardiers*. The assessment of French philosophy as glamorous, frivolous and, above all, unphilosophical is a familiar caricature deriving from a particular strand of the analytic philosophical tradition. These theorists, such as Jean Curthoys and Sokal, are vehemently anti-continental philosophy[17] and Bordwell replicates the tactics and tonality of this faction in his comments on the vagaries of associational reasoning displayed in the work of Guy Rosolato and Raymond Bellour. His criticism of an exchange between them goes as follows: 'the discussion is unintelligible because the connections among ideas meet no canons of reasonable inference.'[18] These canons are set up by analytic models of 'inductive, deductive and abductive reasoning'.[19] Importantly, the device of using selective and truncated quotation in order to ridicule the targeted theorist is a common tactic of the anti-continental faction. The depiction of Rosolato's and Bellour's work as unintelligible and unreasonable borrows from a series of disputes in which continental philosophy has been defined as jargon-ridden and incoherent.

Bordwell's reliance on analytic criteria explains the prevalence of the scientific paradigm in his critique. It underpins his analysis of the 'top-down' nature of 'doctrine-driven' theorising. As a result, Bordwell's argument against theory-driven textual interpretation should not be mistaken for the very common argument that theory simply imposes on the text and that the text should be allowed to 'speak for itself'. Bordwell's argument is that the application of theory to a mere handful of films cannot serve to establish said theory:

> [w]hen theory projects downwards to the datum, the latter becomes an illustrative example. The result may have rhetorical force, as vivid examples often do, but because of the underdetermination of theories by data, a single instance is not particularly strong evidence.'[20]

The language of data clearly indicates the scientific paradigm at stake here. 'Grand theory' thus fails to establish itself because its use of limited numbers of examples lacks sufficient scope. Thus, the objection is *not* that 'grand theory' is inherently top-down and totalising but rather that it fails to establish itself in a sufficiently scientific and top-down way. The introduction to *Post-Theory* endorses the contributors' use of films as data 'to substantiate or illuminate theoretical claims'.[21]

Bordwell's critique of *bricolage* is also reliant on the concept of 'pure' theory. He argues that the deployment of parts of a theorist's work constitutes an illegitimate frag-mentation of the system. Thus the take-up of Lacan in psychoanalytic feminist film theory is seen to be suspect in that it focuses on the imaginary/symbolic dyad and leaves out other aspects such as the real.[22] Bordwell's previous use of the same example in *Making Meaning* clarifies the issue, as it is clear he regards the trio Imaginary/Symbolic/Real as the 'true' Lacanian system.[23] In addition to promulgating incorrect models of philosophical systems, film theorists are accused of being insufficiently theor-etical. This is because they do not attempt to prove the value of their chosen theory over others: 'no film theorist has mounted an argument for *why* the comparatively informal theories of Saussure, Émile Benveniste, or Bakhtin are superior to the Chomskyan par-adigm.'[24] Nor do they attempt logical exposition of their chosen systems. This failure to conform to the scientific method of proceeding via refutation and exposition means that 'grand theory' cannot be regarded as '"pure theory"'.[25]

In the final part of his critique, Bordwell argues that the attempt to 'prove' a theory through the construction of textual interpretations is not valid because interpretations do not constitute a proper test.[26] This is because Bordwell defines interpretation as a 'craft-like' skill. The absolute division between the practical and the theoretical is set up in *Making Meaning*.

> Like an artisan using strategies derived from experience, the critic draws upon a
> repertory of options and adjusts them to the particular task. And this skill no more
> constitutes a theory of cinema than a good bicyclist's know-how amounts to a physics
> of moving bodies or a sociology of recreation.[27]

The critic's skills are said to be constituted through tacit obedience to institutional con-ventions, which in turn, are largely derived from the techniques and practices of New Criticism.[28] Given that interpretation also fails to conform to the scientific model of rule-governed reasoning, there is an implicit parallel between the atheoretical status of interpretation and the untheoretical status of 'grand theory' in *Post-Theory*.

This parallelism can be better understood by looking at Bordwell's arguments con-cerning the status of theorists such as Mulvey and Wollen in *Making Meaning*. In this earlier book, he argues that they are better positioned as critics who create templates for interpretation. Thus Mulvey's 'Visual Pleasure and Narrative Cinema' is said to con-stitute an 'interpreter's exemplar' insofar as her work is seen to crystallise a way of approaching film texts.[29] Bordwell argues that Mulvey utilises a tradition of symptomatic reading in which the text is viewed as fundamentally fissured.[30] Her article is also said to list 'a host of interpretive cues – the look as bearing power and sexual difference, the equating of the camera with the viewer, the notion of woman as fetishised spectacle, plot patterns such as surveillance and punishment.'[31] Importantly, these cues are not said to form a totally original interpretive template.[32] Instead, Bordwell argues that a number of them conform to a traditional critical schema for interpretation.

> It is part of the critic's mapping process to ascribe . . . folk psychological traits to aspects of the film, and this can be done by following particular routines. The critic uses the schema to build up more or less 'personified' agents in, around, underneath, or behind the text.[33]

Mulvey's analysis of the camera and the series of looks across a text are thus read as instantiations of the 'personification schema'.[34]

I have traced Bordwell's analysis of Mulvey's article in some detail in order to demonstrate the way in which her creation of an interpretive exemplar is ultimately shown to conform to a pre-existing critical schema. This conformity means that the theoretical elements of her work are judged to be subordinated to critical practice, thus undermining their validity as theory.[35] Bordwell argues that most critics simply use theory as a rhetorical device to persuade others of the value of their interpretations. He therefore sets up an absolute distinction between interpretive writing in which theory merely functions as rhetoric and 'theoretical writing, which proposes, analyses, and criticises theoretical claims.'[36] Importantly, this distinction serves to place theory itself beyond interpretation.

What is striking about this is the utter incongruity of positioning the major film theorists of the 1970s and 1980s as mere critics who do not do theory at all and simultaneously labelling their work 'grand theory'. According to Bordwell, only Christian Metz actually qualifies as a theoretician.[37] It would seem that the term 'grand theory' is simply applied to any work that refers to a particular tradition in continental philosophy. Yet it is worth noting that the criteria for dismissing 'grand theory' utilise an analytic model of 'pure theory' that is even more abstract, top-down and totalising. Moreover, this vision of 'pure theory' serves fundamentally to unsettle the new model of middle-level research that Bordwell ostensibly endorses. It is hard to see how the work of Vito Russo and Richard Dyer could possibly be said to conform to this scientific paradigm. In the light of this analysis, it becomes clear that the cognitive paradigm that Bordwell endorses as one possible future strategy actually constitutes the 'true theory' of the future given its quasi-scientific status.[38]

If Bordwell's model of a plurality of paradigms for future research is compromised by his vision of 'pure theory', Carroll's article makes the analytic trajectory towards one true theory much more overt. Drawing on *Making Meaning*, Carroll argues that the institutional prevalence of 'Interpretation, Inc.'[39] has resulted in the reduction of film theory to '"theoretically" derived jargon'.[40] This jargon can be understood as the remnants of a theoretical paradigm that has been cut and stretched to fit different films.[41] Carroll then inverts the story, arguing that the needs of 'Interpretation, Inc.' have actually determined which theories get taken up. He comments, '[t]heories with the greatest "weasel factor" are more attractive to scholars concerned primarily with producing interpretations, because such theories will be applicable almost everywhere and in more ways than one.'[42] Carroll, like Bordwell follows an analytic tradition in which continental philosophy is caricatured for being inherently imprecise and ambiguous. This caricature is contrasted with the scientific paradigm of neutral theoretical models that utilise the correct methodology of exposition and refutation.

Like Bordwell, Carroll advocates debate between different theorists in order to establish which of their proffered paradigms is superior.[43] Carroll envisages that such debates will take the form of dialectical argument in which the new theory will demonstrate that it has superseded the previous models.[44] This account of the dialectical process is couched in the language of pragmatism and might be more accurately defined as a commonsensical model of scientific progression. Carroll advocates 'piece-meal' research projects that acknowledge their historical specificity as well as their need for constant revision. However, the revisions that arise out of dialectical debate are also said to constitute 'the successive elimination of error' from the theoretical paradigm.[45] Thus, Carroll offers a teleological model of debate, which could ultimately lead to the creation of one true theory. He admits that this is a possible result: '[p]erhaps one day we will be in a position [to] frame a unified or comprehensive theory of film.'[46] The admission should be regarded as a disingenuous statement of the consequences of the teleological framework of his model of scientific progress.

Carroll explicitly argues that theory should not be political. He criticises Mulvey and others for their 'partisan' deployment of theory to serve the interests of radical film movements.[47] Moreover, he suggests that proponents of 'grand theory' utilise a 'cloak of political correctness' in order to protect their paradigms from proper logical analysis and refutation.[48] Ultimately, aesthetic theories are said to 'underdetermine the political viewpoints with which they are compatible, there is generally no real point in diagnosing them for their political allegiances.'[49] Thus, the politicisation of aesthetics is due to the personal inclination of the theorist rather than being an inherent part of the process of theorising.

Carroll's example of the neutrality of theory is informative in this context. He offers a sketch of a cognitive analysis of the effects of horror films, focusing on the '"startle response"', 'an innate human tendency to "jump" at loud noises and to recoil at fast movements.'[50] This enables him to analyse audience response to horror films without reference to politics or ideology. Carroll comments that a film critic might want to relate this research to the political agendas of the chosen films, arguing that such a political interpretation would be entirely compatible with the cognitive data. However, it is important to note that the political critic is not positioned as a theorist: 'this is a matter of film interpretation, not film theory.'[51] Thus, politics is relegated to the status of personal inclination or critical interpretation and positioned completely outside the realm of pure scientific theorising.

The adoption of dialectical argument as the only mode of theorising can be seen to erase many of the fundamental presuppositions of film theory. Carroll comments that his vision of 'methodologically robust pluralism' might be regarded as aggressively competitive and 'macho'.[52] However, he contends that feminists who offer paradigms said to be better than patriarchal ones are equally embroiled in the competitive process. Here, Carroll reveals a total lack of knowledge of feminist epistemology in which the process of theorising is not simply defined as the annihilation of the other.[53] Importantly, Carroll envisages dialectical argument to be 'a debate between existing rivals ... before a court of fully rational participants, endowed with full information.'[54] This model erases differences between the participants in favour of a spurious democratic abstract rationality. Thus, the considerable body of work in Film Studies focusing on the representational consequences of differential power relations and material social positions is simply swept aside.[55]

2 Theory as Dialectic

While it is clear that Žižek's work constitutes the prototype of the kind of 'grand theory' that Bordwell and Carroll wish to abolish, I have chosen to discuss *The Fright of Real Tears* in the second section because it contains a critique of the paradigm offered in *Post-Theory*. The section will begin with an outline of the major elements of Žižek's critique and then offer a summary of his account of theory as dialectic. I will then examine his methodological practices in some detail in order to call Bordwell and Carroll's conception of the illogical nature of 'grand theory' into question. This will lead into an examination of Žižek's problematic presentation of gender.

Žižek argues that the post-theorists' rejection of 'grand theory' is an erasure of the past that generates a false sense of the possibility of beginning all over again:

> (Post-)Theory starts to behave as if there were no Marx, Freud, semiotic theory of ideology, i.e. as if we can magically return to some kind of naiveté before things like the unconscious, the overdetermination of our lives by the decentred symbolic processes, and so forth became part of our theoretical awareness.[56]

Carroll's vision of a court of fully rational participants clearly erases any role for the unconscious, and indeed emotion, in the process of theoretical debate. At the same time, the vehemence that accompanies and imbues Carroll's conception of this model of debate attests to the presence of considerable emotion. For Žižek, the desire to expunge theory of all political content is yet another unsuccessful attempt to erase the past. This expulsion of the unconscious, emotion and politics from theory is used to sustain a picture of 'the Post-Theorist himself/herself as the observer exempted from the object of his/her study.'[57] Žižek comments that this 'immoderate position of enunciation', i.e. that of the pure objective observer, is entirely at odds with the modest language of middle-range research.[58]

The main thrust of Žižek's critique of the post-theorists is levelled at Carroll's account of theoretical debate. Žižek argues that Carroll's model of scientific progression in which theories are placed in competition with each other is not a dialectical one. 'What Post-Theorists mean by a "dialectical approach" is simply the notion of cognition as the gradual progress of our always limited knowledge through the testing of specific hypotheses.'[59] This process of proceeding via discussion and testing is said to be a long way from classical dialectic. On the Hegelian model, theory is said to progress in a three-fold way: beginning with the assertion of the thesis, which is followed by its negation in the form of the antithesis, and culminating in the final resolution of the two in a synthesis which operates as 'a negation of the negation'. It is this emphasis on the logic of negation that sustains the classical definition of dialectic as an unfolding of theory. Each new system is seen to emerge from turning the previous ones inside out and the final synthesis is said to be inherent to the previous systems and is thus described as 'always already there'.

Žižek also argues that the role of examples and counter-examples within dialectical methodology differs very greatly from Bordwell's and Carroll's accounts. I have argued that the scientism of their approach results in a top-down conception of films as data. Žižek assimilates Bordwell's and Carroll's approach to a more standard bottom-up scientific paradigm, namely the accrual of data and the attempt to reason up from it to theoretical conclusions. He argues that the procedure of collecting multiple examples does not conform to dialectical methodology. Following Hegel, Žižek perceives the relation between theory and examples to be a question of focusing on the one specific instantiation that works to sustain the paradigm: '... the great art of dialectical analysis consists in being able to pick out the exceptional singular case which allows us to formulate the universality "as such".'[60] This formulation is given a specific twist via the logic of negation in which particular emphasis is placed on the function of the counter-example. Thus, the 'exceptional singular case' is the one, which structurally sustains the theoretical paradigm by instantiating the point at which it fails. To rewrite Žižek: 'the domain of rules [would] collapse without its founding exceptions'.[61]

Žižek's emphasis on the structural importance of the counter-example is interesting because it can be seen to constitute a specific inflection of the dialectical paradigm. On Žižek's model, the moment of synthesis constitutes an awareness of the ways in which any thesis is reliant on its antithesis. Accordingly, his work tends to emphasise the structural role of negation per se, rather than moving towards a more positive conception of synthesis in which the work of negation is reconciled and overcome. This reading of dialectic is common in the work of theorists who conjoin Hegel with traditional psychoanalysis, such as Judith Butler, in that the antithesis tends to be reformulated as that which is repressed by the system itself.

This emphasis on negation and repression is clearly demonstrated in Žižek's definition of what is to constitute 'theory proper'. He argues that historical accounts of stylistic innovation in the cinema cannot be regarded as theoretical because they fail to place sufficient emphasis on that which is excluded from the film text.

> We only attain the level of true Theory when, in a unique short-circuit, we conceive of a certain formal procedure not as expressing a certain aspect of the (narrative) content, but as marking/signalling the part of the content that is excluded from the explicit narrative line, so that – therein resides the proper theoretical point – *if we want to reconstruct 'all' of the narrative content, we must reach beyond the explicit narrative content as such, and include some formal features which act as the stand-in for the 'repressed' aspect of the content.*[62]

In this account, synthesis, or the whole text, can only be appreciated by focusing on that which is excluded or repressed. It is the logic of negation that is privileged in that it is the only means of attaining knowledge of the whole.

Žižek clearly presents his paradigm of 'theory proper' in opposition to the post-theorists. His very definition of true theory emerges from a discussion of the theoretical failings of historical accounts of developments in cinema style, an argument that is aimed at Bordwell among others. However, it is worth noting that both sides offer very traditional paradigms of 'true' theory. While the specific philosophical underpinnings of each paradigm are different – Bordwell and Carroll use analytic models and Žižek is resolutely continental – neither side embarks on a critical appraisal of their chosen tradition. This co-option of philosophy as a solution that needs no further justification is clearly problematic. Both sides also draw a rigid distinction between the process of interpretation and the practice of theorising. Žižek can be seen to share the basic tenet of *Making Meaning* in his differentiation between commentary and philosophy. The process of commentary, however critical, is deemed to be purely descriptive thereby ensuring that the practice of close reading cannot be considered as a mode of theorising.[63] This move also ensures that theoretical texts are positioned outside the realm of interpretation.

Both the different sides also offer paradigms that take the form of top-down theoretical models. While Žižek privileges the insights offered by a single counter-example and Bordwell and Carroll stress the importance of multiple data, the structural position allocated to examples is the same. This can be seen in Žižek's brief comment on his use of Kieślowski's films at the beginning of *The Fright of Real Tears*. 'The aim of this book is . . . not to talk *about* . . . [Kieślowski's] work, but to refer to his work in order to accomplish the *work* of Theory.'[64] The films are deemed to be useful only in so far as they serve to illustrate particular aspects of the overarching theoretical system. Thus, in both paradigms, films serve as instantiations of the system or of that which the system represses. As a result, the films are deemed to be irrelevant to the development of the system itself.

I want to examine the ways in which Žižek develops the concept of suture across *The Fright of Real Tears* in order to analyse further his use of examples. I will argue that rather than constituting the afterthought of a top-down system, Žižek's dialectical use of examples can be seen to bring pressure to bear on the Lacanian system itself. However, my reading of Žižek's practices will not be used to sustain a post-theoretical critique of his work as an illegitimate cutting and stretching of the Lacanian mainframe. Instead I will demonstrate the ways in which some of the changes can be seen to conform to patterns of coherence, which require a more careful nuancing of the analytic paradigms of logical argument.

Žižek first defines suture after outlining the structure of hegemony in which society articulates the threat of the 'non-social' by mapping it as an internal component of the social system. This move from radical exterior threat to a contained, albeit differential, element within the social order is said to constitute the logic of suture. Furthermore, the transition is inescapable: 'the very opposition between the symbolic order and its absence has to be inscribed *within* this order, and "suture" designates the point of this inscription.'[65]

The transformatory power of suture is then converted into a cinematic paradigm by focusing on the subject's/spectator's relation to radical alterity and the way in which it is contained by the interplay between two shots. During the first shot the spectator is envisaged in a state of imaginary plenitude, which is jeopardised by a growing awareness of the pictorial frame. The frame emphasises the passivity of the spectator, constructing the film as a show run by the Other. The second shot neutralises this threat by offering an image of one of the protagonists within the diegesis. The first shot is thus reinscribed as a point-of-view shot, the view of the protagonist, and the threat of the Other is effectively sutured in that it is contained within the diegetic world of the film.[66] Importantly, these first definitions of suture clearly present it as a means by which the threat of the Other is contained/covered over.

Žižek argues that the suturing effect of the two shots can be jeopardised by the presentation of the first as a point-of-view shot that is not subsequently owned by a character within the diegesis. He argues that Hitchcock's presentation of physical objects as threatening uses this formula. To take his example from *Psycho*, shot one could be a side view of the protagonist viewing the house and shot two an image of the house as viewed by the protagonist. For Žižek, the first shot is ambivalent, in that it is both an 'objective' view of the protagonist and a 'subjective' point-of-view shot: 'the subject's eye sees the house, but the house – the object – seems somehow to return the Gaze....'[67] This reversal of the subject/object relation is said to be threatening and uncanny because the subject is positioned as the recipient of the gaze of the Other.[68] Importantly, the failure of suture does not jeopardise the Lacanian system itself. Rather, Hitchcock's use of the gaze is read as a 'proper' instantiation of the Lacanian definition. Fundamentally for Lacan, 'the Gaze is on the side of the object, it stands for the blind spot in the field of the visible from which the picture itself photo-graphs [sic] the spectator.'[69]

While Žižek's reading of Hitchcock's texts as exemplary instances of the Lacanian gaze seems to be a clear demonstration of the top-down nature of his theoretical paradigm, it is worth noting that the texts are simultaneously presented as counter-examples because they are used to demonstrate the moment at which suture fails. This endeavour to proceed via a consideration of counter-examples clearly conforms to dialectical methodology. Žižek expands the discussion by using Kieślowski's work to demonstrate the failure of suture in a different way. The Hitchcock texts are seen to jeopardise the subject's attempt to suture the threat of the Other. In contrast, Kieślowski's texts are said to demonstrate the ways in which reality itself is ontologically sutured thereby effecting the return of the Real. Žižek develops the concept of the 'interface' which functions as both the artificial moment that stitches reality together and as a spectral screen through which the threat of the Real can be directly represented.[70] Importantly, the repeated demonstration of the failure of suture at both the enunciative and ontological levels results in its redefinition as an impossibility, an attempt at closure that *necessarily* fails.[71]

The key question to ask at this point is why Žižek finds it necessary to embark on this process of redefinition. At one level, Žižek's answer must be that the future of film theory is ultimately reliant on a 'proper' understanding of the Lacanian frame. Thus, the rebuttal of the definition of suture as closure is a dismissal of the way in which Lacan has been previously used within Film Studies.[72] However, it is interesting to note that the change of definition occurs after the explication of numerous counter-examples and this suggests another answer, namely, that Žižek's reinterpretation of the Lacanian frame is a response to the pressure wrought by the examples themselves. At the very least it is clear that the plethora of counter-examples make the redefinition of suture plausible. Moreover, the development of the concept of the interface occurs in relation to the discussion of specific examples. While Žižek attempts to efface the process of theorising by passing it off as a description of existent textual features, the security of his top-down model is significantly jeopardised at this point. I am not adopting the post-theoretical perspective in which responding to the pressure wrought by examples renders the theory illegitimate. Rather, I am suggesting that the failure of this avowedly top-down model of theorising indicates that examples do not merely function as inert instantiations of theory. I will go on to develop this argument using the work of Michèle Le Doeuff in Chapter 2.

The redefinition of suture from that which contains the threat of radical alterity to that which attests to the impossibility of such containment might seem to constitute an illegitimate cutting and stretching of the Lacanian frame. Carroll argues that such moments of redefinition show the ambiguity of key concepts which sustain the '"weasel factor"' of continental theory.[73] However, I would suggest that the inversion of definition that takes place across Žižek's work is entirely consistent with the centrality of paradox within the Lacanian system. On this model, the cut that founds the subject is also the scar which acts as a reminder of the impossibility of fully attaining a subject position within the symbolic order. Rather than simply being ambiguous, the doubleness displayed by the concepts of suture and the cut is clearly controlled by a logic of negation.

Žižek's development of the concept of the interface is reliant on a model of reasoning by analogy in which the founding structure of subject formation is transferred to the Real. While the post-theorists dismiss analogy as a loose form of association, implying that it is both vague and incoherent, Žižek's use of it in this instance results in an appropriately paradoxical definition, in that the interface both effaces and attests to the existence of the Real. What I wish to stress here is that the post-theoretical insistence that particular forms of reasoning be deemed de facto illegitimate is not at all helpful in evaluating the arguments presented by specific theoretical systems. Judging an argument relies on more than the recognition that it makes use of analogical reasoning; it requires an assessment of how the analogy is used and whether or not it is successful. Thus, analogy must be regarded as a form of reasoning that can be executed more or less well.

An example of a problematic use of analogical reasoning can be seen in Žižek's efforts to compare the structure of suture to the inscription of sexual difference. He begins by arguing that women's internalisation of gender roles conforms to the initial structure of suture as containment: 'to take the elementary example of sexual difference: in a patriarchal society, the external limit/opposition that divides women from men also functions as the inherent obstacle which prevents women from fully realising their potential.'[74] The analogy is complicated further by Žižek's use of the Lacanian formulation of sexual difference in which femininity is defined as the 'not-all' that falls outside 'the phallic function'.[75] As a result, the feminine comes to constitute the 'external limit' that symbolises sexual difference itself. While the positioning of woman outside the symbolic order constructs her as a threat, her radical exteriority is defined as illusory: 'the "appearance" of the feminine position is the mysterious Exception, the Feminine which resists the universal symbolic order, while its "truth" is that *there is nothing outside* the symbolic order, no exception.'[76] This positioning of woman in a space that is pre-defined as impossible, means that the threat that she represents is always already contained. This is consistent with the presentation of the inscription of sexual difference as a form of suture, only now women's internalisation of femininity can be seen to constitute a doubled form of containment.

What is striking about this use of analogy is that it results in a definition of femininity that is clearly inconsistent with the rest of Žižek's position. The final analysis of femininity as a threat that is always already contained is entirely at odds with Žižek's own redefinition of suture as that which acts as a constant reminder of the impossibility of containment. The erasure of the threatening aspect of femininity is the result of an elision of the paradoxical doubleness that characterises all Žižek's other definitions. This inconsistency is due to Žižek's straightforward perpetuation of Lacan's formulations of gender roles and the necessary absence of the sexual relation. The definition of the feminine as a non-threatening Other also follows the Lacanian model in positioning the feminine as a fail-safe device that serves to shore up a system in which masculinity alone functions as the privileged term.[77] Žižek's unthinking reinscription of Lacanian gender categories with all their concomitant problems can be seen to significantly jeopardise his status as a political theorist.

My final objection to Žižek's position is that he constantly presents the Lacanian system as the end point of the dialectical process. As a result, his endless revisions of and additions to the Lacanian frame are constantly covered over and constructed as the return to the 'true' system. This mode of presentation is important because it effaces the ways in which his model is ultimately reliant on interpretation. Žižek offers a particular reading of Lacan, one that emphasises the negative aspects of paradoxical definitions and focuses on the neglected features of the system, such as the Real. In presenting this mode of reading as a result of dialectical logic, Žižek's interpretations are given the status of the 'truth'. However, I would argue that the adoption of dialectical methodology generates particular kinds of reading practices and that the ensuing focus on negation does not reveal the 'truth' but rather the limits of what can be seen using a dialectical lens.

3 Theory as Rhetoric

This section will begin with Nichols' critique of the ahistorical nature of the post-theoretical position, which will also involve examining his reasons for rejecting the terminology of 'grand theory'. Nichols develops his models of theorising in relation to three key concepts: culture, representation and rhetoric. The first two sustain his sense of theory as both perspectival and political and I will compare and contrast this position with those explored in the previous sections. Last, I will address Nichols' definition of theory as rhetoric and his attempt to position it outside the Western philosophical tradition. In contrast, I will demonstrate that Nichols' redefinition of theory has much in common with Irigaray's reconceptualisation of the philosophical tradition, which will involve looking at her critique of Descartes.

Žižek's conception of Lacan as the end point of dialectic can be compared to the post-theorists' conviction that their work marks the starting point of future theorising in that both positions are sustained by a rejection of their own historicity. Nichols argues that the post-theorists' attempts to return to the analytic ideals of 'abstract rationality and democratic equality' erases any conception of cultural and socio-historical specificity.

'They dissociate the theorist from any sense of historical situatedness and allow theory to stand with its feet firmly planted in the air.'[78] While Žižek is concerned that the post-theorists neglect the history of philosophy in order to begin again, Nichols' point is that the process of theorising always takes place within a specific set of institutional and social contexts.

For Nichols, the post-theorists' definition of 'grand theory' as 'congealed dogma' serves to efface the historical specificity of the take-up of different aspects of continental philosophy in Film Studies.[79] I would add that Bordwell's and Carroll's rejection of interpretation as a mode of theorising leads them to postulate that 'grand theory' forms a monolithic block because they have no way of accessing the diversity that is created through a particular conjunction of close textual analysis and critique. Importantly, Nichols argues that the historicity and diversity of 'grand theory' can only be appreciated if the term itself is abandoned.[80] Indeed, the term 'grand theory' acts as a purely pejorative label, which is used to designate allegedly obsolete modes of theorising that have been supplanted by new models, thus promulgating a linear history of theory. In contrast, Nichols offers a short account of developments in film theory in terms of the use of different *conceptual frames*.[81] These developments are said to trace 'a pattern that is neither linear nor predictable', thus creating a fluid sense of emergent histories which reread the past in order to reconfigure the future of theorising.[82]

Nichols' model of theory is fundamentally pragmatic. The criteria for judging the success or failure of the take-up and development of different conceptual frames is that of usefulness. Thus, the key consideration is how far the conceptual frames succeed in explicating the chosen field of examples. The criteria of usefulness can be seen to rely on a demonstration of a 'fit' between the theory and the examples, which the post-theorists have criticised for constituting a loose form of argument. However, such demonstrations clearly utilise logical categories, particularly the concepts of consistency and coherence. Nichols defines theorising as purposeful in that each project is subject to specific ends, which, in turn, set out further categories by which it can be judged to succeed or fail. The sense of the importance of the aims and goals of each theorist means that theorising is defined as fundamentally perspectival. In sharp contrast to the post-theorists' nomination of cognitivism or Žižek's advocation of the Lacanian–Hegelian frame as the one true theory, Nichols' model of pragmatic perspectivalism means there can be no one answer.

This emphasis on multiplicity can be seen in Nichols' definition of the concept of culture as a symbolic economy of diverse social practices, which forms a site of conflict and contest. Importantly, the awareness of differential power struggles means that Nichols' perspectivalism should not be regarded as a complacent advocation of multiplicity. He is well aware of the ways in which theories can serve to efface or to minimise the importance of cultural differences. This means that any perspective can be judged in relation to others in terms of what it includes and excludes from its designated field of vision. For Nichols, the centrality of the concepts of culture and representation means that the process of theorising is always political, in that it feeds into and sediments particular forms of socio-cultural relations:

> Who gets to represent what to whom and why; what image, icon or person shall stand for what to whom are questions in a form that allows issues of visibility and cinematic representation to tie into issues of social and political consequence.[83]

Nichols believes that film theory should take the form of specific projects and his emphasis on particularity results in a model of theorising that is both top-down and bottom-up. The model is closest to being top-down in its utilisation of previous conceptual frameworks in order to theorise 'specific forms, practices and effects'.[84] However, the relation between theory and examples is a feedback loop in so far as the examples continually serve to challenge and alter the theory. The model is most obviously bottom-up when Nichols describes the development of new modes of theorising. 'Contemporary film theory ... *works out from* the specific or particular to tell stories, offer interpretations, make arguments and propose conceptual frames....'[85] In contrast to both the post-theorists and to Žižek, Nichols' explicitly acknowledges the active role of examples in so far as they provide the impetus to theorise as well as generating a sense of the limits of particular conceptual frames.

Nichols' conception of theory as a range of historically located projects which are developed through allowing examples an active role corresponds to what many people have understood by the post-theoretical term 'middle-range theorising'.[86] However, the scientific paradigm is clearly incompatible with the development of radically diverse conceptual frames because it constructs conflict as something that must always be resolved using the allegedly neutral criteria of 'truth' and 'progress'. What is important about Nichols' model is that it facilitates a mapping of the relation between the conceptual frames and socio-historical power relations, thus ensuring that the choice or development of any one particular frame is never seen to be 'neutral' or 'objective'. He therefore allows for conflicts that cannot move towards any smooth resolution. At stake here is the recognition that all theorising is fundamentally political. While Bordwell does attempt to leave a space open for political projects, I have already argued that his underlying theoretical paradigm serves to undermine this possibility. The work of theorists such as Vito Russo and Richard Dyer, whom Bordwell cites as exemplary of middle-range theorising, can clearly be seen to conform methodologically to Nichols' paradigm of political perspectivalism.

Nichols' analysis of rhetoric can be seen to encompass and expand on the definition of theorising as a historical, perspectival process that is generated by his use of the concepts of culture and representation. For Nichols, the classical conception of rhetoric as the art of oratory in which speaking well is defined as persuading and moving the audience, serves as a key means of linking language and the body. Rhetoric can be seen to rely on a 'symbolic economy of corporeal expression' in that it promotes the use of words and gestures in order to effect change in the chosen audience.[87] 'Rhetoric ... aims to move (*movere*) us bodily, ... in our way of seeing and being in the world, not simply to convince only our mind of a truth.'[88] It is this emphasis on materiality and affect that provides the crucial link between rhetoric and specific socio-historical conditions. 'Rhetoric abandons the universal (disembodied) subject of philosophy ... in favour of particular subjects, specific cultures, situated issues.'[89]

Nichols' emphasis on the materiality of theory can be seen to undermine the fundamental oppositions of mind/body and thought/affect, which underpin the Western philosophical tradition. In continually reworking the concepts that philosophy placed firmly outside the parameters of 'true' theory, such as materiality and emotion, Nichols addresses many long-running debates. His analysis of the importance of figurative language can be seen as a response to the traditional distinction between philosophy and poetry, which results in the denigration of the latter.

Famously, Plato expels poets from the Republic because their use of vivid imagery and metre serves to undermine the audience's capacity for logical argument. 'Instead of articulating the true and the real, [poetry] creates a semblance, an appearance, through a colourful glitter of words and rhythms that produce an effect of fascination and a vertigo of the mind.'[90] The denigration of poetry as both distortive, in that it sets up fake images, and superficial has been recently reinscribed in the post-theorists' rejection of philosophers whose writing styles utilise figurative language, such as Nietzsche. Nichols' take-up of rhetoric results in an expansion of the concept of the poetic in that he is concerned to address both visual and verbal images. Importantly, he argues that cultural imagery can be subject to logical analysis because it serves as the means by which particular power relations are inscribed at a social level. In this way, poetry is repositioned as a part of theory and theorising. 'The figurative aspects of language ... become crucial: metaphor and other rhetorical tropes become not the enemies of logic but the allies of knowledge and power.'[91]

Nichols' conception of different kinds of situated knowledges that are created through the reworking of the concepts of materiality, affect and imagery, clearly challenges the traditional conception of philosophy as 'rational, abstract, universal and detached' as well as the equation of philosophical knowledge with objective truth.[92] However, Nichols does not pursue this challenge. He addresses the impossibility of objectivity in his analysis of rhetoric in the documentary, but does not offer a similar critique of objectivity in philosophy.[93] This lack of further critique, coupled with the presentation of rhetoric as a product of a counter-tradition formed by Greek oratory and Christianity, serves to leave the philosophical tradition disappointingly intact.[94] While Nichols briefly references Lichtenstein to argue that the opposition between philosophy and rhetoric has served to sustain a false dichotomy, which has impoverished both sides, the positioning of rhetoric within a separate counter-tradition actually serves to maintain this opposition.[95]

The re-emergence of the philosophy/rhetoric dichotomy in Nichols' work is disappointing given his fundamental reworking of other key oppositions, such as mind/body, reason/emotion and philosophy/poetry. His strategies for reworking the binaries can be paralleled with Irigaray's critique of Western philosophy in *Speculum*. Like Irigaray, Nichols does not simply choose the familiar option of reworking key oppositions by privileging the 'lesser' element in the binary hierarchy. Both theorists choose instead to implode dualities by showing the necessary interpenetration of both aspects. Nichols offers a model of situated knowledges in which materiality, affect and poetry are reinscribed as logical structures. Irigaray's critique of Cartesian dualism focuses on the necessary relation between materiality and thought. Importantly, Irigaray's critique of Descartes makes use of particular rhetorical strategies and I want to use her work to demonstrate briefly how Nichols' model of theorising can be applied to philosophy.

Irigaray's critique of Descartes is based on a traditional reading that focuses on the dualism generated by his opposition of the conscious mind and the non-conscious, machinic body. Throughout *The Meditations*, Descartes systematically subjects the physical world, bodily sensation and even his own thoughts to hyperbolic doubt, arguing that he might be deceived as to the truth of all of them. Famously, this methodology gives rise to the formation of the *cogito*, the one thing that cannot be doubted. Irigaray summarises the founding moment of the Cartesian system in this way: '(it is) I (who) doubt(s), therefore (it is) I (who) am.'[96] She then adds a comment that calls the truth of this founding moment into question, suggesting that the method of reasoning from which it is derived is fundamentally solipsistic. 'But he took good care not to suppose, not to presuppose, that some other "I" might be doubting too.'[97]

Irigaray's critique takes the form of a series of dramatisations that expose the untenable nature of the *cogito*. She offers a parodic re-enactment of the logical sequence of its formation in order to reveal the absurdity of denying all materiality.

> And if the objection is raised that you have to 'breathe' before you can think, and therefore exist, such naivete [sic] will illicit the retort that, whether or not I am breathing, if I am not aware of breathing, nothing can prove to me that I am in fact doing so. Therefore, that I exist.[98]

Irigaray's dramatisations of the failure of the *cogito* serve to draw attention to the rhetorical strategies that Descartes deploys in order to pass off his conclusions as the only possible truth. Her use of parody mimics and sends up the original text, enabling its assumptions and conclusions to be called into question. She thus undermines the distinction between philosophy and rhetoric by exposing the ways in which traditional texts rely on particular rhetorical effects to achieve their status as the undisputed voice of truth. I have positioned Nichols alongside Irigaray because they both make use of the resources of rhetoric in order to reconceptualise the theoretical. The conjunction of both theorists leads to the conclusion that all theories are rhetorical but some acknowledge their strategies more readily than others.

Nichols and Irigaray both offer methodologies, combining techniques that are derived from diverse theoretical positions such as post-structuralism and psychoanalysis, thus sustaining a variety of different modes of theorising. The lack of any single theoretical prototype also ensures that theorising is defined as a process in which everyone can participate. This can be seen as a welcome change from the elitist reinscription of the boundaries of 'proper' theory offered by both the post-theorists and Žižek. The systematic denigration of past theories and theorists that is promulgated by both sides clearly puts theorising back into the hands of the favoured few. In contrast, the celebration of the 'improper' can be seen to generate a means of appreciating the value of past forays into philosophy as well as opening up the possibility of future encounters. At stake here is a democratisation of philosophy that I believe to be fundamental to the future of theorising.

I have chosen to end this chapter by looking at Irigaray's analysis of Descartes because it demonstrates some of the ways in which feminist critique has challenged the philosophical tradition. In contrast to Nichols' paradigm of rhetoric, which is located outside the tradition, Irigaray's critique creates spaces for subversion within philosophy. This is tremendously important because feminist philosophers have drawn attention to the considerable discrepancy between philosophical definitions of 'proper' theory and the 'improper' theoretical practices that are actually instantiated in philosophical texts. Chapter 2 will address the work of two prominent feminist philosophers, Le Doeuff and Irigaray, in order to show how their work sets up different models of theory and theorising, thus providing an alternative solution to the current crisis in film theory. Like Nichols, both these feminist philosophers offer models of theorising that emphasise the ways in which theory both feeds off and informs our experience of the everyday. I agree wholeheartedly with Nichols' proposition that 'Theories 'R' Us'[99] and would add that this means it is incumbent on all of us to recognise and realise the stake we have in the process of theorising.

Notes

1. T. Perkins, 'Who (and What) Is It for?', in C. Gledhill and L. Williams (eds), *Reinventing Film Studies* (London: Arnold, 2000), p. 76.
2. D. Bordwell and N. Carroll (eds), *Post-Theory: Reconstructing Film Studies* (Madison and London: University of Wisconsin Press, 1996), pp. viii, 2.
3. G. Branston, 'Why Theory?' in C. Gledhill and L. Williams (eds), *Reinventing Film Studies* (London: Arnold, 2000), pp. 28–9.
4. D. Bordwell, 'Contemporary Film Studies and the Vicissitudes of Grand Theory', in Bordwell and Carroll (eds), *Post-Theory*, p. 34, fn. 64.

5. While Bordwell and Carroll capitalise the terms Grand Theory to underline their sense of it as monolithic and totalising, I am using lower case and inverted commas to indicate the provisional nature of this label.

6. Bordwell, 'Contemporary Film Studies and the Vicissitudes of Grand Theory', p. 6.

7. Ibid., p. 13.

8. Ibid., p. 14.

9. Ibid., p. 18.

10. Ibid., pp. 19–21.

11. Ibid., p. 19. Bordwell makes the same point in *Making Meaning: Inference and Rhetoric in the Interpretation of Cinema* (Cambridge, MA and London: Harvard University Press, 1989), p. 97.

12. Bordwell, 'Contemporary Film Studies and the Vicissitudes of Grand Theory', pp. 21–2.

13. Ibid., p. 24.

14. Ibid., p. 26. There are two references to *Making Meaning* in this section, pp. 25–6, 34, fns 57, 61.

15. Ibid., p. 20.

16. Ibid., p. 27.

17. Žižek argues that Sokal's attack on continental philosophy involves a caricature of the tradition that can be read as positively parodic. S. Žižek, *The Fright of Real Tears: Krzysztof Kieślowski between Theory and Post-Theory* (London: BFI, 2001), p. 4.

18. Bordwell, 'Contemporary Film Studies and the Vicissitudes of Grand Theory', pp. 22–3.

19. Ibid.

20. Ibid., p. 19.

21. Ibid., p. xvii.

22. Ibid., p. 22.

23. Bordwell, *Making Meaning*, pp. 122, 302 fn. 93.

24. Bordwell, 'Contemporary Film Studies and the Vicissitudes of Grand Theory', p. 22.

25. Ibid., p. 25.

26. Ibid., p. 26. See also *Making Meaning*, pp. 4–7.

27. Bordwell, *Making Meaning*, p. 7.

28. Ibid., pp. 6–7, 23.

29. Ibid., pp. 24–5.

30. Ibid., p. 9.

31. Ibid., pp. 92–3.

32. I therefore disagree with Durant's more optimistic assessment of the status given to interpretive exemplars in *Screen* vol. 41 no. 1, Spring, 2000, p. 16.

33 Bordwell, *Making Meaning*, p. 152.

34. Ibid., pp. 164–5.

35. Ibid., pp. 26–7.

36. Ibid., p. 250

37. Ibid.

38. B. Nichols, 'Film Theory and the Revolt against Master Narratives', in C. Gledhill and L. Williams (eds), *Reinventing Film Studies* (London: Arnold, 2000), p. 42.

39. Bordwell, *Making Meaning*, p. 21.

40. N. Carroll, 'Prospects for Film Theory: A Personal Assessment', in Bordwell and Carroll, (eds), *Post-Theory*, p. 42.

41. Carroll borrows this argument from *Making Meaning* (Bordwell 1989, p. 104).

42. Carroll, 'Prospects for Film Theory: A Personal Assessment', p. 44.

43. Ibid., pp. 49–63.

44. Ibid., pp. 56–8.

45. Ibid., p. 58.

46. Ibid.

47. Ibid., p. 44.

48. Ibid., p. 45.

49. Ibid., p. 46.

50. Ibid., p. 50.

51. Ibid.

52. Ibid., p. 63.

53. I will come back to this issue at the end of Chapter 4.

54. Carroll, 'Prospects for Film Theory: A Personal Assessment', p. 59.

55. Nichols, 'Film Theory and the Revolt against Master Narratives', p. 42.

56. Žižek, *The Fright of Real Tears*, p. 14.

57. Ibid., p. 16.

58. Ibid.

59. Ibid., p. 14.

60. Ibid., p. 26.

61. Ibid., p. 27.

62. Ibid., p. 58.

63. Ibid., p. 9.

64. Ibid.

65. Ibid., p. 32.

66. Ibid., pp. 32–3.

67. Ibid., p. 35

68. Ibid., pp. 34–6.

69. Ibid., p. 34.

70. Ibid., pp. 52–4.

71. Ibid., p. 58.

72. Ibid., pp. 55–8.

73. Carroll, 'Prospects for Film Theory: A Personal Assessment', p. 44.

74. Žižek, *The Fright of Real Tears*, p. 58.

75. In *'Encore'* Lacan maps out a table in which the phallic function producing the divided subject is presented in opposition to the *objet a*, the Other and woman. On entering the Symbolic the male subject is said to take up a relation to the *objet a*, thus ensuring that 'the whole of his realisation in the sexual relation comes down to fantasy'. The effect of the *objet a* is to barricade access to both woman and the Other (symbolised by the barring of the definite article preceding woman and the 'O' of Other), preventing the subject from pursuing a self-annihilating fantasy of holism. The barricaded Others can thus be seen to uphold the phallic economy in that they do not constitute a viable space beyond it. J. Lacan, 'God and the *Jouissance* of the Woman', 'A Love Letter', in J. Mitchell and J. Rose (eds), *Feminine Sexuality, Jacques Lacan and the École Freudienne*, J. Rose (trans.) (London: Macmillan, 1982), pp. 149, 157, 152.
76. Žižek, *The Fright of Real Tears*, p. 91.
77. This is part of Irigaray's critique of Lacan, see L. Irigaray, *Speculum of the Other Woman*, G. C. Gill (trans.) (Ithaca, NY: Cornell University Press, 1985), pp. 134–7.
78. Nichols, 'Film Theory and the Revolt against Master Narratives', p. 42.
79. Ibid., pp. 34–5.
80. I entirely agree with Nichols' argument and the term 'grand theory' is not used again after this chapter.
81. Nichols, 'Film Theory and the Revolt against Master Narratives', p. 35.
82. Ibid.
83. Ibid., p. 45.
84. Ibid., p. 38.
85. Ibid. My italics.
86. Branston, 'Why Theory?', p. 29.
87. Nichols, 'Film Theory and the Revolt against Master Narratives', p. 45.
88. Ibid., p. 46.
89. Ibid.
90. J-P. Vernant, 'The Birth of Images', *Mortals and Immortals*, F. I. Zeitlin (ed. and trans.) (Princeton, NJ: Princeton University Press, 1992), p. 177.
91. Nichols, 'Film Theory and the Revolt against Master Narratives', p. 42.
92. Ibid., p. 46.
93. B. Nichols, *Representing Reality: Issues and Concepts in Documentary* (Bloomington: Indiana University Press, 1991), p. 137.
94. Nichols, 'Film Theory and the Revolt against Master Narratives', p. 46.
95. Ibid., p. 47.
96. Irigaray, *Speculum of the Other Woman*, p. 181.
97. Ibid.
98. Ibid, p. 182.
99. Nichols, 'Film Theory and the Revolt against Master Narratives', p. 48.

2 | The Mirror of Woman

This chapter will examine the work of Michèle Le Doeuff and Luce Irigaray in order to draw out their specific conceptions of theory and theorising. I have chosen to combine Le Doeuff and Irigaray because their different analyses of theorising can be productively interrelated. Both theorists provide different ways of focusing on the crucial role played by images within philosophy. As such, they can be seen utterly to undermine the opposition between philosophy and rhetoric discussed in Chapter 1. I will argue that their critiques of philosophy result in a radical reconceptualisation of theory that has much to offer Film Studies.

I will begin by looking at Le Doeuff's analysis of the use of imagery in philosophy in *The Philosophical Imaginary*. This will involve comparing and contrasting her account of the role of examples with those of the theorists addressed in Chapter 1. Le Doeuff traces the ways in which philosophy is reliant upon the utilisation of images from other socio-historical discourses. I will demonstrate her arguments by providing an analysis of Bram Dijkstra's work on the mirror of Venus. Dijkstra traces the ways in which theoretical work on female narcissism is indebted to key images from both literature and fine art. The focus on the visual images of woman and the mirror is important for two reasons. First, it shows that Le Doeuff's account of literary imagery can be successfully expanded to address visual images, a move that underpins my take-up of her work in relation to film. Second, it is only by tracing the ways in which these images have been theorised that we can begin to reconceptualise the relations between femininity, beauty and superficiality.

Such a reconceptualisation involves combining Le Doeuff's and Irigaray's philosophical methodologies. Section two addresses their accounts of the construction of femininity in philosophy in order to interlink the theoretical and political strategies that they offer. While both theorists emphasise the ways in which theory impacts on the social, their analyses are different and I will argue that each can be used to augment the other. The final section will look at Le Doeuff's and Irigaray's analyses of the different structures of thought which underpin philosophical analyses of femininity. I will draw attention to the ways in which their critiques deploy the imagery of woman and the mirror, in order to set out the starting point for my own analyses.

1 Introducing the 'Philosophical Imaginary'

Le Doeuff begins her analysis of philosophical writing by focusing on a discrepancy between the way in which philosophy is defined and the texts in which it is actualised.

Philosophical discourse is characterised as rational, conceptual, abstract and logical. It is explicitly defined in opposition to literature, myth and poetry. Le Doeuff comments:

> [i]f, however, one goes looking for this philosophy in the texts which are meant to embody it, the least that can be said is that it is not to be found there in a pure state. We shall *also* find statues that breathe the scent of roses, comedies, tragedies, architects, foundations, dwellings, doors and windows, sand, navigators, various musical instruments, islands, clocks, horses, donkeys and even a lion . . .[1]

Le Doeuff's identification of a plethora of images within philosophy is, in itself, not sufficient to disrupt its characterisation as a purely rational discourse. Philosophical writing maintains its logical status by defining the role of the image as merely decorative. Images are said to constitute textual embellishments and, as such, are judged to be extrinsic to any theoretical enterprise.[2] Le Doeuff argues that these assumptions result in two apparently contradictory strategies for dealing with images in philosophy. In the first, the image is seen as heterogeneous to the text, an impure element that must be expelled in order to maintain the writing of 'true theory'. In the second, the image is said to be absorbed within the theoretical project, functioning as an illustration of a particular set of results or a translation of a specific theoretical point.[3]

The first of these strategies is exhibited in Bordwell's *Making Meaning* in which he is concerned to address the relation between film theory and the interpretation of film texts. He poses the key question thus: '[i]n what sense does the interpretation *follow from* the theory?'[4] The very formulation of the question sustains a complete division between the discussion of filmic examples and theoretical writing, presenting interpretation as a parasite of theory. Bordwell outlines two ways in which interpretation may be seen to be entailed by theory, as either a scientific test or a logical deduction, concluding that most film readings do not conform to these categories.[5] He then suggests a weaker connection in which interpretation functions as an illustration, however this formulation is rejected as insufficient because any reading cannot help to establish the truth or falsity of the theory under discussion.[6] This move sustains Bordwell's exclusion of those who offer templates for interpretation from the title of theorist. As a result, *Making Meaning* may be seen to play out a doubled process of exclusion, expelling both interpretation and interpreters in order to sustain the quest for 'pure theory'.

The second strategy can be seen in *Post-Theory*, in which the top-down model of theorising allows for the discussion of filmic examples as data. The examples serve as a means of illustrating specific aspects of the proposed theoretical paradigm and the accumulation of a sufficient quantity can serve to confirm the validity of the system. While it is clear that Bordwell's position has altered between the writing of *Making Meaning* and *Post-Theory*, the designation of filmic examples as mere data means that they are simply absorbed by a theoretical process to which they do not contribute. Le

Doeuff argues that the two philosophical strategies she outlines are fundamentally inter-related.

> In each case there is a common failure of recognition: whether the image is seen as radically heterogeneous to, or completely isomorphous with, the corpus of concepts it translates ... the status of an element within philosophical work is denied it. It is not part of the enterprise.[7]

In sharp contrast to the traditional conception of the image as unphilosophical, Le Doeuff argues that imagery can be seen to constitute productive points of tension within philosophical texts. In this way, focusing on the image is said to provide a means of illuminating the fault lines of any theoretical system.[8] This conception of the disruptive capacity of the image is largely in line with post-structuralism. However, Le Doeuff goes even further, arguing that textual imagery also 'stands in a relation of *solidarity* with the theoretical enterprise itself'.[9] Within Le Doeuff's model, images have a doubled function, working both for and against the theoretical system in which they appear: '*[f]or*, because they sustain something which the system cannot itself justify, but which is nevertheless needed for its proper working. *Against*, for the same reason – or almost: their meaning is incompatible with the system's possibilities.'[10]

The doubled capacity of the image arises from its dual status: it is both a specific element within a philosophical text and a product of a wider socio-cultural context. Le Doeuff argues that philosophy incorporates images drawn from different social fields, social practices and knowledges. Moreover, this process of incorporation involves transformation in that the images are imbued with particular theoretical significance once they are placed within a philosophical context. In this way, the images can be seen to crystallise into a specific formation in order to sustain the concomitant theoretical system. However, the process of incorporation that produces philosophical images can never be completed. The image always retains its previous connections to other socio-cultural contexts and, as a result, maintains its capacity to generate further meanings, some of which will be incompatible with the concomitant theoretical system.

Le Doeuff is concerned to emphasise the ways in which specific socio-cultural images are altered when they are circulated between different discursive fields. 'Certainly this circulation is not an undifferentiated diffusion: what it imposes is rather the requirement, at each stage, to think through the transformations which are produced in a borrowed element by virtue of the act of borrowing itself.'[11] The philosophical take-up of cultural images for theoretical ends is said to result in the creation of a particular vocabulary, which Le Doeuff terms 'the philosophical imaginary'. Moreover, the images that constitute the philosophical imaginary are always seen to be subject to further transformations. These changes can be the result of the use of a single metaphor across a body of work, such as Kant's use of different types of islands.[12] Amendments will also occur when an image is taken from a particular theoretical system and moved to another. Le Doeuff demonstrates this point by charting the ways in which Kant's famous metaphor of the island of truth in *The Critique of Pure Reason* draws on Bacon's earlier work *Temporis Partus Maximus*.[13]

Le Doeuff positions philosophical writing within a series of feedback loops. At one level, the texts can be seen to utilise images from previous philosophical texts, altering and augmenting the philosophical imaginary. At another level, philosophical writing may be seen to draw on other socio-cultural elements in order to create theory. Importantly, both levels offer specific reworkings of images, which, in turn, may be fed back into wider socio-cultural networks. It is this charting of the repeated interpenetration of the theoretical and the social that enables Le Doeuff to argue that philosophical writing does not transcend its historical context. She offers a mode of reading philosophy that combines textual analysis with attention to socio-historical detail.

I want to analyse Bram Dijkstra's work on the literary and artistic representations of woman and the mirror using Le Doeuff's model of multiple feedback loops. This will enable me to demonstrate the ways in which her conception of the philosophical imaginary can be expanded and applied to visual images. Dijkstra's work directly addresses the interpenetration of the socio-historical and the theoretical in that he explores the ways in which early psychoanalysis drew on the artistic and literary models of the time. He argues that late nineteenth-century paintings in which woman is presented as fascinated with her own mirror image formed the basis of Havelock Ellis's conception of female narcissism.[14] Manet's depiction of Zola's heroine, Nana, is one example. Nana is positioned in the centre of the painting, standing sideways-on in front of an oval mirror. Her head is turned to the left 'as if to give the viewer a casual and only mildly curious glance'.[15] Dijkstra comments that the viewer's marginal positioning echoes that of the top-hatted suitor who is just visible at the righthand side of the painting, constructing him as another gentleman caller. 'Manet's message is clear enough: Nana stands self-contained, self-absorbed, largely unmoved by the concerns of the men around her.'[16] Her self-containment is also suggested by the duplication of curved shapes; Nana's rounded belly is visually matched with the soft roundness of the powder puff that she holds in her right hand and the convex curving of her oval mirror.[17]

Dijkstra argues that this image and others like it were formative in the creation of the concept of female narcissism. However, this chain of cause and effect comes to be reversed in the work of Havelock Ellis in that artistic and literary representations are evidenced as proof of the existence of the psychoanalytic complex.[18] This reversal is important because it effaces the substantial amount of theoretical work that is done by the images by covering over the ways in which the theory is ultimately reliant upon a crystallisation of particular representations of femininity.

Dijkstra argues that these representations of woman and the mirror have specific resonances in relation to the wider normative social values of the mid-nineteenth century.

Conventional gender roles set up the male egotist in contrast to the female altruist and the image of the narcissistic woman breaks up this binarism. Narcissa's egotistical self-absorption clearly constitutes a negation of the Victorian ideal of the selfless angel in the house.[19] Dijkstra thus argues that Narcissa symbolises a betrayal of nineteenth-century ideals of femininity and that her egotism was correspondingly represented as both destructive and dangerous.[20] The negative connotations of this figure are also carried over into theoretical work on narcissism. The early sexologists argued that Narcissa's self-absorption constituted a form of autoerotic enjoyment that they deemed to be perverse.[21]

While Freud's later analysis of narcissism owes a great deal to the work of Havelock Ellis *et al.*, his account of Narcissa does seem to offer a more positive characterisation of the figure. Freud begins his paper 'On Narcissism' with an analysis of the megalomania that is suffered by some schizophrenics, in which they divert their attention from the external world and refocus it on themselves. He argues that the symptom of redirecting object libido onto the ego can be seen to constitute a return to an original libidinal state, which existed prior to object cathexis, the state of 'primary narcissism'.[22] In this account, the spectacle of egotistical self-absorption is deemed to be charming rather than dangerous because it reminds the spectator of what they have lost. Freud compares the charm of the narcissistic woman to that of the child, they are both said to possess enviable qualities of 'self contentment and inaccessibility'.[23] Sarah Kofman argues that the narcissistic woman's self-absorption can be seen as tremendously positive in that Freud states that she enjoys 'a blissful state of mind' and 'an unassailable libidinal position'.[24]

Kofman's positive appraisal of Freud's portrait of Narcissa is largely the result of contrasting this figure with the later construction of woman as castrated. However, focusing on the ways in which Freud produces a specific philosophical imaginary can help to draw attention to problematic aspects of his version of narcissism. He goes on to posit that both the narcissistic woman and the child have a capacity for unconcern that makes them similar to 'cats and ... large beasts of prey'.[25] This comparison is interesting because Freud draws on other visual and literary antecedents of the psychoanalytic type in which the narcissistic woman is often described as a feline sexual predator.[26] The image is clearly transformed through its take-up into this theoretical discourse in that the iconography of active female sexuality is used to suggest a childlike capacity for detachment. Freud can therefore be seen to nullify the dangerous qualities that the narcissistic woman was seen to represent through a systematic infantilisation of the figure.

Freud's containment of the narcissistic woman works in a doubled way. In spatial terms the blissful self-absorption of Narcissa is a state of self-reflexive circularity because the libido is focused inwards upon itself. This analysis can be seen to derive its cultural credibility from the prevalence of circular shapes in the paintings of the narcissistic woman, however, the theory can be seen to reconstruct the circle as a space of enclosure. While Freud does discuss the possibility of making narcissistic object choices, woman is only mentioned in relation to the fourth object choice in that she is able to love a child who was once part of herself.[27] Within this context, the infantilisation of the narcissistic woman clearly positions her alongside the child, who acts as the object of desire, rather than the maternal subject. This is important because it feeds into Freud's construction of Narcissa as an example of incomplete psychic development, her lack of object cathexes means that she is unable to progress beyond the bliss of her self-enclosed psychic state. In sharp contrast to the literary presentation of the narcissistic woman as unrelentingly self-seeking, Freud's account eliminates the very possibility of Narcissa pursuing her own desires by characterising her as incapable of forming external object choices.

The theoretical vocabulary of narcissism generated by Havelock Ellis and Freud, among others, has had a wider social dissemination than many other theoretical discourses because of their explicit and implicit references to key artistic and literary images. The terminology of narcissism comes to circulate as a psychological label that is applied to numerous representations of woman and the mirror. The feminist film critic, Janey Place, can be seen to follow in this tradition in her analysis of female characters in film noir. She reads a still from *Gilda* in which the title character gazes into the mirror while applying her perfume with her back to her husband, Ballin, as a representation of 'self-absorbed narcissism'.[28] Rita Hayworth's stance with her weight on her left hip draws attention to the concave line of her waist, which is visually echoed by the curved frame of the mirror as well as being reflected within it. The lush display of curves links the still to the nineteenth-century paintings analysed by Dijkstra.

While Janey Place's reading of the still is clearly consistent with its artistic and literary antecedents, her analysis of the significance of narcissism departs considerably from Freud's account. Her work offers an interesting example of the ways in which the imagery that is taken up to create and sustain a particular theoretical system may also be mobilised against it. For Place, the spectacle of self-absorption operates as a means of portraying the desires and goals of the female protagonist. 'The independence which film noir women seek is often visually presented as self-absorbed narcissism: the woman gazes at her own reflection in the mirror, ignoring the man she will use to achieve her goals.'[29] In this analysis, the positioning of the male protagonist gains importance. Gilda's look into the mirror takes place behind Ballin's back and can therefore suggest her own agenda. Importantly, Place's reading of narcissistic self-absorption as a form of self-interest breaks the Freudian circle of containment and offers a means of beginning to think through the reconstruction of Narcissa as more than an object of desire.

Place's positive assessment of the figure of the narcissistic woman is partly the result of changes in social values. She comments that the exciting *femmes fatales* of film noir are often presented alongside the figure of the domestic woman.[30] However, in contrast to the nineteenth-century theorists' veneration of the domestic angel, Place is clearly disenchanted with the archetype that she characterises as '"good" but boring'.[31] Her reaction is underpinned by first-wave feminist discourses in which the conception of woman as the 'natural' guardian of an idealised domestic space is fundamentally deconstructed. Place acknowledges that her reading of film noir makes use of competing frames of social values. She comments that her assessment of the *femme fatale* as the possessor of an exciting active sexuality is often at odds with the moral framework of these narratives, in which the character is destroyed in order to restore the status quo.[32]

My analysis of the complex ways in which the literary and visual representations of woman and the mirror have informed the philosophical imaginary can be seen to lead to an expansion of Le Doeuff's model of multiple feedback loops. Her model is clearly exhibited by Ellis's and Freud's take-up of cultural imagery and the subsequent circulation of their theoretical vocabulary. Furthermore, each image or concept is clearly transformed by its transition between discourses. Le Doeuff's emphasis on different discursive fields also opens up a way of thinking through the differential development of key images or concepts. Thus, it would also be possible to plot the history of the cultural representation of woman and the mirror charting a trajectory from *fin-de-siècle* literature and paintings to the *femme fatale* of modern film noir. The history of the theorisation of narcissism could be seen to weave in and out of such a cultural history, providing a means of tracing the doubled genealogy of theoretical concepts. I will go on to address the ways in which Freud's analysis of narcissism can be seen to draw on key structures that are delineated in previous philosophical systems in Section 3.

This conception of interweaving histories also serves to sustain the multiple contexts of the images that work both for and against diverse theoretical systems. The doubled capacity of the image means that cultural representations always hold open the possibility of future, different theorisations. As a result, examples can never be used to 'prove' the truth of a theory in any definitive way. On Le Doeuff's model the post-theorists' attempt to accumulate a quantity of examples as a form of corroboration is simply a means of covering over the ways in which they are actually embedded within the theoretical enterprise. For Le Doeuff, a single example is sufficient to form the basis of a particular theory because it comes to constitute a key structure within that specific philosophical imaginary. Like Žižek, Le Doeuff recognises that all examples are not equal and that it is therefore necessary to focus on the ones that play a pivotal role, creating and sustaining the concomitant theoretical system. However, her emphasis on the ways in which the examples permeate the theory also results in a significant difference from Žižek in that she does not privilege the role of the counter-example.

Le Doeuff's analysis of the importance of imagery within philosophical writing enables an appreciation of the ways in which philosophy secures its status as the voice of truth. The suppression of the role played by cultural representations can be seen to play a vital part in this process. Ellis's attempt to read works of art as examples of his psychoanalytic prototype covers over their role in the creation of the theory. This deletion of cultural and historical specificity also enables the theory to gain its 'universal' and 'objective' status. Furthermore, the eradication of specificity enables theory to pass as more than an objective description, it becomes the means of delineating the boundaries between the thinkable and the unthinkable. I have argued that Freud's account of the narcissistic woman's blissful state of self-enclosure derives its cultural credibility from the circular patterns evident in the nineteenth-century paintings. However, his theorisation of such self-absorption as indicative of a lack of object cathexes deploys a scientific vocabulary in order to present his reading as the only valid one. In this way, the narcissistic woman's pursuit of her own desires and goals becomes a theoretical impossibility because the Freudian model of her psychic state renders it unthinkable.

While Le Doeuff is concerned to offer a critique of philosophy, it is possible to draw a more positive picture of what she thinks theory should become. Any theory would have to acknowledge the work that is done by the specific examples, cultural representations and images embedded within it. This would also involve accepting the specificity and the historicity of the theory itself, which would, in turn, ensure that the proposed theoretical claims were seen as limited in their scope. In this way, a theory would always acknowledge its status as intrinsically perspectival in that it would be seen to arise from particular circumstances and to be created in relation to particular debates. Le Doeuff's model has much in common with Nichols' paradigm in that he too stresses the importance of positioning theory within its social context. However, Nichols defines theorising as purposeful, subject to specific ends. This underpins a pragmatic evaluation of the success or failure of each theoretical system in terms of whether or not it achieves its own goals. Le Doeuff is more concerned to demonstrate the tangential and diverse ways in which theories take up and rework the gender politics expressed in socio-cultural discourses.

Both theorists offer ways of reappraising the process of abstraction that is part of any theoretical enterprise. They argue that abstraction cannot be considered to be the means by which a theory is rendered universally applicable. For Nichols, film theory always involves going beyond the single example: '[t]o theorise is to step back, to assemble categories and concepts that will allow us to formulate ideas about film that have greater extension than a single instance.'[33] However, all theories are seen to be limited in their scope. On Le Doeuff's model any theory remains permeated by the imagery that has facilitated its creation. The process of crystallisation that is undergone by the cultural images that are transferred into philosophical discourse is always incomplete and, as a result, they can always be mobilised differently, rendering the theory precarious. Le Doeuff's conception of abstraction can therefore be seen to involve a transformation of form, which does entail an expansion of scope. (I will go on to discuss her analysis of the ways in which specific configurations of femininity come to form abstract structures for philosophical thought in Section 3.) However, the vital role played by the privileged examples/images ensures that any theory is permeated by a sense of its own specificity. Le Doeuff can therefore be seen to share Nichols' conception of theory as perspectival, and explicitly or implicitly, political. However her model also offers a way of viewing theory as *intrinsically* precarious and limited.

2 Le Doeuff and Irigaray Focusing on Femininity

This section addresses Le Doeuff's and Irigaray's analyses of the presentation of femininity in philosophy. Both theorists are concerned to address the role that is played by the concept of the feminine, exploring the ways in which it functions as a means of shoring up specific philosophical systems. However, their accounts of the interaction between the philosophical and the social are very different. I will argue that each theorist offers the other a way out of a particular impasse and will suggest that their accounts could be usefully combined. I will continue to utilise Le Doeuff's concept of the philosophical imaginary and will demonstrate that it facilitates a different understanding of Irigaray's project.

Le Doeuff provides an outline of 'the imaginary portrait of "woman"' that haunts philosophy. She is characterised as:

> . . . a power of disorder, a being of night, a twilight beauty, a dark continent, a sphinx of dissolution, an abyss of the unintelligible, a voice of underworld gods, an inner enemy who alters and perverts without visible sign of combat, a place where all forms dissolve.[34]

Le Doeuff comments that these many configurations of 'a femininity of chaos'[35] serve to demarcate the boundaries of philosophical thought in that they represent that which is unknowable, unthinkable or simply unthinking. Moreover, philosophy polices its boundaries by excluding modes of thought that do not conform to its definition of logic. Thus, the opposition logos/mythos serves to validate the rigorous logic of philosophical argument by contrasting it with the unthinking emotionalism of 'old wives' tales'. The superiority of philosophy is demonstrated by the repeated use of a scenario in which the shadows of superstition provided by such tales are cleared away, revealing the true light of the concept.[36]

The continual process of separation and exclusion, which sets up the boundaries of philosophy, is also essential to its very definition. In this way, the femininity of chaos that has been constructed as the outside of philosophical thought becomes the Other within: '[t]hus shadow is within the very field of light and woman is an internal enemy.'[37] However, Le Doeuff argues that the construction of the feminine as a purely hostile principle is a means of covering over the structural necessity of the role that she plays in the development of philosophical thought. 'Femininity as an inner enemy? Or rather the feminine, a support and signifier of something that, having been engendered by philosophy whilst being rejected by it, operates within it as an *indispensable deadweight* which cannot be dialectically absorbed.'[38]

Luce Irigaray also draws attention to the vital role played by the concept of femininity in philosophy, arguing that it constitutes '[a] reserve supply of *negativity*' which underpins both present and future dialectical systems.[39] Like Le Doeuff, Irigaray outlines the key ways in which philosophy constructs woman as Other:

[T]he feminine will be allowed and even obliged to return in such oppositions as: be/*become*, have/*not have* sex (organ), phallic/*non-phallic*, penis/*clitoris* or else penis/*vagina*, plus/*minus*, clearly representable/*dark continent*, logos/*silence* or idle chatter . . .[40]

However, the inclusion of Freudian and Lacanian oppositions in this list shows a key difference from Le Doeuff. Irigaray is concerned to demonstrate the ways in which the conception of the feminine as negative serves to uphold the position of the male subject. In this way, the Freudian construction of woman as lacking and consequently envious can be seen to create and sustain the value of the phallus. 'Inverse, contrary, contradictory even, necessary if the male subject's process of specul(ariz)ation is to be raised and sublated.'[41]

Irigaray argues that the symmetrical structures of dialectical opposition reveal the particular economy of desire underpinning the construction of the Other. Within the psychoanalytic model, woman functions as a 'mirror charged with sending man's image back to him – albeit inverted'.[42] It is her status as a simple inversion that reveals 'the desire for the same, for the self-identical, the self (as) same', that forms the basis of this 'hom(m)osexual' economy.[43] Irigaray's use of a Lacanian frame means that this model of desire is always intrinsically linked to the structures of representation. As a result, woman's construction as lack can be seen to present her as 'a *hole* in men's signifying economy'.[44] Irigaray summarises the bleak implications of this positioning of woman thus: '[o]ff-stage, off-side, beyond representation, beyond selfhood'.[45]

Both Irigaray and Le Doeuff argue that the images of femininity appearing within philosophy have a very specific role and consequently they should not be taken to represent every aspect of the feminine. However, they arrive at this conclusion in very different ways. Irigaray argues that it is possible to challenge the construction of woman as Other by recognising that the feminine forms a separate sexuate economy of desire and representation. The attempt to delineate 'two syntaxes' within the confines of the current masculine economy of representation requires that attention be paid to the significance of the spaces between the lines.[46]

Spaces that organise the scene, blanks that sub-tend the scene's structuration and that will yet not be read as such. Or not read at all? Not seen at all? Never in truth represented or representable, though this is not to say that they have no effect upon the present scenography. But fixed in oblivion and waiting to come to life.[47]

For Irigaray, delineating the feminine economy is a process of recovering that which philosophy has erased and rendered unthinkable. As a result, the feminine is always already there and yet it is also that which needs to be created in the future because it has to be brought back to life.

In sharp contrast to Irigaray's vision of a pure femininity that can be recovered from the depths of the masculine symbolic, Le Doeuff emphasises the multiple and diverse constructions of femininity that exist across different discourses. Le Doeuff comments that the philosophical conception of the chaotic feminine formed a contrast with the other representations that were available to her, enabling an appreciation of its limitations.

> The icon of the feminine in philosophical texts is not a universal notion. It is indeed formulated in conjunction with some rather common phallocratic prejudices, found in opinions, everyday behaviour and social practices extending far beyond the sphere of the learned few, but its specificity – not to say strangeness – seemed clear to me, no doubt because my personal sociological trajectory has also taken me through places in society where another image of the feminine is proposed for, or imposed upon, women's self-identification.[48]

While I think Le Doeuff is right to stress the diversity of discursive constructions of the feminine, her analysis of the way in which philosophy fails to secure its version of a femininity of chaos as the only one can be seen to undermine her own position. She goes against her model of the repeated interpenetration of the philosophical and the social in order to argue that the circulation of this specific imagery is limited.

> As for the possibilities of such an element having progressively become absorbed into a more collective imaginary, that is another story. The sphere of influence of the gender-dichotomies created by philosophy is actually very limited. This notion of woman as sphinx and chaos is surely current today only among certain factions of the ruling class.[49]

This statement contains a contradiction of an assertion that I have quoted elsewhere, namely that we are always 'within philosophy, surrounded by masculine–feminine divisions that philosophy has helped to articulate and refine'.[50] It is therefore worth ascertaining why Le Doeuff treats this specific imagery differently.

At stake here is the link between a femininity of chaos and the figure of the mad woman. Le Doeuff demonstrates that the concept of feminine irrationality sustains masculine rationality, which is then credited with the power to define the feminine position. As a result, woman becomes the privileged exemplar of madness while simultaneously being deprived of the ability to articulate and to understand her own state. The mad woman is thus constructed as a site of non-knowledge. Le Doeuff's emphatic rejection of this imagery serves to differentiate her work from that of other French feminists, such as Cixous, who have attempted to use the iconography of madness as a way of demarcating a space beyond patriarchy. In contrast, Le Doeuff points out that the designation of woman as 'a dear being without reason' only occurs within patriarchal societies and rightly concludes, 'it is being a little too generous always to credit power with the privilege of reason'.[51]

Le Doeuff's attempt to vanquish this particular construction of the feminine by arguing that it constitutes 'a fantasy-product of conflicts within a field of reason that has been assimilated to masculinity' is linked to her position as a female reader of philosophy.[52] In order to read herself into the philosophical project, Le Doeuff refuses to ally herself with that which the text explicitly excludes. Consequently, she argues in favour of a clear distinction between the philosophical construction of a femininity of chaos and real women. 'This is, in other words, to say bluntly that women (real women) have no reason to be concerned by that femininity; we are constantly being *confronted* with that image, but we do not have to recognise ourselves in it.'[53] While this refusal of recognition is entirely understandable, the argument is problematic because it can be used to undermine the key link between the philosophical and the social that Le Doeuff fights so very hard to establish. The argument that philosophical conceptions of woman are not applicable to real women is frequently used by theorists who wish to deny the very obvious implications of their gendered imagery.

If Le Doeuff's system is to be applied consistently, it is necessary to examine the ways in which the imagery of a femininity of chaos is utilised within other social discourses. Barbara Creed suggests that this imagery can be seen in contemporary horror films. She argues that the presentation of female protagonists as a locus of violent disorder draws on mythic representations of femininity and violence, specifically the figures of Medusa and the Bacchae.[54] Moreover, she traces the ways in which these filmic reworkings of the myths both feed into and disrupt the psychoanalytic construction of woman as Other.[55] This involves examining the psychoanalytic transformation of myths into theoretical doctrine while also focusing on the elements that are lost during the process of crystallisation. Importantly, Creed's work on horror suggests that the philosophical construction of a femininity of chaos constitutes a well-worn 'imaginary pathway'[56], which continues to inform the discourses of contemporary culture.

Le Doeuff's model of theory may also be used to trace the ways in which the construction of the feminine as irrational and chaotic draws on material from different theoretical systems. Irigaray's extensive critique of psychoanalysis in *Speculum* draws attention to its considerable debt to the Western philosophical tradition. In the chapter entitled 'Any Theory of the "Subject" Has Always Been Appropriated by the "Masculine"', she gestures towards a number of the key sources of the Freudian and Lacanian models.

Subjectivity denied to woman: indisputably this provides the financial backing for every irreducible constitution as an object . . . As a benchmark that is ultimately more crucial than the subject, for he can sustain himself only by bouncing back off some objectiveness, some objective. If there is no more 'earth' to press down/repress, to work, to represent, but also and always to desire (for one's own), no opaque matter which in theory does not know herself, then what pedestal remains for the existence of the 'subject'? If the earth turned and more especially turned upon herself, the erection of the subject might thereby be disconcerted and risk losing its elevation and penetration. For what would there be to rise up from and exercise his power over? And in?[57]

The psychoanalytic construction of woman as Other can be seen to draw upon the Hegelian dialectic of master/slave. Like the slave, woman is said to constitute a crucial 'benchmark' because the subject is ultimately reliant upon her functioning as an object. The construction of femininity as an opaque matter, which has no generative capacity of its own, is Aristotelian.[58] The analysis of the subject's transcendence is a reference to Kant and is also consistent with Irigaray's dramatisation of the repression of materiality that is required to sustain Descartes' *cogito*. The predominance of phallic imagery in the last three sentences clearly serves to link Cartesian transcendence with the subject of psychoanalysis. Indeed, the image of the earth turning 'upon herself' can be seen as a reference to female autoeroticism, which Freud argues must be given up in favour of the vaginal orgasm, thus securing the potency of the male subject.

Irigaray positions psychoanalysis as the logical successor of a Western philosophical tradition in order to challenge the ways in which its key concepts are presented as ahistorical and universal.

You refuse to admit that the unconscious – your concept of the unconscious – did not spring fully armed from Freud's head, that it was not produced *ex nihilo* at the end of the nineteenth century, emerging suddenly to reimpose its truth on the whole of history . . . The unconscious is . . . interpreted as such within a tradition. It has a place within, by and through a culture.[59]

Moreover, she is particularly concerned to demonstrate that the Lacanian reworking of Freud constitutes an ossification of psychoanalysis into its most repressive form.[60] This is because the limits of the Freudian model come to be constituted as the very conditions of representation.

You would constantly reduce the yet-to-be subjected to the already subjected, the as yet unspoken or unsaid of language [*langage*] to something that a language [*langage*] has already struck dumb or *kept silent*. And so . . . aren't you . . . the agents . . . of repression and censorship ensuring that this order subsists as though it were the only possible order ... ?[61]

Irigaray's work on psychoanalysis is important because she constructs it as *applied* philosophy. This point can be translated into Le Doeuff's terms in that psychoanalysis can be seen as a means by which the philosophical imaginary is absorbed into the collective imaginary. It constitutes a point at which a number of the gender dichotomies promulgated by philosophy impact directly upon wider social discourses because it is used in the diagnosis of real people. Irigaray constantly stresses the ways in which the Lacanian construction of woman impacts upon the lives of real women in order to demonstrate the psychic cost of trying to live within the symbolic order.

> Love and desire between women and in women are still without signifiers that can be articulated in language [*langue*]. The result is paralysis, somatization, non-differentiation between one woman and another, enforced rejection or hatred, or at best 'pretence' [*faire comme*].[62]

Furthermore, Irigaray demonstrates that this psychic state of '*déréliction*' is enforced as the norm by the school of Lacanian psychoanalysis.

While I have argued that Irigaray's work provides a means of upholding Le Doeuff's model of the repeated interpenetration of the philosophical and social, it is also the case that Le Doeuff acts as a vital counterbalance to Irigaray. Although Irigaray is aware of the many ways in which the Lacanian model attempts to pass itself off as universal, she tends to present the existence of alternative psychic economies as a possibility that has yet to be theorised.

> Whatever you may think, women do not need to go through the looking glass to know that mother and daughter have a body of the same sex. All they have to do is touch one another, listen to one another, smell one another, see one another – without necessarily privileging the gaze ... But these two women cannot speak to each other of their affects in the existing verbal code, and they cannot even imagine them in the ruling systems of representations.[63]

This quotation begins to delineate a possible model of female–female relations based on the neglected senses of touch, hearing and smell and then falls back into an analysis of the Lacanian construction of woman rather than addressing the ways in which this alternative economy might challenge the very concept of a single symbolic order.

Le Doeuff can be seen to provide a way out of Irigaray's impasse in that she insists upon the heterogeneity of diverse socio-cultural discourses, thus undermining the possibility of a single symbolic order. Le Doeuff offers a complex model of patriarchy as a dissipative system in which different socio-cultural discourses can generate and transform particular iconographies of femininity, which may or may not work to sustain misogynistic imaginary pathways. In this way, psychoanalytic constructions of the feminine can be seen to reinscribe the gendered iconography promulgated by different philosophical systems; however, the model of woman as Other still exists alongside different socio-cultural constructions of femininity. For Le Doeuff, political analysis consists of a tracing of intricate connections between discourses, sustaining an awareness of the ways in which such interconnections serve to hold open alternative possibilities as well as closing them down.

3 Structures of Femininity

While both Irigaray and Le Doeuff draw attention to the construction of the feminine as chaotic Other which occurs repeatedly within philosophical texts, they are also concerned to elucidate different structures of thought which work alongside the dialectical model. To this end, both theorists examine the structures which underpin the ways in which femininity is presented in particular philosophical works. Le Doeuff provides a detailed analysis of Pierre Roussel's text, *Système physique et moral de la femme*, which was originally published in 1777. She argues that his model of woman's body–space can be seen to produce 'new, abstract intellectual structures'[64] which are taken up by other theorists. For Irigaray, the patriarchal model of dialectical opposition is reliant upon a particular staging of the appearances of femininity. She outlines a repeated scenario in which the generative capacity of the maternal body is repressed and appropriated by the masculine economy. I will begin with Le Doeuff's analysis and will use her theoretical vocabulary to address the ways in which Irigaray's dramatisation of a repeated scenario goes beyond her stated aim of simply 'jamming the theoretical machinery'.[65]

Le Doeuff argues that the underlying structure of Roussel's text is that of the 'chiasma'. This is defined as 'the denial of a quality "X" to an object or place which common sense holds it actually to possess, with the compensating attribution of that same quality to everything but that object or place.'[66] Roussel's analysis of sexual difference is said to begin with a denial, in that he argues that the female's pubis does not possess greater mobility than the male's and concludes that the pubis does not constitute a site of sexual differentiation.[67] Le Doeuff argues that this degenitalisation of sexual difference results in its wider dissemination in that every aspect of women's lives and bodies is then presented as proof of their difference. Thus, Roussel's reasoning can be seen to correspond to the structure of the chiasma. 'Silence as to the literal meaning, a void at the centre; metonymic proliferation everywhere else.'[68]

Roussel follows tradition in constructing woman as 'the sex', and presenting procreation as her *raison d'être*. Le Doeuff comments on the metonymic proliferation of woman's procreative role. 'By degrees it comes to inform all the other parts and functions of woman's body, as well as her "moral" and relational existence.'[69] Her body is defined as elastic, 'more apt to yield to external impulses', and she is said to possess a greater 'tactile sensitivity', which means that her sensory impressions are vivid and detailed.[70] However, she is confined within the vividness of the present moment, unable to apply herself to the study of science, or to comprehend political matters or moral principles. Her inability to concentrate also ensures that she is not able to create or even to appreciate Fine Art.

Roussel may be said to construct woman as an art object rather than an artist. He argues that her graceful, curving, soft body is beautiful. In this, he can be seen to take up a gendered conception of beauty that was common in the eighteenth century. Edmund Burke's work *A Philosophical Enquiry into the Origin of Our Ideas of the Sublime and the Beautiful* was published in 1757 and provides a useful summary of the key aesthetic terms of this era. He argues that an object would be said to be beautiful if it possessed one or more of the following qualities: gradual variation in form or colour (expressed in curving rather than angular lines), gracefulness and elegance, smallness, powerlessness and fragility.[71] However, for Roussel, the aesthetic category of the beautiful is subsumed by the biological demands of procreation. 'A beautiful woman is thus one whose elastic, rounded body proclaims her aptitude for maternity'.[72] Woman's attractiveness is said to be nature's way of ensuring the conservation of the species and, as a result, her beauty is constructed as a biological imperative. Time spent acquiring the skills that will enable her to be beautiful and pleasing is also constructed as her natural occupation.

Importantly, Le Doeuff argues that Roussel's account of what constitutes feminine attractiveness corresponds to the structure of the chiasma. For Roussel, an attractive woman will be seen to combine two sets of opposing qualities: feminine modesty and beauty enhanced by coquetry. Taking up his energic delineation of these qualities as 'two motors',[73] Le Doeuff characterises each as a directional force. Modesty is constructed as 'a negative, *centred* psychological disposition' which has a centripetal, inward movement, while beauty and coquetry are seen as 'positive outward faculties, centrifugal effects of sex'.[74] Le Doeuff argues that these two forces correspond to the two aspects of the chiasma, constituting denegation and metonymic proliferation respectively. 'Womanly modesty can be understood here as the mirror-image, the emblematic projection of Roussel's own constant negative practice – the void at the centre, the silence about the "place".'[75] The final part of the sentence clearly refers to Roussel's lack of commentary on the female genitalia located at the pubis. Moreover, the line 'the silence about the place' can be read as a reference to a later icon of feminine modesty, the angel in the house, who was the gentle, quiet keeper of the hearth. Le Doeuff goes on to argue that Roussel's construction of woman's 'yielding beauty', which acts as a continual reminder of her procreative role, is an overt demonstration of metonymic proliferation: 'this body dispersed about its own surface, is a mirror of metonymy.'[76] Interestingly, it is the female body that is reduced to two dimensions and constructed as pure surface. Le Doeuff's critique of Roussel draws attention to the way in which his theories reconstruct woman as a mirror, a point to which I will return later.

While Roussel constructs feminine modesty and beauty as two different directional forces, they are both seen to serve the same ends, namely to render woman pleasing to man. Le Doeuff links the capacity to be pleasing to the concept of feminine altruism. 'To please and, through sentiment, to prefer another to oneself. In either case, the same virtue: alienation. A woman does not live or act for herself but, spontaneously, for the other.'[77] Le Doeuff argues that Roussel can be seen to consolidate Rousseau's account of gender relations, presenting feminine altruism and dependency as the necessary counterpart to masculine individualism and independence.[78] Importantly these accounts of woman's dependency serve to contain her within the domestic sphere, in that she is said to lack the mental capacity to take on a public role. For Le Doeuff, Roussel's work offers an enormously influential image of 'a womanhood enclosed in itself'.[79]

Le Doeuff's account of Roussel also provides a means of thinking through the theoretical antecedents of Freud's narcissistic woman. In Section 1 I suggested that the characterisation of Narcissa's self-absorption as a state of enclosure has credibility because of the prevalence of circular shapes in the artistic presentations of this figure. While Freud's account is congruent with the patterns within these images, his analysis clashes with the literary and artistic representation of Narcissa as self-seeking and decadent. Le Doeuff's analysis of Roussel provides a means of tracing the origins of this clash. Her construction of feminine modesty as a negative, centripetal movement is clearly very close to Freud's conception of woman's narcissistic libido as turned in upon itself. Indeed, the dynamic of narcissistic autoeroticism can be seen to reproduce the centripetal movement of modesty without the accompanying centrifugal movement of beauty. Freud's analysis of Narcissa's blissful state can therefore be seen to follow a well-worn imaginary pathway in that her pleasure in her own beauty serves to deprive her of any relation to exteriority and the wider social sphere.

Tracing the philosophical antecedents of Freud's Narcissa is useful because it explains his inability to address her more dangerous aspects. He draws on a model of feminine self-enclosure that is created through combining the key characteristics of beauty, modesty and altruism. While Narcissa can be seen to possess the first of these characteristics, she does not conform to Roussel's/Rousseau's ideals of feminine altruism and dependence. Indeed, on their model, she clearly usurps the masculine domain of egotism and independence. Freud's take-up of their conception of beauty and self-enclosure has the effect of mapping Narcissa on to the very figure to which she was diametrically opposed during the nineteenth century. She becomes the unlikely companion of the angel in the house in that both may be said to display the same lack of relation to exteriority. Freud's failure to present Narcissa as a desiring subject can be seen to consolidate a philosophical tradition in which woman is defined as being for others.

Le Doeuff argues that Roussel's analysis of feminine attractiveness raises some key questions. Do the complementary structures of denegation and metonymic proliferation serve to 'incite the desires of man and render them more durable, as the text affirms, or doubly to efface a disagreeable object?'[80] The structure of the chiasma can be seen to play a fundamental role in later theorisations of feminine beauty. The connection between denegation and beauty is asserted later by Freud, in that woman is said to seek different forms of adornment in order to cover over her status as a mutilated creature. On the Lacanian model, woman is not required to efface her disagreeable lack. Instead, she herself is effaced and reconstructed as pure masquerade. Žižek plays out the logic of this move most clearly. Woman cannot function as an exception to the symbolic order because there is nothing outside that order. She does not possess a 'narcissistic secret treasure that escapes the male Master's universal grasp, … the truth of it is that *there is no secret*, that femininity is a masquerade concealing nothing'.[81] This move constructs femininity as a series of roles, paralleling the structure of metonymic proliferation, which, in turn, sustains the Lacanian concept of desire as a never-ending process. Woman becomes a play of mirroring surfaces, the ultimate desirable object, because she can never be fully possessed or known.

While Le Doeuff characterises the metonymic aspect of the chiasma as a mirror, she also describes the overall balance between the outward and inward movements as a visual structure. She argues that Roussel's analysis of woman can be seen to constitute a pictorial system because the many facets of femininity are derived from a central predicate, in this case the maternal function. Le Doeuff compares the structural role of the central predicate to that of the 'vanishing point' of a painting. This can be defined as an imaginary point that orientates the viewer's gaze that is often positioned centrally on the horizon line where the lines of perspective converge.[82] In one sense the maternal function may seem to constitute a point of disappearance because its omnipresent quality is sustained by Roussel's postulation of the absence of genital difference. However, the vanishing point may be said to constitute a chiasmic structure insofar as it both organises the gaze by drawing it into a specific point and also serves to lead the eye back outwards. Le Doeuff connects the visual arts of painting and sculpture by examining the prudish practice of adding fig leaves to classical statues.[83] The fig leaf serves to draw the eye in but also baffles the gaze, thus drawing the eye out to view the figure in its entirety. Importantly, Le Doeuff argues that the chiasma comes to constitute a privileged form of spatial logic: 'the chiasma may well be, for the spatial imagination, what dialectical logic is for the conceptual.'[84]

Le Doeuff's redefinition of the chiasma enables her to trace the ways in which this abstract structure is used in other theoretical systems. However, she also addresses the clusters of concepts around this particular structural form. Thus the theme of woman's lack of relation to exteriority is explored alongside the chiasmic structure, which also sustains this conception of femininity. Importantly, the focus on both content and form enables Le Doeuff to trace a sophisticated series of imaginary pathways across different theoretical discourses right up to the present day. For example, she examines the ways in which

Evelyne Sullerot's writing on embryology in the 1970s presents spatial aptitude as a key mode of sexual differentiation, concluding that the 'imaginary schema' used to describe the development of the embryos is the same as Roussel's: 'woman enclosed in her interiorist cocoon, man with his relation to exteriority. "Inherent", staying-always-close-to-itself, developing without external influence: the female embryo is already a house-wife.'[85]

The methodological practice of defining an abstract structure and tracing its use across a series of different philosophical texts is evident in both Le Doeuff's and Irigaray's work. Irigaray dramatises a repeated scenario within Western philosophical discourse in which the generative capacity of the maternal body is repressed and appropriated in order to sustain the presentation of each particular philosophical system as its own point of origin. She offers a complex analysis of Plato's myth of the cave, arguing that it can be seen as 'a metaphor of the inner space, of the den, the womb or *hystera*'.[86] However, the myth is said to offer an account of the origin of philosophy that marks the crystallisation of the hystera as a metaphorical space, which can only generate false images. Irigaray's critique uses detailed textual analysis to generate particular critical images, which she uses to augment and unpick Plato's mythology. Her reading emphasises the ways in which his system is reliant upon the containment of particular metaphors and she goes on to trace the possibilities that he wishes to exclude from the philosophical imaginary.

Irigaray notes that the topography of the cave is notoriously difficult to map. The prisoners in the cave are chained to one wall so that they can do nothing but stare at the shadow play on the opposite wall, which forms flickering images that they mistake for reality. The shadows are said to be caused by objects held by men travelling up and down a passageway. The passage is hidden behind 'a curtain wall ... like the screen at puppet shows'[87] and is positioned behind the prisoners and in front of a fire. Irigaray argues that the prisoners are thus effectively positioned between two screens, which can be seen to constitute axes of symmetry, and proceeds to demonstrate this point by swinging the topography of the cave on its axes.

> They [the prisoners] are condemned to look ahead at the wall opposite, toward the back wall of the cave – the back which is also the front, the fore – toward the metaphorical project of the back of the cave, which will serve as a *backcloth* for all the representations to come.[88]

Irigaray's focus on the cave's multiple capacity for reflection and inversion sets up a key metaphor in her critique. Plato's hystera is compared to a concave mirror: '*this cave is already, and ipso facto, a speculum.*'[89]

The topography of the cave is said to be orientated towards the passageway that opens onto the outside world.[90] The true philosopher is the one who breaks free of his chains and clambers out of the cave into the dazzling sunlight. The sun is said to represent the Form of the Good, a figure of eternal truth. It also acts as a template for the fire, which is 'lighted by the *hand of man* in the "image" of the sun',[91] and symbolises the world of phenomena. Phenomena are said to be imitations of the eternal Forms. In contrast, the shadow play on the cave wall has no direct relation to the world of the Forms because it is caused by the fire and is therefore said to constitute an imitation of an imitation. Irigaray comments on the reversals that sustain the hierarchical presentation of the relations between the Forms, phenomena and the shadow play. 'For if the cave is made in the image of the world, the world ... is equally made in the image of the cave. In cave or "world" all is but the image of an image.'[92]

For Irigaray, Plato's cave operates as a specular mirror, providing a simulation of reproduction that produces 'fake offspring'. Her critique links the shadow play on the cave wall to the eternal Ideas, presenting both as imitations.

> This cave intercepts the games of copula in a miming of reproduction and in each figuration of the inner space the image of the Sun engenders sham offspring. This mime simulates offspring beyond appeal and recall, pretends to defer them by/for some kind of amnesia. Irretrievably. For has reminiscence not always already engaged in rapturous contemplation of the Idea? The eternally present Idea? Target, or vanishing point, and death, that dominates this preliminary education.[93]

This imitation of reproduction marks the moment at which Plato appropriates the position of the maternal/material point of origin. The presentation of the Ideas as always already there serves to construct his system as self-generating. The Ideas may be said to constitute the 'vanishing point' of the system because they act as both the end point of the philosophical quest for knowledge and the original concepts that serve to create the possibility of the quest. Plato's account of knowledge as the recollection of the soul's prior acquaintance with the Forms can be seen to create a further series of inversions in that the end is the beginning and the point of death is also the moment of birth. For Irigaray, the world of the Forms is part of the relay of mirrors begun within the cave in that it is said to operate as both a projection screen and a mirage of origin.

While both Le Doeuff and Irigaray use the imagery of the mirror and the vanishing point in order to formulate their respective critiques of Roussel and Plato, it is important to appreciate that the images set up different constructions of femininity. In Le Doeuff's critique, woman is constructed as both vanishing point and mirror, drawing the gaze into a central point of denegation, then dispersing it across a series of reflective surfaces. On this model, the construction of woman as mirror is explicitly linked to the ways in which feminine beauty has been theorised. By contrast for Irigaray, the metaphor of Plato's cave silvers over the hystera, replacing it with a self-contained relay of mirrors, which create and sustain the new vanishing point of the eternal Ideas. In this analysis woman is positioned on the other side of the looking glass. She becomes the point beyond the vanishing point, an unacknowledged ground whose generative capacity is co-opted and suppressed by the system. Irigaray uses the mirror imagery in order to expose Plato as a conjurer whose model of absolute truth is reliant upon a considerable sleight of hand.

Irigaray's way out of the cave involves drawing attention to the way in which the central images work to exclude specific possibilities. She argues that Plato's use of the sun as a metaphor of knowledge of the good sets up a particular imagery of light that comes to constitute a key pathway within the philosophical imaginary. While the transition from the shadows into the sunlight is said to dazzle the prisoner, Irigaray argues that the material dangers presented by the figure of the dazzling sun are overcome by the development of a specific vocabulary in which light becomes a metaphor for a cool, detached rationality.

> But the consuming contact of light will also be avoided by paying attention to *forms* alone ... Direct vision means looking directly ahead, of course, but it also means doing so through an optical apparatus that stands between man and light and prevents light from *touching* him at all. Reason – which will also be called natural light – is the result of systems of mirrors that ensure a steady illumination, admittedly, but one without *heat* or brilliance. The everlasting correctness of things seen clearly, perceived rightly, has banished not only the darkness of night but also the fires of noon.[94]

This analysis of viewing correctly links the screen at the back/front of the cave with the membrane at the back of the eye, presenting both as specular mirrors which silver over the materiality of the hystera and the ocular cavity respectively. The comparison links Plato's mythology of light to Descartes' *Optics*. The mirror at the back of the eye is said to constitute a barrier, which prevents the light from touching the I/eye, ensuring that the subject is never positioned as the object of the illuminating rays. Irigaray argues that these constructions of correct vision serve to set up and perpetuate an imaginary pathway in which the key metaphor of the natural light of reason is systematically secured through the elimination of other images, which would sustain a different analysis of the possible relations between the sun and the concave mirror.

Irigaray is therefore concerned to draw attention to the dazzling, blinding capacity of the sun in Plato's myth of the cave. She links this image of the sun to another story, the legend of Archimedes' defeat of the Roman fleet by using vast concave mirrors to set fire to their ships. 'And the sun, in its incandescence, joins together with a burning glass ... and sets the fleet of the whole nation aflame....'[95] The motif of the burning glass is used to symbolise that which lies outside the visual economy of reason established by Plato *et al*. In this way, the legend of Archimedes is linked to the figure of the female mystic who is said to form a '*miroir ardent*' when uttering prophecies in an ecstatic state.[96] Irigaray's imagery stresses the materiality of light, explicitly linking it to the twin dangers of combustibility and emotional excess. Her deployment of the image of the burning glass can be seen to set up a number of different imaginary pathways which, in turn, gesture towards the possibility of other theoretical systems in which reason and vision could be constructed differently.[97] Importantly, this understanding of the moments in which Irigaray's work reaches beyond critique is made possible through the take-up of Le Doeuff's concept of the philosophical imaginary.

I have chosen to combine Le Doeuff and Irigaray because they provide the methodologies which underpin my project. The former offers a means of tracing the development of particular imaginary pathways and abstract structures, noting the changes that are effected by the movement between different social and theoretical contexts. I will go on to focus on three key theoretical structures presented by the figure of the woman and the mirror. The first structure is binary opposition in which woman is positioned as man's mirror image, acting as both his inverse and his inferior. On this model, she becomes the object that secures the subject. The second structure is that of circular self-enclosure set up by philosophical analyses of womanly modesty and altruism as well as visual representations of feminine vanity. The third is the movement of dispersal presented by the construction of woman as a mirror of metonymy. I have departed from Le Doeuff by presenting the movements of denegation and metonymic proliferation as separate structures. All three will be used in the analyses of Nietzsche, Derrida and Baudrillard in Chapters 4, 5 and 6.

My methodology will also include Irigarary's strategy of utilising neglected features of specific images to think through the possibility of new conceptual frames. I will deploy this strategy to focus on key aspects of Baudrillard's figure of the seductress in Chapter 6, developing the conceptual implications of the figure across Chapters 6 and 7. While this will involve using the means by which Irigaray arrives at the figure of the 'miroir ardent', I will not be taking up the motif of the burning mirror. This is because Irigaray also uses it to indicate the destruction of the specular economy of representation, carrying out her threat 'to set fire to fetish-objects and gilded eyes'.[98] By contrast, I want to think about how such objects and I/eyes might be seen differently.

My point can be demonstrated by returning to Dijkstra's analysis of Manet's picture of Nana. For Dijkstra, Nana's casual gaze out of the painting indicates her lack of interest in the concerns of her gentlemen callers, showing her self-absorption. In this way, the quality of her exterior gaze is defined by her state of self-enclosure, sedimenting the imaginary pathway begun by Roussel. However, it is possible to view Nana's gaze differently. Manet's painting stands out among those collected by Dijkstra because the protagonist does not simply gaze into the mirror. Thus, her look outwards can be seen as a gesture towards exteriority, which suspends her state of self-absorption. Nana's smile as she regards the viewer out of the corner of her eye is one of recognition. It is an amused acknowledgement of her own desirability, which is reflected in the gaze of the viewer rather than the mirror itself. Her smile suggests that she is well able to understand the desires and concerns of her gentlemen callers and, furthermore, that she has chosen to keep them waiting. Thus, her gaze outwards has a dismissive quality, indicating her enjoyment of the power she has over others. Manet's portrait of Nana is interesting because the protagonist can be seen to mobilise her own objectification in order to use it as a locus of power for herself, thus breaking out of the circle of self-absorption.

This example indicates the ways in which I intend to look at the theoretical capacity of filmic images of Marlene Dietrich presented in three films: *The Scarlet Empress*, *The Devil Is a Woman* and *Shanghai Express*. I will go on to address the work of two other stars: Rita Hayworth and Nicole Kidman in the final chapter. While glamorised images of woman have been used to support theoretical systems, such as those advanced by Mulvey, de Lauretis *et al.*, they can also be seen to constitute an imaginary resource insofar as the images denote the possibility of different kinds of theorisations. I will use detailed textual analysis in order to trace the ways in which specific filmic images serve to sediment well-worn imaginary pathways, marking the re-emergence of the structures of chiasmic and binary logic. However, I am concerned to draw attention to the images that set up the possibility of different theorisations, specifically Dietrich's characters, Concha Perez and Shanghai Lily, showing how they can open up other pathways – the roads that film theory has not yet taken.

Notes

1. M. Le Doeuff, *The Philosophical Imaginary*, C. Gordon (trans.) (London: Athlone Press, 1989), p. 1.
2. Ibid., pp. 1–2.
3. Ibid., p. 7.
4. D. Bordwell, *Making Meaning: Inference and Rhetoric in the Interpretation of Cinema* (Cambridge, MA and London: Harvard University Press, 1989), p. 4.
5. Ibid., pp. 4–5.
6. Ibid., pp. 5–6.
7. Le Doeuff, *The Philosophical Imaginary*, p. 7.
8. Ibid., p. 3.
9. Ibid., p. 6.
10. Ibid., p. 3.
11. Ibid., p. 4.
12. Ibid., p. 9.
13. Ibid., pp. 9–12.
14. B. Dijkstra, *Idols of Perversity: Fantasies of Feminine Evil in Fin-de-Siècle Culture* (New York and Oxford: Oxford University Press, 1986), pp. 136–7, 146.
15. Ibid., p. 140.
16. Ibid.
17. Ibid., pp. 140–3. Dijkstra discusses the significance of the use of curved lines and the prominence of round and oval mirrors in a number of paintings.

18. Ibid., p. 147.
19. Ibid., p. 145.
20. Ibid., p. 146.
21. Ibid., pp. 145–7.
22. S. Freud, 'On Narcissism', *The Standard Edition of the Complete Works of Freud*, vol. 14 (London: Hogarth Press, 1961), p. 75.
23. Ibid., p. 89.
24. Ibid. S. Kofman, *The Enigma of Woman*, C. Porter (trans.) (Ithaca, NY: Cornell University Press, 1985), p. 61.
25. Freud, 'On Narcissism', p. 89.
26. Dijkstra, *Idols of Perversity*, pp. 291–9.
27. Freud, 'On Narcissism', pp. 89–90.
28. J. Place, 'Women in Film Noir', in E. A. Kaplan (ed.), *Women in Film Noir*, rev. edn, (London: BFI, 1998), p. 57.
29. Ibid.
30. Place reads Gilda as a *femme fatale* but I argue that she does not really conform to key features of this archetype in my analysis of *Gilda* in Chapter 7.
31. Ibid., p. 60.
32. Ibid., pp. 47–9.
33. B. Nichols, 'Film Theory and the Revolt against Master Narratives', in C. Gledhill and L. Williams (eds), *Reinventing Film Studies* (London: Arnold, 2000), p. 34.
34. Le Doeuff, *The Philosophical Imaginary*, p. 113.
35. Ibid., p. 114.
36. Ibid., p. 115.
37. Ibid.
38. Ibid. My italics.
39. L. Irigaray, *Speculum of the Other Woman*, G. C. Gill (trans.) (Ithaca, NY: Cornell University Press, 1985), p. 22.
40. Ibid.
41. Ibid.
42. Ibid., p. 51.
43. Ibid., p. 26.
44. Ibid., p. 50.
45. Ibid., p. 22.
46. Ibid., p. 139.
47. Ibid., p. 138.
48. Le Doeuff, *The Philosophical Imaginary*, p. 4.
49. Ibid., pp. 113–14.
50. Ibid., p. 101. This quotation occurs at the beginning of the chapter in which Le Doeuff explores the construction of a femininity of chaos.

51. Ibid., p. 116.

52. Ibid.

53. Ibid.

54. B. Creed, *The Monstrous Feminine: Film, Feminism, Psychoanalysis* (London and New York: Routledge, 1993), Chapters 8 and 9, pp. 105–38.

55. Ibid., Chapter 11, especially pp. 156–66.

56. Le Doeuff, *The Philosophical Imaginary*, p. 165.

57. Irigaray, *Speculum*, p. 133.

58. Ibid., p. 162.

59. L. Irigaray, 'The Poverty of Psychoanalysis', in M. Whitford (ed.), *The Irigaray Reader*, D. Macey and M. Whitford (trans.) (Oxford: Blackwell, 1991), p. 80.

60. Ibid., pp. 83–4. Irigaray argues that the Freudian model was originally far more open.

61. Ibid., p. 82.

62. Ibid., p. 101.

63. Ibid.

64. Le Doeuff, *The Philosophical Imaginary*, p. 139.

65. L. Irigaray, 'The Power of Discourse and the Subordination of the Feminine', in *This Sex Which is Not One*, C. Porter and C. Burke (trans.) (Ithaca, NY: Cornell University Press, 1985), p. 78.

66. Le Doeuff, *The Philosophical Imaginary*, p. 140.

67. Ibid., pp. 145–6.

68. Ibid., p. 140.

69. Ibid., p. 142.

70. Ibid., p. 143.

71. E. Burke, *A Philosophical Enquiry into the Origin of Our Ideas of the Sublime and the Beautiful* (Oxford: Oxford University Press, 1990), pp. 102–6, 109. Burke argues that the assertion that a particular object is beautiful is not the result of rational judgment but is rather the product of sensory impressions of the objective qualities that the object possesses.

72. Le Doeuff, *The Philosophical Imaginary*, p. 144.

73. Ibid., p. 149.

74. Ibid.

75. Ibid.

76. Ibid.

77. Ibid., p. 154.

78. Ibid., pp. 154–5.

79. Ibid., p. 157.

80. Ibid., p. 186, fn. 28.

81. S. Žižek, *The Fright of Real Tears: Krzysztof Kieślowski between Theory and Post-Theory* (London: BFI, 2001), pp. 91–2.

82. Le Doeuff, *The Philosophical Imaginary*, p. 144.

83. Ibid., p. 151.

84. Ibid.

85. Ibid., p. 167. For the whole discussion of Sullerot's *Le Fait Feminin*, see pp. 161–7.

86. Irigaray, *Speculum*, p. 243.

87. Plato, *The Republic*, D. Lee (trans.) (London: Penguin, 1987), p. 317.

88. Irigaray, *Speculum*, p. 245.

89. Ibid., p. 255.

90. Ibid., p. 246.

91. Ibid.

92. Ibid.

93. Ibid., p. 255.

94. Ibid., p. 148.

95. Ibid., p. 148.

96. Ibid., p. 191.

97. For an interesting analysis of light as glare see B. Bolt, 'Shedding Light for the Matter', *Hypatia Special Issue: Going Australian: Reconfiguring Feminism and Philosophy* vol. 15 no. 2, Spring 2000, pp. 202–16.

98. Irigaray, *Speculum*, p. 143.

3 | Venus of Stone

This chapter will examine Gaylyn Studlar's work *In the Realm of Pleasure: Von Sternberg, Dietrich and the Masochistic Aesthetic*. I will focus on her attempts to move beyond the logic of binary opposition in order to establish a gender-free, egalitarian aesthetic model. Studlar argues that any attempt to base feminist theory on sexual specificity simply reproduces the traditional oppositions of subject/object and active/passive.[1] She is particularly critical of Mulvey's famous analyses of visual pleasure arguing that the pivotal positioning of the castration complex affects the subsequent analyses of voyeurism and fetishism resulting in a visual economy that excludes the female viewer.[2] In contrast, Studlar argues that the psychic economy of masochism can provide an egalitarian account of spectatorship and signification. This chapter will use Le Doeuff's and Irigaray's techniques in order to examine Studlar's new system and to judge how far she succeeds in creating a gender-free model. The first section will outline the theoretical concepts that underpin the masochistic aesthetic. I will argue that Studlar continually positions the masculine as standard, thus resulting in the retention of one half of the binary rather than actually undermining the structure. This will be followed by an assessment of the ways in which Studlar uses key theoretical source material in order to account for the continual re-emergence of the very structure she tries to abolish. The second section will look at the application of the masochistic aesthetic to a specific film text. Each theory can be seen to function as a frame that stakes out a specific field of vision and this will be demonstrated by analysing Studlar's reading of *The Scarlet Empress*.[3]

1 Gender and the Masochistic Aesthetic

Studlar contends that her presentation of masochism is based on 'Coldness and Cruelty' by Gilles Deleuze.[4] In this work, Deleuze uses psychoanalysis in order to analyse the writings of Sade and Sacher-Masoch. In turn, he also uses the literary texts to interrogate Freud's conception of sado-masochism,[5] concluding that the sadist and the masochist construct two completely 'separate dramas'.[6] Studlar follows Deleuze in her characterisation of masochism as a specific psychic economy in which the figure of the oral mother plays a formative role. However, in 'Coldness and Cruelty' the mother is said to facilitate the *construction* of an alternative Symbolic. 'The masochist experiences the symbolic order as an intermaternal order in which the mother represents the law under certain prescribed conditions; she generates the symbolism through which the masochist expresses himself.'[7] In contrast, Studlar argues that the figure of the oral mother is located within the imaginary.[8] The mother is therefore said to inspire the masochist's *rejection* of the symbolic. Studlar's presentation of a maternal imaginary means that her position is far closer to Kristeva than the Deleuzian source material. I will go on to address other points of divergence between Studlar and her major source at the end of the section.

Studlar defines masochism as the desire to return to the pre-Oedipal.[9] The masochist is said to desire to return to an initial state of symbiosis with the mother. This desire requires the disavowal of her/his 'phallic inheritance', the psychic changes wrought by the castration complex.[10] As a result, the masochist will disavow her/his knowledge of sexual difference, rejecting genital sexuality. S/he will also ignore the edicts of the super-ego.[11] By turning from the father, the child goes back to an economy in which s/he desired and identified with the mother.[12] Within the pre-Oedipal, the mother functions as both 'love object and controlling agent'[13] and this dual role evokes an ambivalent response. Importantly, the pre-Oedipal image of the mother is said to be totally at variance with her later characterisation as deficient. For the masochist, 'the maternal figure represents a femininity "posited as lacking nothing." '[14]

Studlar argues that the masochist's desire to return to the pre-Oedipal is paradoxical. The attempt to recreate a state of symbiosis with the mother requires the obliteration of the boundaries of the self. In this way, the desire for the pre-Oedipal is the desire for death.[15] As a result, the masochistic subject must ensure that consummation will always be deferred.[16] Furthermore, the enjoyment of pain can only be sustained if the love object is constantly positioned as unattainable. Pleasure is gained through the thwarting of the desire for symbiosis. Masochistic gratification is therefore dependent upon the separation of the subject and the object.[17] The necessity for complete differentiation is overlaid by the desire for fusion. This double movement is sustained by an erotic investment in suspension of consummation. Unlike sadism, which requires endlessly repeated acts of penetration and ultimately the negation of its object, masochism is said to sensualise waiting and disappointment.[18]

Studlar maintains that masochism has two strategies which ensure the constant suspension of consummation. First, desire is controlled by a dialectical interplay of presence/absence.[19] The mother is positioned as an elusive figure and the reversals of her appearance/disappearance serve both to evoke and evade desire. This scenario is taken from the pre-Oedipal *fort/da* game, in which the child replays the drama of maternal separation.[20] For Studlar, the masochist's re-enactment of the game illustrates both the desire for fusion and the enjoyment of loss.[21] The second means of prolonging desire is masochism's association with theatricality. In the original novels of Sacher-Masoch, masochism is presented as a contract between two consenting parties. Each agree to play their role in the fantasy.[22] Masochistic 'posturing' results in a displacement of the function of play. 'Masochism's emphasis on performance ... means that the fantasy is aesthetically savored purely for itself.'[23] The investment in theatricality for its own sake acts as a distancing device. It serves to avert the dangers of symbiosis by displacing the goal of masochistic desire and allowing pleasure to be gained from the 'aesthetics' of suffering.

Studlar contends that masochism is the desire to return to a 'prephallic, prelinguistic, pregenital stage of development'.[24] This construction of the pre-Oedipal is familiar, it constitutes a realm prior to the assimilation of difference. However, Studlar privileges the imaginary, reading it as a stage of polymorphous sexuality, which has the potential to undermine the dimorphism imposed by the Symbolic.[25] The radical power of the pre-Oedipal is said to lie in the bisexual nature of infantile sexuality. This is illustrated by the child's capacity for multiple cross-gendered identifications. Bisexuality, in the form of fantasised hermaphroditism, is postulated to be the aim of infantile desire: 'the human goal seems almost invariably to be *both* sexes'.[26] Studlar contends that the wish 'to cross the anatomical boundaries of gender identity may be interpreted as a primitive, literal representation of the wish to subvert the polarised gender-role stereotypes fostered by a patriarchal society'.[27]

The suggestion that the pre-Oedipal constitutes a realm in which gender identities can be transgressed relies on a tacit reworking of the moment of entry into the Symbolic. If the infant can be regarded as bisexual rather than polymorphously sensual, a process of sexual differentiation must have already taken place. This means that the imaginary no longer constitutes a realm beyond difference.[28] Studlar never addresses this issue. She simply pits the multiplicity and fluidity of the pre-Oedipal against the ossified dialectic of the Symbolic. Sexual difference, in terms of possession/lack, is dissolved by the infantile desire 'to be *both* sexes'.[29] This desire is also said to constitute the foundation of cinematic spectatorship. Film provides a fantasy that the spectator accesses via mobile, cross-gendered identifications, thus achieving temporary fulfilment of his/her repressed bisexuality.[30]

It is clear that Studlar takes up the concept of the pre-Oedipal in order to avoid promulgating binary structures. However, her use of the imaginary mother/child dyad as the basis for infantile bisexuality is problematic. While it is true that both sexes take the mother as primary love object, Studlar's reading is based on the experiences of the little boy. This can be seen in her definition of the masochistic ideal, i.e., symbiosis with the mother, as a state in which 'gender identity is transmutative and triumphantly bisexual'.[31] It is only the boy's union with the mother that exhibits cross-gendered identification. For the little girl, the pre-Oedipal is a homoerotic organisation, in which she both loves and desires to become the mother. Kaja Silverman has suggested that this form of the mother/daughter relation constitutes the basis for female/female identification in avant-garde cinema.[32] In Freud's analysis of the development of the girl, she becomes bisexual because the change of love object moves her from original homoeroticism to obligatory heterosexuality. As a consequence, the pre-Oedipal cannot be seen to provide both sexes with the latent bisexuality that is said to underpin cinematic spectatorship.

While Studlar attempts to move beyond binary structures, their hierarchical logic re-emerges in her accounts of the psychic mechanisms of masochism, which clearly take the male as standard. This flaw is evident in her analyses of fetishism and disavowal. Although she argues that both these psychic mechanisms come into play before the castration complex and cannot be associated with the presentation of woman as lack, they are still based on the boy's projections. The male child's fetishisation of the female takes the form of the fantasy of the phallic mother. This is read as a denial of sexual difference, which enables the boy to disavow his separation from the maternal figure.[33] The equation of knowledge of sexual difference and the splitting of the mother/child dyad is straightforwardly Lacanian. However, the form taken by that knowledge is no longer possession/non-possession of the phallus. The boy is said to desire bisexuality in order to be able to give birth.[34] As a result, the fantasy of the phallic mother is read as 'the male child's projection of his own wish for bisexuality'.[35]

Studlar can be seen to take up the boy's construction of the maternal figure as an 'idealized wholeness'[36], making it emblematic of the pre-Oedipal itself. The imaginary is seen as a symbiotic space allowing the constant fusion/confusion of gender identities. However, the figure of the phallic mother is a specifically male projection. The girl does not have to appropriate the ability to give birth. Furthermore, the disassociation of the moment of separation from the mother and the intrusion of the phallic third term means that the girl does not appear to have access to a construction of sexual difference. For the girl, the pre-Oedipal dyad is devoid of maleness. She may construct the mother's ability to give birth as a parthenogenetic capacity. There would be no need for her to project an image of fantasised hermaphroditism and indeed no means for her to create such a fetish. Studlar has to provide an account of an alternative process of sexual differentiation in order to explain how the girl might come to construct the pre-Oedipal as bisexual realm.

Ultimately, masochism can only constitute a means of escape from an identity that is gender specific. The masochist's rejection of the superego is an attempt to regain a state in which identity formation is fluid. He desires to abandon the rigid tripartite construction of id/ego/superego for a symbiotic relation in which the ego/ego ideal are intermingled.[37] However, the imaginary can only be constructed as an ideal realm by a subject whose boundaries of identity are firmly established within the Symbolic. This conception of subjectivity as complete differentiation is a masculine model. Within traditional psychoanalytic frameworks, women are constructed as lack, ensuring that they cannot access the Symbolic in a straightforward way. As a result, they are already said to have a privileged relation to the imaginary. Luce Irigaray argues that this means women suffer from 'déréliction', 'a state of fusion which does not succeed in emerging as a subject'.[38] Women do not have access to the state of complete individuation that is the basis of masochistic desire. Importantly, Studlar's account of masochism makes it clear that the attempt to bypass gender categories in favour of dispersed bisexuality simply serves to privilege masculinity once again. As Rosi Braidotti comments, '"multi-plicity" ... that does not take into account the fundamental asymmetry between the sexes is but a subtler form of discrimination.'[39]

I have argued that Studlar's analysis of masochism sets up the imaginary as a means of escaping masculinity. The male masochist's desire to return to the position of the powerless infant in the pre-Oedipal dyad is an obvious evasion of traditional construc-tions of masculinity as dominance. In this way, the desire for symbiosis is said to constitute a 'rejection of the father's sexuality'.[40] The masochist escapes the demands of the superego by taking the 'idealized wholeness' of the mother as his ego ideal. Stud-lar comments that patriarchal norms are reversed because 'the masochistic male defines himself in relation to the female.'[41] The assumption that the fetishistic construction of the phallic mother can be equated with the female is problematic. Moreover, the pres-entation of masochism as radical is obviously gendered. A woman who adopts a position of powerlessness before the pre-Oedipal mother is not greatly reconstructing patriarchal notions of femininity. The traditional features of passivity and submission will still be pre-sent despite the change of love object.

Studlar's argument that the masochistic aesthetic offers a radical reworking of gen-der roles actually rests on the figure of the pre-Oedipal mother. The construction of the maternal figure as both authoritative and nurturing is said to challenge the traditional equation of femininity and castration because the former presents a femininity that lacks nothing.[42] Importantly for Studlar, the figure of the pre-Oedipal mother operates as a symbol of idealised wholeness, which the boy wishes to imitate. As a result, the phallic mother may be seen to constitute the masochist's ideal ego. While Studlar claims that this reading is based on Deleuze,[43] it is here that she departs from her source material. In 'Coldness and Cruelty' the mother constitutes the means by which 'the ideal ego of parthenogenetic rebirth' is created, however, the ideal itself is said to be 'a new Man devoid of sexual love'.[44] Deleuze argues that the 'mother image' functions as a mirror through which the masochist realises the death of the superego and his concomitant rebirth as a desexualised subject: '[t]he narcissistic ego contemplates the ideal ego in the maternal mirror of death'.[45] By constructing the mother image as a mirror of death, Deleuze makes it clear that it is the masochistic subject who does the work of project-ing the ideal ego. Within the Deleuzian framework the mother image becomes the silvering on the back of the mirror, which enables the masochist to realise his own psy-chic progression. Studlar's attempt to rework the mother as the ideal ego can therefore be read as a repositioning of the figure as a perfect mirror image, which offers a glimpse of an idealised wholeness that the masochistic subject can never attain.

Importantly, Studlar's attempt to change the role played by the mother image does not alter the power structures that are apparent in the Deleuzian model. Taking the phal-lic mother as the ideal ego simply moves the maternal role from the depths to the surface of the mirror. The maternal function remains the same – she is vital to the masochistic subject's process of self-creation. Studlar assumes that the substitution of an all-power-ful maternal figure in place of the traditional image of the castrated woman would have the effect of undermining the binary opposition of subject/object. However, the perfect mirror image presented by the pre-Oedipal mother is ultimately said to be the product of the boy's fantasised bisexuality.[46] The maternal mirror can thus be seen as a screen, which gains delineation from the fantasies that are projected onto it. The mother's forms of mutilation or plenitude are the projections of the desires of the boy. As a result, the two different characterisations of the fetish can both be seen to rely on the same binary structure, the traditional division between the subject and the object of desire.

Studlar's tacit reliance on binary structures becomes overt when she outlines the relation between the pre-Oedipal and the cinematic apparatus. Studlar takes up Bertram Lewin's concept of the 'dream screen',[47] a blank surface onto which the sleeper projects dreams. The gendered power structure maintained by the division between the dreamer and the screen is absolutely clear. The screen is said to represent the maternal breast, the first site of falling asleep. The loss of ego boundaries in sleep enables the infant to ident-ify with images projected onto the breast/screen.[48] The infant/dreamer's experience of a 'primal state of visual unity'[49] is taken to be the psychic basis of identification between the spectator and the film image. In this way, the cinema and the dream screen are said to offer the temporary and partial fulfilment of the desire for symbiosis.[50] The pleasure of cinematic spectatorship clearly conforms to the doubled structure of masochism. The desire for fusion is gratified by identification with the film image. At the same time, the necessary separation is sustained by the distance between the viewer and the screen as well as the different physical status of the spectator and the cinematic illusion.[51]

The final chapter really highlights the key problem with Studlar's attempts to create a gender-free system. The psychoanalytic concepts that she takes up are imbued with the dialectical framework she wishes to dismantle. Indeed it can be argued that the very structure of masochistic desire requires a rigorous maintenance of the difference between subject and object. The masochistic subject has to invest in an endless defer-ral of consummation and thus requires an ever-elusive object of desire. This model of desire as yearning for symbiosis with the unattainable maternal object is fundamentally Lacanian. While Studlar argues that masochism inverts the traditional Lacanian model because the subject turns away from the Symbolic back to the imaginary, she does not alter the standard definitions of both realms. The attempt to treat the pre-Oedipal as the 'true' location of identity formation[52] does not constitute a radical reworking of the system because the characterisation of the phallic mother and her construction as the ultimate object of desire remain the same. Importantly, it is Studlar's strategy of refus-ing to address the ways in which the theories she takes up are already gendered that results in her continual promulgation of binary structures.

I have argued that Studlar's perpetuation of a Lacanian account of desire frames the figure of pre-Oedipal mother as object. However, the Deleuzian source material also contains the maternal figure in that he explicitly argues that the torturess/oral mother does not constitute an authoritative subject. She belongs 'to masochism, but without realizing it as a subject; she incarnates instead *the element* of "inflicting pain" in an exclusively masochistic situation.'[53] The masochist is said to seek out women whom he can educate to play the role of torturess.[54] While Sacher-Masoch's heroes seek women with a particular aptitude for this role, it is important that they cannot achieve it without instruction. The gulf between the female characters and their performance as the torturess, for example Wanda's reincarnation as the titular Venus in furs, charts their slow subsumption into the role that is proscribed by the masochist's fantasy.[55] Studlar's attempt to rework the pre-Oedipal mother as ego ideal does not alter the perimeters of the staging. However, the failure of her endeavours to reconstruct the maternal figure as a subject does draw attention to the ways in which Deleuze's theoretical model works to completely circumvent this possibility.

The theoretical models of masochism may be said to offer a specific crystallisation of the figure of the torturess/oral mother, defining her as a key element within the masochist's fantasy. However, it is possible to turn back to the work of Sacher-Masoch in order to look at the myths and images that accrue around the character of the torturess. The beginning of Severin's manuscript from *Venus in Furs* makes reference to the myth of Pygmalion and Galatea. In the Greek myth, Pygmalion is said to have been so disgusted by the wanton behaviour of the women in his town that he creates a statue of his perfect partner, 'an ivory maid',[56] a vision of beauty and innocence. He names the statue Galatea and having fallen in love with his work he wishes for a wife like her when he attends the festival of Venus. On returning home he kisses the statue and his wish is granted when she comes to life in his arms. In *Venus in Furs*, Severin falls in love with a statue of Venus: 'Often at night I pay a visit to my cold, cruel beloved; clasping her knees, I press my head against her cold pedestal and worship her.'[57] The contrast between Pygmalion's and Severin's ideals and the sentiments which accompany them is clear; the former desires a pure maiden, the latter worships the goddess of love. The masochistic staging of the myth also departs from the classical version in several ways. The transformation from statue to woman is incomplete: 'her hair still seems made of marble and her white dress gleams like moonlight – or is it satin?'[58] In this way the ideal woman retains the qualities of hardness and coldness which were worshipped in the marble figure. The other change is the description of Pygmalion's response. Instead of embracing the figure, Severin takes flight from his Venus, hearing her mocking laughter around him as he runs away.

Unlike the magical metamorphosis of Galatea, the transformation of Severin's Venus is revealed to be a joke. Severin mistakes Wanda for his statue come to life. However, Wanda is actually attempting to imitate a photograph that Severin had left in a book that he lent to her.[59] The photograph of Titian's portrait entitled 'Venus with the Mirror' adds further strands to the imagery associated with the torturess. The Venetian woman is said to gaze into the mirror, 'coldly inspecting her majestic charms'.[60] The description combines a sense of narcissistic self-absorption as well as an additional element of coldness and calculation. The furs in which Venus is enveloped are said to represent 'the tyranny and cruelty that are common to beautiful women'.[61] They are symbolic of a state of nature, which was said to have free rein in women because they were the less civilised sex.[62] The imagery that collects around the torturess works in two distinct and different directions. The restaging of the myth of Galatea emphasises role-play and imitation, indeed, Wanda congratulates herself on her own performance commenting, 'I have a certain talent for playing despotic roles....'[63] In contrast, Wanda's later comments to Severin present her take-up of the role of torturer as a return to a state of primitive nature: 'I am aware of dangerous forces lurking within me, ... You are awakening them, and it will do you no good.'[64]

The juxtaposition of the imagery of high culture and brute nature that surrounds the torturess does not appear in the theoretical models offered by Deleuze and Studlar. They focus on the high levels of performance in the masochistic scenario, ultimately positioning the male subject in control of the stage. Dijkstra's reading of *Venus in Furs* follows this model by drawing attention to Wanda's reluctance to become Severin's fantasy figure. However, he also addresses her presentation as nature, arguing that this enables Severin to express the anti-civilised aspects of his own character: 'Wanda is to be ... his own suppressed, bestial nature rising to the surface.'[65] This analysis of nature does not affect the binary structure of subject/object that is at stake in all the theoretical models. However, it should be noted that the exclusion of the imagery of nature or its inclusion purely as a motif of Severin's desires obliterates any way of ascertaining what anti-civilised desires Wanda might be expressing by taking up the role of torturess. All three theorists make it impossible to ask the question: 'Why does Wanda choose to become Venus in furs?'

The beginning of Severin's manuscript sets out Wanda's options, which conform to well-worn imaginary pathways. The choice is either Holbein's angel in the house, or Titian's Narcissa; Pygmalion's Galatea or Severin's Venus. Both sets of roles are clearly presented as male fantasy. However, the power to define a role is not synonymous with the power to delineate all the pleasures and privileges that might accrue from instantiating it. At stake here is the necessity of mapping the masochistic scenario from the side of the object of desire. This involves finding an answer to Irigaray's famous question '[b]ut what if the "object" started to speak?'[66] Wanda may be said to take up the role of the torturess because it enables her to express desires that cannot be acted out in the other roles offered to her. Importantly, these desires are not animal instincts but socio-historical constructions. Wanda presents 'the serene sensuality of the Greeks' as a 'natural' state, however, its construction as a primitive idyll relies on a modern dichotomy between the pagan and the Christian.[67] Wanda's idealisation of the Greeks' alleged freedom of sensual expression makes sense of her decision to take up the role of Venus and in so doing she also offers a critique of Christian matrimony and monogamy, becoming a truly dangerous force.

Ultimately, telling the story of the masochistic object of desire requires the use of Le Doeuff's methodology to focus on those aspects of the images that are not crystallised within the theoretical discourses. In this way, Wanda's mocking laughter at Severin's flight from his Venus is indicative of her appreciation of the humorous aspects of the masochistic scenario, showing her distance from it even while she is immersed within it. The marbled coiffure of the living Venus suggests a propensity for turning back into stone, a feature that might be used to deliberately evade unwanted embraces. Narcissa's cold inspection of her charms in the mirror suggests a distance from her own image that would enable her to control its effects. These elements of cool rationality constitute the most disruptive features of the torturess because they attest to her ability to manipulate the role to her own advantage. I will return to this during the film reading.

2 *The Scarlet Empress*

This section examines the ways in which Studlar's masochistic aesthetic frames her reading of *The Scarlet Empress*. I have chosen to focus on this particular film from the Sternberg/Dietrich cycle because the protagonist, Catherine the Great, is also a motif in *Venus in Furs*. Sacher-Masoch refers to her as one of the archetypal torturesses[68] and Wanda is compared to her when appearing in furs.[69] I will begin by addressing Studlar's analysis of signification within the masochistic aesthetic, focusing on her account of the role of spectacle. Studlar characterises masochistic texts as narratives of suspended desire whose dramatic intensity is constituted in moments of stasis and yearning: '[m]asochism's perverse pleasure extends into the spectacle of decorative and erotic excess that displaces conventional narrative "progress" with the lingering voluptuousness of masochistic suspense.'[70] While this analysis enables her to move beyond Mulvey's focus on linear narrative and the consequent denigration of spectacle, I will argue that Studlar's account of signification is ultimately compromised by her model of desire. I will then go on to address the way in which the gendered framework of the masochistic aesthetic stakes out a specific field of vision in order to draw attention to the elements that form the blind spots in Studlar's reading of *The Scarlet Empress*. This will draw attention to key elements of the film: such as the characterisation of the Empress and the presentation of Catherine II, which will then be mobilised to create a different theoretical reading.

The narrative of *The Scarlet Empress* unfolds in a series of tableaux. The pictorial composition of the many scenes in the Russian palace is overwhelming in its complexity. Andrew Sarris argues that this is the most visually sumptuous film of the Sternberg/Dietrich cycle.[71] The baroque, cluttered nature of the images explains the use of intertitles to convey aspects of the narrative.[72] For Studlar, the density of the images prevents the titles from acting as the text's latent meaning. The intertitles after Catherine has

given birth to an heir present her sudden transformation into a politically astute courtesan as a foregoing of her youthful ideals. However, Studlar argues that the logic of
the images tells a different story in that the motifs that convey Catherine's pursuit of
power are set up in the first sequence of the film.[73]

In this sequence the child Sophia is being examined by a doctor who recommends
that she be placed 'in harness' for about a year. The servants comment on his prescrip-
tion after he has left saying that the 'horse doctor' is also the court executioner. Sophia
then asks if she can become a hangman when she grows up. Her tutor begins to read
her some Russian history concerning Czars and Czarinas who were hangmen. The next
images are connected by a series of wipes from right to left like the turning leaves of a
book. The sequence depicts a variety of acts of sexual cruelty and torture. It ends with
a medium shot of a bell ringer who is pulling the bell rope frenziedly. The scene culminates in a long shot of a man who is tied up and suspended upside down functioning
as the clapper of a huge bell. This image dissolves into a high-angle long shot of the
adult Sophia on a swing in the garden surrounded by her friends. Studlar argues that
the visual motifs 'such as the motion of swinging, the bell, the tortures, the galloping
horses of the cossacks [sic], occur with increasing frequency and thematic intensity in
Sophia's adult life.'[74] She thus reads Catherine's pursuit of power as the realisation of
her infantile desire to become a hangman.[75]

Studlar's mode of reading makes use of motifs that are dispersed across the text in
order to construct the meaning of the film. She charts the way in which the original
'fusion of bell clapper/Sophia' is played out in different contexts.[76] The movement of the
incense burners in the wedding sequence mimics the movement of the swing. It is accompanied by the sound of bells. The bells ring out again to announce the birth of an heir
to the throne. At the end of the film Catherine becomes the 'repulsively enthusiastic bell
ringer/torturer' of the first sequence.[77] There is a medium shot of her pulling the bell
rope in a state of frenzied triumph. The peal of bells wakes Peter and acts as a signal to
his executioner who is one of Catherine's lovers. Through these textual associations the
bell rope which she pulls to announce Peter's death also constructs her as a hangman.

Studlar's readings make use of the non-linear organisation of Sternberg's films to
articulate a different model of textuality. Unlike Mulvey for whom linear narrative functions as *the* form of signification, Studlar focuses on the signifying capacity of visual
metaphors. A metaphor, such as the dissolve between the images of the bell clap-
per/Sophia, is said to function as 'a "screen memory", a fetish that suspends immediate
meaning, frustrates knowledge, and waits on the play of restatement and repetition.'[78]
This form of imagistic organisation is therefore said to create a 'density of delayed meaning'.[79] The linear temporality of the film is disavowed in order to sustain a synchronous

Dietrich as Catherine the Great wearing the high toque hat and fur-trimmed jacket typical
of the torturess. Publicity still for *The Scarlet Empress*

reading of the textual motifs.[80] Studlar parallels the process of waiting for a motif to be repeated with the masochistic dynamic of suspended desire.[81] She therefore argues that this model of signification belongs to the pre-Oedipal and suggests that it exhibits the logic of dreams.[82]

I find Studlar's method of reading to be an extremely useful way of approaching the Sternberg/Dietrich cycle. However, her analysis of metaphoric structuring as a form of signification which 'leads directly to and from the regressive infantile fantasy of masochism' is problematic.[83] She presents Sternberg's complex visual style as the result of unconscious primary processes of thinking. This prevents her from addressing social issues, such as film censorship, which had a material effect on the form of Sternberg's films. Studlar argues that *The Scarlet Empress* makes oblique references to the legend of Catherine's death in which she was said to have been crushed when the stallion with which she was attempting intercourse slipped from its harness over her bed.[84] Studlar traces the imagery of Catherine/bed/horse across the text: beginning with Sophia's being put into harness and ending with Catherine's triumphant ride up the palace stairs on her white stallion. 'The child tended by the horse doctor is transformed, by dream logic, into a woman whose bedroom adventures are so polymorphous as to include bestiality.'[85]

While I would agree that *The Scarlet Empress* sustains this reading, I would suggest that the use of 'dream logic' can be seen as a technique that enabled the film to evade censorship. Given that the previous Dietrich/Sternberg collaboration, *Blonde Venus*, had been subjected to three rewrites, any direct representation of Catherine's infamous sexual proclivities would have been out of the question.[86] Lea Jacobs' book, *The Wages of Sin: Censorship and the Fallen Woman Film 1928–42*, charts the censors' increasing intervention in the processes of production during the early 1930s.[87] She argues that censorship during this era can be seen as a 'constructive force' that shaped 'film form and narrative'.[88] Jacobs reads Sternberg's elliptical style as a mode of representation that grew out of the conditions of studio production.[89]

I would argue that Jacobs' analysis is important because she constructs Sternberg's visual style as a different form of signification rather than a form of regression. If the oblique imagery of the cycle is viewed as the result of studio production, then these films can be seen to negotiate ways of signifying differently. At stake here is the possibility of thinking about different symbolic systems. Studlar does generate an awareness of the signifying potential of the cycle's imagistic organisation. However, her insistence that these organisational structures constitute primary processes considerably affects the political potential of her project. The cycle becomes a way of escaping symbolic structures, thus consolidating their status by presenting them as the only form of socio-cultural organisation.[90]

The difference between the theorists can be seen in their respective analyses of Sternberg's style. For Jacobs, the opaque images of the cycle construct the possibility of representing forms of female eroticism which had been banned by the censor.[91]

Studlar reads the diffuse nature of the images as the result of masochistic 'supersensu-alism'. Eroticism is said to be played out across different textual elements, such as the *mise en scène*, because of the impossibility of consummating masochistic desire. As a result, textual density becomes the expression of one form of infantile libidinal organis-ation. While Studlar does occasionally comment on the political implications of the representation of woman in these texts, she can only do so by departing from her theor-etical system.[92] The cycle is seen to offer the opportunity of escaping into the pre-Oedipal: '[t]hese films do not pay homage to nature or political agendas but to fan-tasy, to desire, and to the magical thinking of primary process.'[93]

Ultimately, Studlar's framework reduces the play of imagistic processes of significa-tion to the endless recycling of the masochistic fantasy. This reduction can be seen in her definition of visual metaphor as a mode of textual organisation which delays mean-ing in the same way as the masochist defers the consummation of desire.[94] The definition has the effect of equating the function of imagistic organisation with the role of the figure of woman in the masochistic fantasy. The structure of metaphor is the same as the role of woman in that both are ambivalent, elusive and unattainable.[95] However, the meaning of the visual image is ultimately contained within the structure of the male masochist's desires.

For Studlar, the films of the Sternberg/Dietrich cycle replay the infantile fantasy of masochism. Dietrich is set up in the role of torturess. Male protagonists such as La Bessière, Don Pasquale and Alexei play the role of the masochist.[96] Studlar reads the first two characters as representatives of Sternberg himself.[97] The films are therefore said to play out the fantasies of their director, constructing Dietrich as Sternberg's creation.[98] In this way, Studlar frames the Sternberg/Dietrich cycle within the terms provided by the classical Galatea myth: male creator and female art object. She also takes up a key fea-ture from Sacher-Masoch's version. The end of *The Scarlet Empress* is said to celebrate Catherine's transformation into the torturess, which is constructed as a metamorphosis into stone:

> Carried on the shoulders of the army she has seduced, dressed in the pure white
> uniform of a Cossack officer, she takes the throne to become the cold, ambivalent
> mother figure in the logical conclusion to the masochistic tale. Elevated to the position
> of relative good in a corrupt system, Catherine becomes a woman of stone.[99]

In *Venus in Furs*, the cold torturess is said to retain features of the marble from which she is first formed. Studlar expands on this, arguing that the masochistic contract requires the torturess to be a statue.[100] However, the transformation into stone is pre-sented as a reflection of the desires of the male masochist. Studlar does not address the ways in which the capacity to change back into stone might be utilised by the torturess for her own ends, an issue that I will address later in this chapter.

Studlar reads *The Scarlet Empress* as a 'masochistic tale'. She argues that the narrative follows the pattern of Sacher-Masoch's novels in which a woman is educated into the role of torturess by the masochistic hero.[101] Studlar draws a parallel between Wanda's education in *Venus in Furs*, and Catherine's transformation. She argues that 'Catherine's assumption of power and her desire for revenge are the result of her manipulation by, then of, a [patriarchal] system personified by Alexei.'[102] This analysis of the film clearly positions Alexei's role as pivotal. In Studlar's reading 'Count Alexei, Master of the Hunt … is quickly transformed into a figure of masochistic suffering.'[103] She argues that he is first forced into the role of impotent onlooker during Catherine's wedding.[104] His later meeting with Catherine on the stairs is preceded by a medium shot of him standing by a statue of the martyred Saint Sebastian. For Studlar, this juxtaposition consolidates Alexei's construction as the masochistic hero. Like the saint, he has become 'the willing victim in a pact of suffering'.[105] 'In pursuing Catherine, Alexei is martyred to love. His desire intensifies as Catherine pursues others.'[106]

I want to analyse the wedding sequence in detail. While I agree that Alexei comes to be presented as powerless, I will demonstrate that this is a consequence of his relation to the Empress rather than to Catherine. Studlar contends that Alexei is presented as

Catherine's final transformation into the torturess. Still from *The Scarlet Empress*

'the helpless child-lover' during this sequence.[107] She parallels his role as the spectator of Catherine's marriage to Peter with the child's position as an impotent viewer of the primal scene. This analysis of the sequence is presented as a challenge to Mulvey's work.[108] Studlar maintains that Alexei's 'impassive stare' at Catherine cannot be constructed as a 'controlling male gaze'.[109] His look is said to coincide with a decline in his control over Catherine's future and therefore cannot be read as a celebration of his power. I will argue that the close-ups of Alexei suggest a different reading of the film's narrative.

The first shot of the wedding sequence is a long shot across the sumptuously decorated cathedral. The Empress enters from behind a screen and climbs the stairs into the pulpit. The camera is positioned on a crane approximately level with the pulpit. It pans right slightly and then moves down and across the cathedral, giving a high-angle long shot of the crowd of white-robed, orthodox priests who are chanting the ceremonial music. The angle emphasises the Empress's height above the crowd and therefore suggests her control over the spectacle. There is a cut to a medium shot of Alexei, which is followed by a long shot of a side row of the aisle. The camera pans left as Catherine and Peter complete their procession to the altar, their progress obscured by a square canopy of veiling, its top edges decorated with swathes of netting, dark tassels and loops of cord. The couple process to the end of the canopy and kneel in front of the altar between the veils, which are fastened like two curtains on either side of them. The immersion of Catherine and Peter within the decoration of the *mise en scène* clearly constructs them as spectacle.

There is a series of close-up shots during the marriage ceremony. The close-up of Peter as he receives the bread from the priest shows him grinning inanely, while jerkily turning his head from side to side as if to take everything in, his mechanical movement contrasting with Catherine's stasis. The next shot is a close-up of Catherine, her eyes are downcast and the glowing flame of the candle that she is holding adds radiance to her veiled face. This is followed by a close-up of Alexei, whose dark hair and black, fur-trimmed coat are visible, his eyes in shadow as he gazes at her impassively. The juxtaposition of the two shots sets up a contrast between Catherine's radiance and innocence and Alexei's political/sexual experience, a standard use of the gendered imagery of light and dark.[110] Narratively, Alexei's duplicity has been instrumental in bringing about the wedding ceremony. Unlike Studlar, I would suggest that this first juxtaposition presents Alexei as a figure of power. Moreover, as he is viewing the spectacle and Catherine's eyes are downcast, the two close-ups would seem to conform to Mulvey's gendered division between the male subject of the gaze and the female object.

The editing moves rapidly between tighter close-up shots of Catherine and Alexei, presenting an extreme close-up of Catherine's face from her forehead to her mouth. In this shot her veil seems to gild her face, its fine texture is just visible across the bridge of her nose. She looks up and left towards Alexei, and then upwards towards the ceiling

and casts her eyes down again as if appealing for help – even for divine intervention. The candle flame gutters, as she breathes increasingly heavily, suggesting a state of frozen panic. There is a cut to a close-up of Alexei gazing back at her impassively, followed by another close-up of Catherine's face and jewelled headdress. Her eye movements become more rapid and she moves her head slightly while glancing about, suggesting her growing awareness of her entrapment within the ceremony. The film cuts back to a close-up of Alexei, his eyes in shadow as he looks down. The sudden change in his expression suggests both sorrow and regret, undermining the previous suggestion of his power over Catherine. He looks up again and there is a cut to a long shot of the Empress in her pulpit, her positioning in the top right corner of the screen emphasising her control over the spectacle. The editing clearly suggests that she also controls Alexei.

The concluding shot of the ceremony is a close-up of Peter's and Catherine's hands as the priest exchanges their rings, tying a chiffon handkerchief around their hands in a visual representation of the bonds of matrimony. There is a cut back to the high-angle long shot used at the beginning of the sequence. The camera retraces part of its initial movement in reverse, moving back to the long shot of the Empress, which dissolves into a close-up of the Empress's head and shoulders. This is the last shot of the sequence which began with her appearance, a repetition that clearly indicates her control over events. The final close-up of her satisfied, smiling face is taken from a low angle, consolidating her status as the director of the ceremony.

I have chosen to discuss this sequence in detail because it foregrounds the limitations of the field of vision constructed by the masochistic aesthetic. By reading *The Scarlet Empress* as a re/play of Sacher-Masoch's *Venus in Furs*, Studlar constructs the film as a two-hander. The narrative is said to follow Alexei's transformation of Catherine into the figure of the torturess. As a result, the analysis of the wedding sequence focuses exclusively on the exchange between Alexei and Catherine and omits the figure of the Empress. This omission is strange given the Empress's structural importance within the sequence. However, I would argue that this exclusion is necessary in order for Studlar to sustain the presentation of Alexei as the pivotal figure in Catherine's transformation. Within the narrative it is the Empress herself who takes on the role of educator, saying that she will show Catherine how to be an obedient Russian wife. Her lessons in obedience, such as making Catherine wait on other servants, form an ironic contrast with her own role as a sexual/political *intriguante*. The scene in which she sends Catherine down to send in Alexei is reversed later in the film when Catherine sends him down to let in her lover. For Studlar, this reversal shows that 'Catherine has been educated by Alexei's betrayal and the cruelties of the system.'[111] However, it seems clear that Catherine has taken up the Empress's methods as well as moving into her bedroom. Studlar

The Empress in control of the proceedings. Still from *The Scarlet Empress*

cannot explore the mirroring relation between the female characters because it constitutes a blind spot within the heterosexual frame set up by the masochistic aesthetic.

Studlar suggests that the wedding sets up a number of motifs that are played out
across the text of *The Scarlet Empress*.[112] I want to explore the way in which the veils
that are presented during this sequence take on different connotations as the film progresses. The canopy over the aisle reappears in the sequence in which Catherine is
presented with a jewelled necklace as a reward for producing an heir. The chiffon handkerchief which binds the couple's hands at the end of the ceremony forms one of
Catherine's accoutrements in her later pursuit of political power. I will also address Mary-
Ann Doane's analysis of the function of veiling in the film in which she argues that the
veil presents Catherine as an enigma, ultimately constructing her as an unattainable
object of desire.[113] In contrast, I will examine the motif of the veil in order to demonstrate the ways in which it is used to suggest Catherine's mobilisation of her
objectification for her own ends.

The sequence in which Catherine is presented with her reward is very short. It begins
with a long shot of a huge, sumptuously decorated door, which is opened by the maid.
An emissary enters, wanting to see Catherine, and the camera pans right as he crosses
the bedroom, providing a long shot of her lying in bed. The marital bed was previously
seen in a ceremonial blessing; however, it has now been transformed into a four-poster
by the addition of a canopy of veils. The familiar patterning of the elaborate frame and
the dark tassels, hanging from the top, indicate that this is the wedding canopy. The
camera continues to pan right positioning the bed as the centre of light in the dark
room. There is a cut to a medium shot of the ladies-in-waiting clustered at the door, followed by a long shot taken through the veiling at the end of the bed in which the
emissary presents Catherine with the necklace. The statue of the Madonna and child at
the bedhead fills the righthand side of the screen during the presentation. It represents
Catherine's role as mother, given that she is never actually shown with her child during
the film. The emissary then withdraws.

The next image is a medium shot of Catherine taken from the lefthand side of the
bed. She is filmed through the veil, holding up the jewelled necklace so that it twists,
catching the light. There is a cut to a close-up of Catherine as she drops the necklace
and turns her head away from the camera. The grain of the netting forms a dark grid
across the screen, obscuring her face. The close-up dissolves into a pattern of ringing
bells, their sound recalling those at the beginning of the sequence, which announced
the birth of an heir to the throne. The bells dissolve into a crowd of people running and
cheering in celebration. This image dissolves back into the close-up of Catherine, who
turns back towards the camera, and the sequence fades to black.

Mary-Ann Doane and Studlar offer two opposing readings of this particular sequence.
For Doane, the close-up of the veil covering Catherine's face serves to heighten her presentation as erotic spectacle:

As the camera increases its proximity to the veil, the veil and the screen it becomes
seem to become the objects of desire. The veil mimics the grain of the film, the material
substrate of the medium, and becomes the screen as surface of division, separation,
and hence solicited transgression.... The woman is revealed as no longer simply the
privileged object of the gaze in the cinema but the support of the cinematic image. Yet
... the foregrounding of the grain, the positioning of the woman as screen – all of this
merely heightens the eroticism, makes her more desirable ...[114]

The veil is said to provide the separation between subject and object that is essential to
the Lacanian account of desire. Veiling Catherine simply enables her to function as the
unattainable object. Doane suggests that any attempt to construct Catherine/Dietrich as
a subject would involve imagining 'what Dietrich's return look might be, from behind
the veil'.[115] In contrast, Studlar reads the separation and distance provided by the veil
as a means of frustrating the gaze, which prevents Dietrich from functioning as an
object: '[t]he camera cannot penetrate the gauze mask.'[116] The veil functions as a mode
of concealment, which covers over Catherine's infantile motives for pursuing political
power.[117] She reads the dissolve into the ringing bells as a reminder of the visual
metaphor of bellringer/hangman set up in the film's first childhood sequence.[118]

I want to argue that any reading of the veil in the reward sequence needs to be constructed in relation to the way in which veiling is presented during the wedding
ceremony. In my analysis of the wedding, I suggested that the long shot of the canopy
of veils over the aisle functioned to construct the couple as part of the spectacle. Catherine is doubly veiled both by the canopy and her bridal costume. The extreme close-ups
of Catherine during the wedding ceremony show her bridal veil shimmering slightly as
she breathes, gilding her face. Her short, rapid breaths and eye movement suggest a
state of frozen panic. The transparency of the veil serves to display her expression while
acting as a symbol of her entrapment. Doubly veiled, Catherine is twice trapped: both
within the spectacle of the Empress's ceremony and as its spectacularised erotic object.

The long shot of the canopy at the wedding can be compared with the two long shots
of Catherine's bed. They all present the canopy as virtually transparent, the veils serving
to soften the view of the bride and groom and the statues at the bedhead. The medium
shot of Catherine in her bed is taken from the side, her face turned towards the camera, she stares impassively at the necklace as it twists in the light. Studlar comments that
Catherine's thoughts are difficult to assess.[119] However, the contrast between her wild
eye movements at the wedding and this impassive, steady gaze suggests an increase in
her power. This is consistent with her transition from innocent virgin to mother. In the
following close-up the veil becomes a dark grid covering over her face. At one level this
suggests entrapment, having given birth to an heir Catherine is now firmly ensconced
within the Russian court. However, in contrast to the bridal veil, which displayed her
frightened expression, this veil conceals her quiet stillness.

Catherine drops the necklace, which the emissary had presented to her as a sign of the Empress's satisfaction at the production of an heir. This gesture can therefore be read as a rejection of the Empress and the role of royal 'brood mare' that the Empress had forced her to play. It is also a fitting response, as Catherine has not produced a legitimate heir but a bastard. Catherine then turns her face away from the camera, the movement heightening the way in which the grid-like veil functions as a mode of concealment. The very canopy that had served to present her bridal procession as spectacle becomes the means by which she evades the gaze. Catherine's movements – dropping the necklace and turning away – are important because they suggest a refusal to function as the object of the Empress's spectacle. For Doane, it would be necessary for Dietrich/Catherine to return the look in order for her to cease to function as an object. However, this suggests that the only way to escape objectification is to assume the role of subject and the associated power of the gaze.[120] A close reading of the sequence shows that the use of the veil to evade the gaze coupled with the gesture of turning away represent Catherine's refusal of her previous role as object.

This short sequence forms a pivotal point. Catherine goes on to present herself as spectacle in order to gain political power. It is as if the refusal of the role of object gives her the power necessary to mobilise the terms of her own objectification. Rather than operating as the spectacular object of someone else's show, she is now in control of staging herself. This reversal is represented by the veil motif. At the end of the marriage ceremony, Catherine's and Peter's hands were bound together by the tying of a chiffon handkerchief. In her appearance directly after she has received the Empress's gift, Catherine is costumed in a white, hooped dress with extravagant feather trimmings and carries a plain chiffon handkerchief. She meets a priest who informs her that the Empress is dying and offers her the political support of the Church. Catherine refuses his aid saying that she has 'weapons that are far more powerful than any political machine', while lifting her chiffon handkerchief up to her face, covering her nose and mouth, and raising her eyes suggestively above the veil. The blatant gesture clearly indicates the nature of her weaponry and her new-found use of innuendo shows her awareness and control of her own sexuality. Importantly, her comments present her sexual gesture as a knowing performance that is adopted to gain specific political ends.

Catherine then encounters Peter who is exercising his Hessian troops indoors. There is an establishing shot of his troops marching around the room, encircling Catherine and her ladies-in-waiting. Catherine is the centre of the light, her white dress contrasting with the soldiers' dark uniforms. The film cuts to a medium close-up of her as she sits impassively, watching the soldiers, and then to a medium shot of Peter. This is followed by a re-establishing shot in which the soldiers point their bayonets at the ladies-in-waiting who run off, leaving Catherine alone in a circle of glinting blades. The

Catherine's lavish feather-trimmed costume. Publicity still for *The Scarlet Empress*

next two medium close-ups of Catherine show the end of Peter's sword pointed at her heart. The point plays with the feather trim of her dress as he congratulates her on providing an 'unexpected addition to the family'. She thanks him calmly and pushes her chiffon handkerchief over the end of his sword. There is a cut to a medium shot of Peter as he pulls the sword away, the handkerchief waving at its tip, and commands his troops to leave.

Throughout this scene, Catherine is presented as calm and confident, unlike her frightened ladies-in-waiting. Peter's oblique reference to her infidelity is met with smiling thanks. Catherine's Freudian use of her chiffon handkerchief is an ironic reference to Peter's refusal to consummate their marriage. Once it is caught at the sword tip, the veil becomes the lady's favour. It has been presented to the husband who has not enjoyed her favours, thus concealing her infidelity. The ironic nature of this particular play with the veil constructs it as an emblem of Catherine's duplicity. Her gesture reverses the very trope that indicated the sacred bonds of matrimony. The reversal connects her new-found power to stage herself to her ability to dissemble.

The next presentation of the veil motif builds on its construction as an emblem of duplicity and sexual power. An intertitle shows a proclamation ordering the people to pray for the Empress. There is a long shot of the people kneeling followed by a tracking shot of religious icons being carried through a church. The dark, sombre images correspond with the slow, dirge-like background music. The sequence of the Empress's death is cross cut with another sequence in which Catherine is presented with a white handkerchief tied across her eyes, playing blind man's buff in the palace gardens. There is a dissolve from the dark church to an aerial shot of the garden, linking the events in time. The garden is a space of frivolity and light. The rapid tempo of the background music emphasises the whirling movements of the players. The camera moves across and down culminating in a high-angle medium shot of Catherine as she tries to catch someone. The cross-cutting sets up contrasts between darkness/light and death/life. The game players appear unconcerned about the fate of the Empress.

There is a cut to a long shot of the priests praying inside the church, which is juxtaposed with a medium shot of Catherine who has been successful in catching a Hussar officer. As she hugs him, another officer presses close behind her, positioned between them she raises her hands to pat both of their faces, before pushing up the lacy blindfold and glancing knowingly from one to the other. The game reveals Catherine's liaisons within the Court. However, its careless frivolity is undermined by the knowing nature of her glance. Her look suggests that the officers were not caught at random and that therefore her liaisons are also the products of deliberation. The cross-cutting between the sequences continues. There is a long shot of a priest pulling the bellrope in the church tower in order to announce the Empress's death. This is followed by a high-angle long shot of the garden in which the officers disperse leaving the ladies alone on hearing the sound of the bell.

The film cross cuts between a medium shot of the bell ringer and a high-angle medium shot of Catherine. She removes the blindfold and looks up, then glances downwards as she twists the white, lacy handkerchief in her fingers. This momentary gesture betrays her perturbation at the Empress's death. In the previous scene, Peter told Catherine of his plans to replace her with the Countess Elizabeth. Catherine quickly shakes the handkerchief, smoothing it out, changing her expression to a slight smile as she looks up. These movements use the veil to disguise her agitation. The smile displays her apparent lack of concern, like the game of blind man's buff. However, the angle of her chin and the set nature of her expression also convey determination, suggesting that her smiles and games have a serious purpose. She will later make use of her lovers in order to control the army.

The image of Catherine is superimposed over the image of a large ringing bell. The first image eventually dissolves into the second. This link between Catherine and the bell is a reversal of the first dissolve from the bell-clapper to Sophia on the swing. In the first sequence, the movement of the clapper became Sophia's swinging movement, suggesting that her future was controlled by others. In this later sequence, the movement of the bell contrasts with Catherine's stasis, showing an increase in her power. She glances down twice but her head remains in the same position. This eye movement is important because Catherine cannot afford to display her pursuit of power. She must operate in a covert fashion using the veil to display her charms and cover her motives. I want to end by looking at the function of the veil in the scene in which Catherine rejects Alexei.

The exchanges between Catherine and Alexei in this scene present them both as duplicitous. Alexei enters Catherine's new bedchamber. There is a medium shot of Catherine standing in front of her white, veiled bed wearing a black, hooped dress, which has a luxurious feather trim across the shoulders and hips. Alexei is positioned in the foreground, forming a dark shadow on the right of the frame. He thanks Catherine for the privilege of being allowed to see her. She dryly replies that she believes he'd 'had that privilege before' and Alexei responds saying that his visits to the Empress were in a purely advisory capacity. There is a cut to Catherine's face as she asks him to send the courtiers waiting outside the room away. The marked contrast between the suggestive drawl in which she delivers this request and the clipped intonation of her previous statement implies that her seductiveness is assumed. The mask of seduction can be seen as a response to Alexei's lie, giving their exchange the form of bluff and counterbluff and thus emphasising the way in which they are both playing roles.

On Alexei's return there is a long shot of Catherine striding up and down the centre of the bedroom. The hooped skirt of her dress is made of diaphanous black material, which veils a darker, slim fitted underskirt. Her movement causes the loose-fitting feather trim to fall from her right shoulder revealing her back. In her next appearance in a two-shot with Alexei she lifts her right arm out of the encircling feathers so that they fall from one shoulder. The dress clearly displays Catherine's body and is quite remarkable for its ability to fall off without ever falling down! The tactile surfaces of the feathers and the veils are clearly seductive. However, the patterning of the feather trim combines short, thick, dark plumage with fine white plumes, which stand slightly proud of the dark background, resembling a sprinkling of snowflakes across dark fur. This combination of seduction and coldness is used in many of Sacher-Masoch's descriptions of the torturess.

Alexei's presentation during the scene becomes increasingly sinister. This begins with the very first shot in which he forms a dark shadow on the righthand side of the screen. Catherine moves out of the two-shot and there is a cut to a medium shot of her lying on the bed flicking the veil with her hands so that its patterned folds move across her smiling face. This is followed by a medium shot in which Alexei's head is positioned in front of a statue of the devil, making the horns on the statue appear to come out of his head. He moves off screen, providing a clear view of the statue's face. This image dissolves into a medium shot of Alexei taken through the veiling of the bed. Studlar argues that this odd use of a dissolve links the scene with the first encounter in the Empress's bedroom where Catherine found out Alexei was the Empress's lover.[121] Catherine's earlier moment of recognition was presented by a close-up of the shadow on the secret door, which dissolved into a close-up of her face and shoulders. On that occasion, she

Two-shot of Catherine and Alexei with the devil head statue in the background. Still from *The Scarlet Empress*

closed her eyes in an anguished refusal to believe what she already knew. For Studlar, the repetition suspends the narrative's temporal progress creating the frozen, static quality of the masochistic aesthetic.[122] However, I want to argue that both dissolves represent Catherine's thought processes. The second dissolve between the devil's head and the medium shot of Alexei shows Catherine's opinion of him. The medium shot is taken through the veil, which clearly suggests that it represents her gaze. These images conflict with Alexei's protestations of loyalty and devotion. The mode of presentation, the dissolve, suggests a continuity between Catherine's recognition of Alexei's affair and her later construction of him as demonic.

During this scene the visual emphasis on the darkness of Alexei's hair and clothing echoes his presentation in the wedding sequence. While Catherine no longer behaves like an innocent victim, the dissolve suggests she has not forgotten or forgiven him for his duplicity. There is a close-up of Catherine following the dissolve. She moves the white veil of the bed behind her, looking seductively at Alexei over the feathered trim on her left shoulder, before pulling the veil back over her face. These gestures give her seductive look a theatrical quality – positioning it between the opening and closing of stage curtains. There is a cut to a medium shot of Alexei taken through the veil and the camera moves down with him as he bends over the bed to kiss Catherine. The veiling screens them from the camera until Catherine's fist pulls it away, revealing their embrace. She then sits up, pushing Alexei away, the movement taking both of them off screen. Her hand reaches back to return the veil to its former position. Catherine's play with the veil has the effect of staging the embrace for the camera. The motion that reveals the embrace turns into the movement that pushes Alexei away, making the veil a means by which she both entices him and keeps him at a distance.

The scene continues and Catherine gets Alexei to blow out the candles as she had done for the Empress. The next shot of Catherine alone is a medium shot of her lying back on the bed with her knees raised covering herself with the veil. Doane argues that this scene:

> traces a movement from a moment where the woman controls the veil, moves in and out of its folds in order to lure the male, to a tableau where her very stillness mimics her death in representation, her image entirely subsumed by the veil.[123]

In contrast, I want to argue that the last two close-ups of Catherine in this scene serve to consolidate her power. This involves comparing the way in which veiling is used in this scene with the other presentations of the veil within the text of *The Scarlet Empress*. Catherine's stillness suggests her transformation into stone and thus presents another reworking of the masochistic version of the Galatea myth.

The first close-up shows Catherine's head and shoulders fringed with the black and white feathers as she flicks the veil with her hand. Her tone is impassive as she instructs

Alexei to let in her visitor. The first couple of phrases are a direct repetition of the instructions that the Empress had given her. This shows Catherine's assumption of the Empress's methods of controlling people and highlights her key role as educator. Catherine delivers the speech without looking at Alexei, smiling slightly as she gazes steadily ahead. The close-up forms a sharp contrast with the close-ups during the wedding sequence in which her eye movement betrayed her perturbation and signalled an appeal for aid, which Alexei had to ignore. In both of these last close-ups her unwavering gaze indicates that she can ignore Alexei because she no longer needs his help. Unlike Doane, I read Catherine's increasing impassivity and stillness as emblematic of her increasing power. Her lack of movement also suggests that it is the moment at which she fully assumes the tactics of Empress in that she becomes a woman of stone.

My reading of Catherine's metamorphosis into stone differs from Studlar's in two ways. For Studlar, the point of transformation is Catherine's final appearance in a white Cossack uniform.[124] Moreover, she argues that the metamorphosis of the torturess simply reflects the desires of the masochistic subject. In contrast, I am arguing that Catherine's transformation occurs earlier and that the rejection scene shows her becoming stone in order to thwart Alexei's desires and ambitions. He is clearly seeking to have the same status that he enjoyed with her predecessor and she utilises the Empress's tactics in order to refuse him. Thus her construction as stone does not reflect Alexei's desires but rather constitutes an expression of her own reservations about his character, presented by the dissolve, and her political decision to exclude him from her power base. Importantly, *The Scarlet Empress* reworks the imagery from Sacher-Masoch's version of the Galatea myth, providing an example of the way in which the torturess might utilise the capacity to turn into stone for her own ends.

My reading of *The Scarlet Empress* utilises textual detail, specifically the focus on the veil motif, in order to trace patterns of reversals that cannot be seen through the binary frame of the masochistic aesthetic. The last close-up of the rejection scene shows Catherine's face as she continues to play with the veil. Unlike the close-up of the canopy in the reward sequence, which formed a dark grid across the screen, this veil traces delicate patterns of light across her face. The lace patterning resembles the curves of flower petals and creates a cocoon of light, which clearly serves to display her. However, the foregrounding of the pattern means that Catherine is less visible than she was in the close-ups of her bridal veil. The opaque nature of the lace therefore both displays and conceals her, acting as a visual representation of her manipulation of her own staging in order to gain power. I have argued that Catherine's rise to power makes use of the doubleness of the veil. It becomes a favour that was never bestowed, a blindfold that blinds others as to the nature of her moods and motives. In this final scene, the veil is used to stage a dissimulation of seduction itself. The kiss is not a prelude to intimacy but a final baffling of Alexei's ambitions. The veil that begins as a lure becomes a cocoon of light, which encloses Catherine's still, marble face.

I have argued that *The Scarlet Empress* generates imagery that has the potential to disrupt the theoretical frameworks set up by Deleuze, Studlar and Dijkstra. All three provide an account of the torturess as the object within the masochistic scenario. Their analyses eliminate the disruptive aspects of the imagery associated with the torturess, specifically the emphasis on distance and cool rationality, which suggest her power to manipulate the role to her own advantage. In contrast, *The Scarlet Empress* retains the disruptive aspects of the imagery in that Catherine's ability to control and exploit her own staging enables her to gain power. Moreover, the film gives the torturess a distinct motive for taking up the role, providing a way of mapping her desires and aims. The filmic imagery opens up the possibility of different crystallisations into theory, setting up a new kind of subject, one who attains subjectivity through the mobilisation of its own objectification. This does not deconstruct binary structures but opens them up to further and more complicated permutations. The object who becomes a subject does not occupy the same position or follow the same route as the subject who is defined in opposition to the object. In turn, this suggests that the male masochist's decision to abandon his status as subject should be mapped as a desire to become a new kind of object. Importantly, utilising Le Doeuff's methodology enables an appreciation of the ways in which the filmic imagery provides the means to challenge and change the established theoretical models.

Notes

1. G. Studlar, *In the Realm of Pleasure: Von Sternberg, Dietrich and the Masochistic Aesthetic* (Urbana and Chicago: University of Illinois Press, 1988), p. 32.
2. Ibid., pp. 2–3.
3. Josef von Sternberg, Paramount, 1934.
4. G. Deleuze, 'Coldness and Cruelty', in *Masochism*, J. McNeil (trans.) (New York: Zone Books, 1991).
5. Ibid., pp. 37–45.
6. Ibid., p. 45.
7. Ibid., p. 63.
8. Ibid., p. 102. This is the only quotation from 'Coldness and Cruelty' that might support Studlar's reading: '[t]he law has become essentially maternal, leading to those regions of the unconscious where the three images of the mother hold supreme sway.' Deleuze makes *no* direct reference to the imaginary or to the concept of symbiosis.
9. Studlar, *In the Realm of Pleasure*, p. 15.
10. Ibid., p. 17.
11. Ibid., p. 18.
12. Ibid., p. 17.
13. Ibid., p. 15.

14. Ibid., p. 15, quoting Deleuze, 'Coldness and Cruelty', p. 59.
15. Studlar, *In the Realm of Pleasure*, p. 26. Studlar's analysis of the desire for death is similar to Kristeva's. However, for Deleuze, masochism constitutes a form of the 'Death Instinct' because it is based on disavowal. The refusal to acknowledge the mother's castration enables the masochist to construct an ideal 'world of dreams'. Deleuze, 'Coldness and Cruelty', pp. 32, 35.
16. Studlar, *In the Realm of Pleasure*, p. 27.
17. Ibid.
18. Ibid., pp. 20, 21, 27.
19. Ibid., p. 108.
20. S. Freud, 'Beyond the Pleasure Principle', *On Metapsychology and the Theory of Psychoanalysis* (London: Penguin, 1991), pp. 283–7.
21. Studlar, *In the Realm of Pleasure*, p. 126.
22. Ibid., p. 22.
23. Ibid., p. 25.
24. Ibid., p. 29.
25. Ibid., p. 32.
26. Ibid., p. 33. Quoting L. Kubie, 'The Drive to Become Both Sexes', in H. J. Schlesinger (ed.), *Symbols and Neurosis: Selected Papers of L. S. Kubie* (New York: International Universities Press, 1978), pp. 195, 202.
27. Studlar, *In the Realm of Pleasure*, p. 35.
28. Other theorists such as Lou Andreas-Salomé and Luce Irigaray have tried to re/construct the imaginary as a differentiated space.
29. Studlar, *In the Realm of Pleasure*, p. 33. Quoting Kubie, 'The Drive to Become Both Sexes', pp. 195, 202.
30. Studlar, *In the Realm of Pleasure*, pp. 34–5.
31. Ibid., p. 32.
32. K. Silverman, *The Acoustic Mirror: The Female Voice in Psychoanalysis and Cinema*, (Bloomington and Indianapolis: Indiana University Press, 1988), pp. 120–5.
33. Studlar, *In the Realm of Pleasure*, p. 41.
34. Ibid., p. 41.
35. Ibid., p. 42.
36. Ibid., p. 43.
37. Ibid., p. 17.
38. M. Whitford, 'Rereading Irigaray', in T. Brennan (ed.), *Between Feminism and Psychoanalysis* (London: Routledge, 1989), p. 112. The quote is her translation of Luce Irigaray, *Ethique de la Différence Sexuelle* (Paris: Editions de Minuit, 1984), p. 70.
39. R. Braidotti, *Patterns of Dissonance*, E. Guild (trans.) (Oxford: Blackwell and Polity Press, 1991), p. 121.

40. Studlar, *In the Realm of Pleasure*, p. 43.
41. Ibid.
42. Ibid., p. 15.
43. Ibid., p. 211, fn. 68.
44. Deleuze, 'Coldness and Cruelty', p. 128.
45. Ibid., p. 131.
46. Studlar, *In the Realm of Pleasure*, pp. 15, 5, 6.
47. Ibid., p. 178.
48. Ibid., pp. 178–9.
49. Ibid., p. 179.
50. Ibid., p. 184.
51. Ibid.
52. Ibid., pp. 35, 185.
53. Deleuze, 'Coldness and Cruelty', p. 42. My italics.
54. Ibid., p. 41.
55. B. Dijkstra, *Idols of Perversity*, pp. 372–3.
56. Ovid, *Metamorphoses*, 2nd edn, 2 vols, G. P. Goold (ed.), F. J. Miller (trans.) (London: Heinemann, 1984), p. 83.
57. L. von Sacher-Masoch, *Venus in Furs*, in *Masochism*, J. McNeil (trans.) (New York: Zone Books, 1991), p. 153.
58. Ibid., pp. 156–7.
59. Ibid., p. 158.
60. Ibid., p. 149.
61. Ibid.
62. Dijkstra, *Idols of Perversity*, pp. 372–3.
63. Sacher-Masoch, *Venus in Furs*, p. 163.
64. Ibid., pp. 183–4.
65. Dijkstra, *Idols of Perversity*, p. 373.
66. Irigaray, *Speculum*, p. 135.
67. Sacher-Masoch, *Venus in Furs*, p. 159.
68. Ibid., p. 146.
69. Wanda appears dressed in an 'ermine-trimmed jacket and an ermine Cossack's toque, high and round, such as Catherine the Great liked to wear'. Ibid., p. 206.
70. Studlar, *In the Realm of Pleasure*, p. 134.
71. A. Sarris, *The Films of Josef von Sternberg* (New York: Museum of Modern Art, 1966), p. 37.
72. This technique is normally used in silent films.
73. Studlar, *In the Realm of Pleasure*, p. 121. The shot analysis provided throughout is my own.
74. Ibid.

75. Ibid.
76. Ibid., p. 145.
77. Ibid.
78. Ibid., p. 144.
79. Ibid., p. 148.
80. Ibid., p. 141.
81. Ibid., p. 144.
82. Ibid., pp. 148, 153.
83. Ibid., p. 148.
84. Ibid., p. 155.
85. Ibid., p. 156.
86. L. Jacobs, *The Wages of Sin: Censorship and the Fallen Woman Film 1928–42*, (Madison: University of Wisconsin Press, 1991), p. 88.
87. Ibid., p. 21.
88. Ibid., p. 23.
89. Ibid., pp. 88, 105.
90. Studlar, *In the Realm of Pleasure*, p. 91.
91. Jacobs, *The Wages of Sin*, pp. 102–4.
92. Studlar, *In the Realm of Pleasure*, pp. 82–3.
93. Ibid., p. 91.
94. Ibid., p. 144.
95. Derrida's analysis of woman as a figure of language and meaning is discussed in Chapters 4 and 5.
96. Studlar, *In the Realm of Pleasure*, pp. 67, 118.
97. Ibid., p. 118.
98. Ibid., p. 200.
99. Ibid., p. 83.
100. Ibid., p. 125.
101. Ibid., p. 165.
102. Ibid.
103. Ibid., p. 67.
104. Ibid., p. 133.
105. Ibid., p. 152.
106. Ibid.
107. Ibid., p. 134.
108. Ibid., p. 132.
109. Ibid., p. 133.
110. R. Dyer, *White* (London: Routledge, 1997), pp. 131–9.
111. Studlar, *In the Realm of Pleasure*, p. 165. She analyses this reversal on pp. 152, 154, 166.

112. Ibid., p. 134.
113. M-A. Doane, *Femmes Fatales: Feminism, Film Theory, Psychoanalysis* (London: Routledge, 1991), pp. 54, 72.
114. Ibid., pp. 72–4.
115. Ibid., p. 75.
116. Studlar, *In the Realm of Pleasure*, pp. 165–6.
117. Ibid., p. 165.
118. Ibid., pp. 148–9.
119. Ibid., pp. 165–6. Studlar relates the motif of the necklace to the miniature that Alexei had given Catherine.
120. The reasons that Doane postulates returning the gaze as the only means of escape from the binary of subject/object are explored in Section 1 of Chapter 5.
121. Studlar, *In the Realm of Pleasure*, p. 154.
122. Ibid.
123. Doane, *Femmes Fatales*, p. 53.
124. Studlar, *In the Realm of Pleasure*, p. 83.

4 | Mapping the Roads Not Taken

In Chapter 3 I indicated those elements of Sacher-Masoch's reworking of the figure of Galatea that are not crystallised into the theory of masochism offered by Studlar. Galatea's capacity to become a Venus of stone can be read as a means of linking the figure to a cool rationality, giving her the ability to manipulate her image for her own ends. This mapping of becoming stone constitutes a change to the philosophical imaginary which, in turn, reverberates through the theoretical model, necessitating its reworking. Chapter 3 can therefore be seen to focus on the creation of new imaginary pathways through the interplay between socio-cultural imagery and theory. By contrast, Chapter 4 will focus on theory, outlining elements of Nietzsche's philosophical writings that do not conform to well-worn imaginary pathways in order to show how his work can be used to think about the roads not taken. This will involve tracing Nietzsche's use of the figure of woman in a number of his accounts of the relation between art and truth.

The analyses of Nietzsche's writings will also delineate the ways in which they draw on and inform other theoretical systems, creating key points of intersection. Le Doeuff's own model of imaginary pathways that gain their cultural credibility through repetition over time bears a distinct resemblance to Nietzsche's analysis of the way in which metaphors become truths in 'On Truth and Lies in a Non-moral Sense':

> What then is truth? A movable host of metaphors, metonymies, and
> anthropomorphisms: in short, a sum of human relations which have been poetically and
> rhetorically intensified, transferred, and embellished, and which, after long usage, seem
> to people to be fixed, canonical, and binding. Truths are illusions which we have
> forgotten are illusions.[1]

Le Doeuff's methodology of tracing the permutations of the imaginary pathways in order to question and dismantle their status as a cultural 'given' can also be seen to draw on Nietzsche's critique of truth. This chapter will examine Nietzsche's writings in order to extrapolate the features that underpin and augment the theoretical framework developed across this book. This will involve utilising Sarah Kofman's work on Nietzsche in order to develop the conception of theory as perspectival in the final section.

While drawing attention to those elements of Nietzsche's writings that serve to open up the roads not taken, Chapter 4 also addresses the elements that serve to sediment well-worn imaginary pathways. These two approaches form the basis of Sections 1 and

2 respectively, both of which examine the gendered imagery that sustains some of Nietzsche's accounts of art and truth. Section 1 will focus on the definition of the Dionysian and Apollinian[2] in his early work, *The Birth of Tragedy*, which I will argue offers an interesting variation on the theme of woman as a symbol of mere appearance. This will be related to the presentation of Baubô in *The Gay Science*. Section 2 will address the ways in which the contrast that is drawn between the Dionysian and the Christian in *The Twilight of the Idols*[3] and *The Will to Power*[4], impacts on the representation of gender. I will demonstrate that Nietzsche's later construction of the dynamics of artistic creativity replicates aspects of chiasmic and binary logic, resulting in the sedimentation of a familiar imaginary pathway. The chronological approach I have adopted here serves to separate Nietzsche's arguments into distinct epochs but this should be seen as an aid to clarity, rather than a rigid demarcation.

Sections 3 and 4 will address two different commentaries on Nietzsche, focusing on Derrida and Kofman respectively. Derrida's famous reading in *Spurs* sets out three different configurations of woman and truth that are said to occur in Nietzsche's work. Derrida's examination of key tropes results in their crystallising differently because he also links the figures of woman to *différance*, his own analysis of the continual movement of meaning in language. While this produces images of woman that appear more positive than some of those offered by Nietzsche, I will demonstrate that Derrida's reading serves to perpetuate the structures of chiasmic and binary logic.

The final section will address Kofman's article on Baubô, whom she reads as representative of both Nietzsche's perspectivalism and the dynamic of the eternal return. While Kofman does take up some aspects of Derrida's methodology, I am concerned to focus on those features of her work that depart from the deconstructive framework. This will involve focusing on her account of the eternal return in order to demonstrate the ways in which it offers an alternative to the structures of chiasmic and binary logic. I will utilise aspects of her work in order to offer a different reading of the encounter between Baubô and Demeter as a metaphor for an affirmative perspectivalism, building on Kofman to create new imaginary pathways.

1 Woman as Affirmation

This section will begin with an outline of the contrast between the Apollinian and the Dionysian that is set out in *The Birth of Tragedy*. I will provide an overview of their respective definitions and interrelations and will then go on to analyse the use of gendered imagery in the depiction of each realm. My analysis will draw attention to the ways in which the gendered characterisation of the two realms departs from traditional binary hierarchies and also sets up a rather different account of the relation between the beautiful and the sublime. This will be followed by an examination of a key passage from *The Gay Science*, which offers two different constructions of truth in the form of Isis and Baubô. I will argue that the figure of Baubô can be related to the images of women in *The Birth of Tragedy*.

The Birth of Tragedy revolves around the two key figures of Apollo and Dionysus, who, Nietzsche argues, constitute the two Greek gods of art. Each is said to rule over a specific art form: sculpture and music respectively.[5] The Apollinian is characterised by measure, order and calm – it is the realm of dreams and plastic images. The Dionysian is excessive, chaotic and terrifying – a state of intoxication and self-forgetfulness.[6] The terror of the Dionysian is also the result of its representing an insight into the nature of life. 'Excess revealed itself as truth.'[7] For Nietzsche, it is Attic tragedy alone which acts as the vehicle for the Dionysian truth.[8] These plays reveal 'that life is at the bottom of things, despite all the changes of appearances, indestructibly powerful and pleasurable'.[9]

The Apollinian and the Dionysian are characterised dialectically: order/chaos, light/darkness, yet they also display a mutual interdependence. While Nietzsche privileges the Dionysian as 'the substratum' and 'the eternal and original artistic power', he also suggests that it is impossible to remain within this realm and therefore that the Apollinian is necessary to life.[10] As 'the veil of Maya', the Apollinian represents the principle of individuation – the self that is obliterated by the state of Dionysian ecstasy.[11] The veil comes to symbolise all illusion and indeed exemplifies the necessity of art as illusion in the face of the terrible truth of life. The revelation of

> primal unity, eternally suffering and contradictory, also needs the rapturous vision, the pleasurable illusion, for its continuous redemption. And we, completely wrapped up in this illusion and composed of it, are compelled to consider this illusion as … empirical reality.[12]

Famously, 'it is only as an aesthetic phenomenon that existence and the world are eternally justified.'[13]

In *The Birth of Tragedy*, the artistic illusion that constitutes the possibility of life is positioned against the Socratic construction of a 'truth' that lies beyond appearances. Socrates' method of enquiry is seen as a process of uncovering which sets up the dialectic of illusion/truth and surface/depth. For Nietzsche, Socrates and science present illusion as error, a move that serves to conceal the utterly fictitious nature of their own concept of 'truth'.[14] While it might be objected that the Dionysian itself operates as the truth beyond the veil in *The Birth of Tragedy*,[15] Nietzsche makes efforts to characterise this realm as another illusion. Writing of Raphael's *Transfiguration*, he comments, 'here is the reflection of the contradiction, the father of things. From this mere appearance arises … a new visionary world of mere appearances.'[16] The mutual interdependence of both realms of illusion means that their relation is never presented in terms of truth versus error. Indeed, Nietzsche argues that it is the Apollinian that gives us access to the Dionysian: '[o]f this foundation of all existence – the Dionysian basic ground of the world – not one whit more may enter the consciousness of the human individual than can be overcome again by this Apollinian power of transfiguration'.[17]

Having sketched out some of the key moves from *The Birth of Tragedy*, I will now focus on the use of gendered imagery in the characterisation of the *Apollinian* and *Dionysian*. Nietzsche's first presentation of the relation between the two artistic powers is sexualised: 'the continuous development of art is bound up with the *Apollinian* and *Dionysian* duality – just as procreation depends on the duality of the sexes, involving perpetual strife with only periodically intervening reconciliations.'[18] Given that both these Greek deities are male, woman cannot be said to occupy one half of the binary in a straightforward manner. However, I will demonstrate that it is the Apollinian that is characterised through references to the figure of woman. *The Birth of Tragedy* can therefore be seen to depart from the traditional depiction of woman as chaos that feminist theorists have identified within Western philosophy in that it does *not* position woman within the excessive, chaotic Dionysian realm.[19]

Nietzsche's presentation of woman as a key figure of the Apollinian is possible because his conception of Apollo substantially re/works the god's traditional role. As a result, his account differs very greatly from Bachhofen's famous construction of the patriarchal lawgiver. This construction is based on a reading of the *Orestia* in which Apollo is presented as the key figure in the transition from a matriarchal to a patriarchal economy.[20] Importantly, the Apollo of *The Birth of Tragedy* is not the lawgiver but a general figure of order and calm. Nietzsche also diverges from classical representations of the god by crediting him with the additional roles of god of the visual arts, dreams and appearance/illusion.[21] It is the last of these unprecedented extensions of the Apollinian that results in the feminisation of this realm. The few references to female mythological figures in *The Birth of Tragedy* usually occur within the context of characterising the Apollinian. The first description of this realm as 'the veil of Maya'[22] is a reference to the Hindu goddess of illusion. The veil of appearances is 'the smile of Helen' – pleasurable, charming and beautiful.[23] The invocation of Helen of Troy entirely omits the destructive capacity of the beauty inherent in the famous description of 'the face that launch'd a thousand ships'.[24] Instead, the beautiful is envisaged as a soothing veil of appearances, which covers over the terror of the Dionysian and thus affirms the value of life for the subject that returns to it.

> This is the true artistic aim of Apollo in whose name we comprehend all those countless illusions of the beauty of mere appearance that at every moment make life worth living at all and prompt the desire to live on in order to experience the next moment.[25]

In this way, Apollinian art is said to function as 'a saving sorceress', preventing resignation in the face of excess.[26]

If Nietzsche's extension of the role of Apollo results in the feminisation of this realm then it is his editing of the Dionysian that compounds its presentation as masculine. According to historical and literary evidence, the followers of Dionysus were usually female. During the festivals these women, known as bacchantes or maenads, were said to roam the hills in a state of frenzy. The Dionysian cults were savagely suppressed in Roman times because the lawless festivities were said to constitute a threat to the state.[27] The exclusion of the bacchantes from *The Birth of Tragedy* is noted by Silk and Stern who simply state, 'Nietzsche has given us his *Bacchae* without the maenads.'[28] The exclusion is sustained by the presentation of the phallus-laden satyr chorus as the key means of accessing the state of Dionysian frenzy. Nietzsche argues that in viewing attic tragedy, members of the Greek audience lost their boundaries of individuation by identifying with the satyr chorus. 'In this magic transformation the Dionysian reveller sees himself as a satyr, *and as a satyr, in turn, he sees the god*'.[29] This vision of the god, Dionysus, is given form by the Apollinian in that it is a visual image. For Nietzsche, Greek tragedy is constructed by a particular dynamic in which 'the Dionysian chorus ... ever anew discharges itself in an Apollinian world of images'.[30] The ejaculatory basis of this energic model clearly makes use of male body imagery, compounding the masculinisation of the Dionysian.

Nietzsche's presentation of the Dionysian and Apollinian as masculine and feminine respectively is partly the result of his drawing on the gendered distinction between the sublime and the beautiful that was established during the eighteenth century. The definition of the Dionysian as a terrifying realm, which threatens the loss of individuation, utilises features of the sublime. Burke argues that both categories arouse specific emotional states, defining the sublime as that which produces a state of terror, incapacitating the spectator.[31] In contrast, '[t]he appearance of *beauty* effectively causes some degree of love',[32] a response that is clearly consistent with Nietzsche's use of Helen of Troy as a motif of the Apollinian. Burke also argues that specific characteristics of the mind can be categorised in this way: sublime attributes include fortitude, justice and wisdom; while those of the beautiful include compassion, kindness and generosity.[33] Within this context, Nietzsche's image of Apollinian art as a saving sorceress feeds into the traditional categorisation of the beautiful in that her acts exhibit the appropriate emotional qualities of compassion and kindness.

However, Nietzsche's utilisation of the categories of the sublime and the beautiful also constitutes a significant departure from the tradition set up by Burke *et al*. The emphasis on the interrelation between the Dionysian and Apollinian is entirely at odds with Burke's model in which the sublime and the beautiful are not intertwined. Indeed, each category constitutes a specific emotional response, which is caused by a particular type of object. Importantly, Nietzsche's image of the Apollinian as a saving sorceress ascribes two new functions to the beautiful. First, it constitutes the only way out of the nausea/terror evoked by the sublime. Second, the beautiful is ultimately the sole means of accessing the sublime because the experience of terror can only be remembered and recounted from within the Apollinian.

The presentation of the beautiful as the way out of the sublime differs significantly from Kant's account. In the Kantian model the beautiful and the sublime are subjective feelings, which will be experienced in the same way by all those whose mental faculties are correctly ordered. These subjective states are not caused by the qualities of specific objects; instead both beauty and sublimity are defined as forms of 'mental attunement' that 'must be sought only in the mind of the judging person'.[34] The beautiful is defined as the free play of the imagination in relation to the understanding. The sublime is the exhaustion of the imagination through the demands of reason: 'If [a thing] is excessive to the imagination (and the imagination is driven to [such excess] as it apprehends [the thing] in intuition), then [the thing] is … an abyss in which the imagination is afraid to lose itself.'[35] This mental abyss is the point at which the imagination fails causing feelings of terror. However, the terror is abated by the recognition that the failure of the imagination is the result of an attempt to expand the domain of reason. 'Yet at the same time, for reason's idea of the supersensible [this same thing] is not excessive but conforms to reason's law to give rise to such striving by the imagination.'[36] For Kant, it is reason that provides the means to overcome the subjective feeling of terror. He follows the traditional gendering of the sublime in that it is the male subject alone who is able to master fear by the use of pure reason.

Nietzsche's presentation of the beautiful as the key means of accessing and escaping the sublime is the result of his undermining the category of pure reason, demonstrated in his attack on Socratic rationality.[37] The characterisation of the Apollinian in *The Birth of Tragedy* can be seen to deploy the romantic rhetoric that imbues the traditional philosophical equation of the feminine and the beautiful, however, the imagery is used to sustain a new aesthetic model and thus crystallises differently. While Nietzsche's motif of Helen of Troy corresponds to Burke's characterisation of the beautiful as that which generates feelings of love, the fleeting quality of Helen's smile also symbolises the transitory illusion that is life itself. In the same way, the image of Apollinian consciousness as a veil of Maya that envelops and soothes can be compared to Kant's definition of the beautiful as a pleasurable state of 'restful contemplation'.[38] The key difference is that for Kant the pleasures offered by the beautiful constitute a form of dalliance, time away from the real work of expanding the domain of pure reason. While for Nietzsche, envelopment within the veil of beauty creates the individuation necessary for the contemplation of Dionysian insights, moreover its soothing power transforms nausea into affirmation. Nietzsche's characterisation of the Apollinian draws on the philosophical imaginary only to subvert it, thus playing out a joke in which the last laugh is on Burke, Kant *et al*. While Helen, Maya and the sorceress emerge from a tradition that emphasises the transitory nature of 'mere' appearances, within *The Birth of Tragedy* they attest to the *necessity* of such illusions and ultimately represent the possibility of affirming life as illusion.

The issue of the relation between illusion and truth is an important theme in much of Nietzsche's work. Having set out the key role allocated to woman as illusion in *The*

Birth of Tragedy, I now want to examine the reworking of the Apollinian in the later writings. This will involve tracing Nietzsche's take-up of the contrast between the Socratic and the Apollinian and I will begin by tracing the continuities presented in his work before addressing the ways in which the Apollinian is ultimately displaced. In *The Gay Science*, the opposition between the Socratic deception that is absolute truth and an Apollinian revelling in fictionality is presented in the form of two very different images of woman: Isis and Baubô. Each figure is used to represent a particular approach to truth: the veiled Isis acts as a trope for the attempt to uncover truth, while Baubô's body-writing is a symbol for choosing to stop at the surface.

Nietzsche's take-up of the story of Isis can be seen a response to Kant and his contemporaries such as Schiller. They told of the veiled statue of Isis, which was positioned in the inner sanctum of the temple. The base of the statue was inscribed: 'I am all that is, that was and that shall be and no mortal has lifted my veil.' In Schiller's poem a young novice steals into the temple, breaks into the sanctum and tears away the veil of Isis. He is found dead the next morning. While Schiller romanticises the priest who was brave enough to die in his attempt to uncover the hidden truth, Kant warns against lifting the veil because it symbolises the limits of human understanding.[39] Nietzsche's critique elides their differences, attacking both theorists for the sexualised imagery that underpins their quest for truth by presenting them as harbingers of bad taste.

> And as for our future, one will hardly find us again on the paths of those Egyptian youths who endanger temples by night, embrace statues, and want by all means to unveil, uncover, and put into a bright light whatever is kept concealed for good reasons. No, this bad taste, this will to truth, to 'truth at any price', this youthful madness in the love of truth, have lost their charm for us: for that we are too experienced, too serious, too merry, too burned, too *profound*. We no longer believe that the truth remains truth when the veils are withdrawn; we have lived too much to believe this.[40]

For Nietzsche, the quest to uncover the truth is based on an opposition between truth and illusion in which the latter is downgraded and simply equated with error. The Egyptian youths seeking the body beyond the veil are seen to make the same mistake as Plato who sought the eternal Forms beyond the realm of mutable appearances. In his later work, *The Twilight of the Idols*, Nietzsche suggests that the construction of the true world of the forms is 'a circumlocution for the sentence: "I, Plato, *am* the truth".'[41] The attributes of truth, reality and goodness credited to the world of forms are simply the reverse of those possessed by the world of appearances. Kant is seen to follow Plato in his presentation of a truth beyond this world, albeit one that can never be fully known. Importantly, Nietzsche argues that both Plato and Kant utilise the conception of a world beyond in order to construct their ethical systems, which are encapsulated in the Form of the Good and the categorical imperative respectively. Thus the true world is revealed to be nothing more than 'a moral–optical illusion', a projection, which ultimately serves to sustain a particular system of values.[42]

In *The Gay Science*, Nietzsche contrasts the lack of decency in the quest for truth that strives to remove the veil from the body of Isis with the respectful acceptance of the value of mere appearances that is represented by the 'bashful' figure of Baubô.

> One should have more respect for the bashfulness with which nature has hidden behind riddles and iridescent uncertainties. Perhaps truth is a woman who has reasons for not letting us see her reasons? Perhaps her name is – to speak Greek – *Baubô*?

> Oh, those Greeks! They knew how to live. What is required for that is to stop courageously at the surface, the fold, the skin, to adore appearance, to believe in forms, tones, words, in the whole Olympus of appearance. The Greeks were superficial – *out of profundity*.[43]

Nietzsche's brief reference to Baubô in this context is partly humorous given that her role in Greek mythology consists of a single story in which she is said to have flashed at the earth goddess Demeter! Baubô comes to the aid of Demeter during her search for her daughter, Persephone, who was kidnapped by Pluto and taken down to the underworld. Disguising herself as an old woman, Demeter searched for nine days and nights without stopping to eat or drink.[44] Eventually becoming exhausted she decided to rest under a tree and was then approached by another elderly woman, Baubô, who offered her a drink of mint and barley-water. Disconsolate, the goddess refused it and in response Baubô lifted her skirt to reveal her pudenda and a drawing of Dionysus's face on her stomach. She moved her hand, making the face grimace, thereby causing Demeter to laugh. The goddess then accepted the drink and went on to bargain with Pluto, eventually recovering the company of her daughter for at least eight months of each year.[45]

Baubô's display is clearly the reverse of the coy gestures traditionally associated with maidenly modesty, offering another example of the way in which Nietzsche subverts feminine archetypes. She is read as a figure of nature's bashfulness because her gesture serves to baffle the sexualised imagery that underpins the philosophical quest for the hidden truth. Baubô lifts her skirts to reveal a portrait of Dionysus on her belly. This is not an 'indecent' gesture because her flesh acts as yet another surface. For Kofman, Baubô's gesture undermines the sexualised logic of surface/depth or decent/indecent by revealing that: 'behind the veil, there is another veil, behind a layer of paint, another layer.'[46] Baubô's bashfulness also implies that the acceptable gestures of feminine modesty, such as veiling and downcast eyes, serve to create and sustain the concept of indecency.

Baubô can be linked to the 'whole Olympus of appearance' presented in *The Birth of Tragedy* in that she lifts the Apollinian veil to reveal the Dionysian as image, and therefore as another realm of mere appearances. While Baubô spans both sides of the

Apollinian/Dionysian divide, she can still be seen as the successor of Helen, Maya and the sorceress because she too is associated with affirmation. Kofman's analysis of the affirming power of Baubô's gesture augments the Apollinian conception of affirmation, namely the acceptance and enjoyment of life as illusion, by linking it to the dynamic of the eternal return. I will discuss the ways in which she develops this point in the third section. Importantly, the different configurations of woman as illusion set up in *The Birth of Tragedy* and *The Gay Science* offer Helen, Baubô *et al.* roles that subvert the imagery and expectations set up by well-worn imaginary pathways. As a result, these figures can be seen to constitute a different set of possibilities, the roads not yet taken, one of which will be explored at the end of the chapter.

2 Woman as Degenerate

I want now to trace the ways in which Nietzsche's later works can be seen to fall back into the imaginary pathways that he had previously subverted. This will involve examining his analysis of art in *The Twilight of the Idols* and the notes on art in *The Will to Power*. Importantly, the later works do not attempt to replicate the complex double binary in which the Socratic was pitted against the Apollinian/Dionysian. The non-hierarchical interweaving structure of the second binary is abandoned in favour of a series of more traditional oppositional structures, specifically the Christian versus the Dionysian. The aesthetic category of the Apollinian is far less evident, partly because the production of art, or life-affirming illusion, is incorporated within the Dionysian. These affirming fictions are contrasted with the empty productions of Christianity. The opposition of Christian/Dionysian also sustains a further contrast between romantic and tragic artists. I will begin by outlining the presentation of these oppositions and go on to draw out their gender implications.

The contrast between the Socratic and the Apollinian that is presented in *The Birth of Tragedy* is the difference between the deception that is absolute truth and overt fictionality. This is reworked in *The Gay Science* in that Isis and Baubô are said to represent two different approaches to truth. In *The Will to Power*, the Socratic/Christian quest for truth is presented as the opposite of the Dionysian. Furthermore, the terms of the opposition are no longer that of deception versus illusion, or uncovering versus remaining at the surface, but rather the degenerate versus the affirmative. Christianity is no longer criticised for its construction of a particular version of absolute truth, but rather for promulgating a 'sickly' mode of living.

> The antagonism between the 'true world', as revealed by pessimism, and a world possible for life – here one must test the rights of truth. It is necessary to measure the meaning of all these 'ideal drives' against *life* to grasp what this antagonism really is: the struggle of a sickly, despairing life that cleaves to a beyond, with healthier, more stupid and mendacious, richer, less degenerate life. Therefore it is not 'truth' in struggle with life but *one* kind of life in struggle with another.[47]

Kofman comments that Christianity constitutes a perversion for Nietzsche because it is 'the "choice" of values other than those that affirm life. It is a will to death, to nothingness.'[48] Furthermore, the will to nothingness is conceptualised as a lack of the will to power and therefore seen to indicate a fundamental lack of creativity:

> The belief that the world as it ought to be *is*, really exists, is a belief of the unproductive who do *not desire to create a world* as it ought to be. They posit it as already available, they seek ways and means of reaching it. 'Will to truth' – *as the impotence of the will to create.*[49]

The illusion of paradise promulgated by Christianity is thus characterised as a projection that arises out of emptiness.

Importantly for Nietzsche, the opposition between the degenerate and the affirmative is the result of their basis in different energic states. 'In regard to all aesthetic values, I now employ this fundamental distinction: I ask in each individual case "has hunger or superabundance become creative here?"'[50] Christianity as the will to truth is impotent, it is inherently degenerate because it constitutes a state of will-lessness.[51] By contrast, the Dionysian is 'an *explosive* condition', a state of 'overflowing fullness'.[52] The artist as genius 'flows out, he overflows, he uses himself up, he does not spare himself – and this is a calamitous, involuntary fatality, no less than a river's flooding the land'.[53] This 'pressure of abundance'[54] is an exaggerated version of the original model of discharge that characterised the Dionysian in *The Birth of Tragedy*.

The contrast between the two energic states of hunger and superabundance is also directional. Kofman comments that Nietzsche constructs Christianity as a perversion of nature because it constitutes a turning away from life.

> Drives change goals, turn back against themselves, become denatured and in turn denature all that is living. This is a *reflexive movement*, no longer a direct discharge. It correlates with the invention of a fictitious, abstract world that one has placed beyond nature, made *super*natural, and set down as the origin of the world here below. Such a world inverts the relations of cause and effect, perverts reasons, and is a symptom of the corruption of nature.[55]

The reflexive, circular movement of turning away is characterised as a symptom of degeneracy because it is a subversion of the outward-flowing, centrifugal nature of direct discharge.

The different energic dynamics of degeneration and affirmation are also represented by the figures of the romantic artist and the tragic artist respectively. Nietzsche defines the romantic artist as someone 'whose great dissatisfaction with himself makes him creative – who looks away, looks back from himself and from his world'.[56] The act of looking away constitutes a gesture of self-enclosure and is thus a rejection of life. It forms a clear contrast with the openness of the tragic artist who is defined as 'the one who says Yes to everything questionable, even to the terrible – he is *Dionysian*.'[57] The acceptance of all aspects of life mirrors the centrifugal dynamic of overflowing insofar as both are seen to involve a movement outwards towards the world.

Nietzsche builds on the oppositional framework of Christian/Dionysian, degenerate/affirmative, romantic/tragic in a discussion of artistic styles. Romantic art is characterised as lesser because it aims to please and is thus subordinated to the values of others. In contrast, the grand style of classical art 'disdains to please; . . . forgets to persuade; . . . it commands; . . . it *wills* – '.[58] The true artist channels the will-to-power regardless of the effects of his work and such art 'repels; such men of force are no longer loved – a desert spreads around them, a silence, a fear as in the presence of some great sacrilege – '.[59] Within *Thus Spake Zarathustra* the journey into the desert is seen as the initial step towards the creation of new values.[60] Here the motif of the desert is linked to sacrilege, indicating that the tragic artist is one who breaks with tradition and creates his own values.

Nietzsche characterises classical taste as a scornful rejection of all things romantic: 'hatred for feeling, heart, *esprit*, hatred for . . . imitations, as well as for the brief, pointed, pretty, good-natured'.[61] In setting up the pleasing and the pretty as the absolute antithesis of the Dionysian, Nietzsche can be seen to reject the tropes of femininity that were previously extolled as key features of the Apollinian in *The Birth of Tragedy*. The beautiful and the charming are no longer allocated vital roles in the production of art and corresponding affirmation of life. Indeed the juxtaposition of '*esprit*' with 'imitations' presents the spirit as a bad copy of the will-to-power, demonstrating a reversion to a traditional devaluation of the beautiful and the charming as 'mere' appearances. Nietzsche's feminised definition of romantic art is only one example of the ways in which he links the feminine and the degenerate in his later work.

The three key aspects of the degenerate that I have outlined are: an energic state of hunger or impotence, a dynamic movement that constitutes a reflexive turning away from the world and the subordination of the process of creation to the production of that which is deemed to be of value by others. Nietzsche's vicious characterisation of female writers provides an extreme example of his linking of femininity to a degenerate hunger that is utter emptiness. 'The literary female: unsatisfied, excited, *her heart and entrails void*, ever listening, full of painful curiosity, to the imperative, which whispers from the depths of her organism, "*aut liberi aut libri*" [either children or books].'[62] Unlike the projections of Christianity, it is not the perverse nature of the values extolled in the works of female writers which display the intrinsic lack of the will-to-power, but rather that their desire to write at all is seen as a betrayal of the female instinct to reproduce.[63] While this suggests that pregnancy would be the only available expression of the will-to-power in women, the attempt to link it to the dynamic of affirmation is highly problematic.

The presentation of affirmation as a state of overflowing in both *The Twilight of the Idols* and *The Will to Power* draws attention to the gendered nature of the underlying dynamic. The model of overflow is described in terms of a sudden discharge, resulting from the 'pressure of abundance',[64] and explicitly related to the male body when in a state of arousal: '(Physiologically: the creative instinct of the artist and the distribution of semen in his blood –)'.[65] The ejaculatory imagery that sustains this conception of affirmation cannot simply be mapped onto the female body in a state of pregnancy without making considerable changes to the theoretical system. I will look at the ways in which pregnancy is used as a motif in Nietzsche's presentation of the eternal return in Section 4.

Rather than being linked to the state of direct discharge that is affirmation, woman is used as a symbol of perverse reflexivity in *The Will to Power*. This focus on directional dynamics provides a vital theoretical context in which to read Nietzsche's most famous comments on feminine modesty. His remarks also position the practice of modesty as a process that is parallel to the cultivation of beauty.

> Woman, conscious of man's feeling concerning women, assists his efforts at idealization by adorning herself, walking beautifully, dancing, expressing delicate thoughts: in the same way she practices modesty, reserve, distance – realizing instinctively that in this way the idealizing capacity of the man will grow . . . Given the tremendous subtlety of woman's instinct, modesty remains by no means conscious hypocrisy: she divines that it is precisely an actual naïve modesty that most seduces a man and impels him to overestimate her. Therefore woman is naïve – from the subtlety of her instinct, which advises her of the utility of innocence. A deliberate *closing of one's eyes to oneself* – .[66]

The final sentence can be read as an extreme version of the degenerate dynamic of turning away from the world. It references a typical gesture of feminine modesty, the downcast eyes which look away from the world, transforming it into the circular reflexive movement of 'closing of one's eyes to oneself'.

Nietzsche's presentation of this reflexive dynamic clearly draws on Roussel's analysis of the directional dynamics of feminine modesty, which are said to take the form of a strong centripetal movement.[67] Both conceptions of modesty as an inward movement clearly conform to Le Doeuff's delineation of the first aspect of chiasmic logic in which the eye is drawn in inexorably towards the vanishing point. Indeed, Nietzsche's version of modesty may be said to emphasise the self-abnegation at stake in the logical structure of denegation. For Roussel, modesty and beauty constitute two different forces, moving in opposite directions that are united by a common aim, that of rendering woman pleasing to man. Nietzsche presents modesty and beauty as parallel processes, both working in the same perverse circular direction and to the same ends – woman renders herself as an ideal object in order to persuade others to fall in love with her.

Nietzsche's analysis of the purpose of cultivating modesty and beauty also conforms to another aspect of degeneracy, namely subordination to the values of others. This particular perversion is used to explain the lack of great works produced by female artists and in this case it takes the familiar form of woman's desire to please.

> Would any link at all be missing in the chain of art . . . if the works of women were missing? . . . woman attains perfection in everything that is not a work: in letters, in memoirs, even in the most delicate handiwork, in short in everything that is not a *métier* – precisely because in these things she perfects herself, because she here obeys the only artistic impulse she has – she wants to *please* – [68]

The process of creating delicate handiwork can be linked to the previous comment on woman's cultivation of delicate thoughts in that both are part of a programme of self-perfection that is synonymous with objectification. Importantly, the links that are drawn here between beauty, modesty and being pleasing combine to re-establish the traditional depiction of woman's altruistic nature that is set up by both Roussel and Rousseau.[69] Nietzsche's later work can therefore be seen to draw on both theorists, resulting in the sedimentation of a well-worn imaginary pathway in which femininity is defined as being for others and contrasted with masculine independence.

This imaginary pathway is most apparent in Nietzsche's analysis of creativity and takes the form of the familiar binary of object/subject. Woman's self-perfection marks her *transformation* into an art object, which will be valued by others. In contrast, man '*perfects* an object ('idealises it')' by putting into it 'everything . . . that he honors and esteems', thus expressing his own values and affirming his status as a subject.[70] The binary is the result of the gendering of the underlying dynamic of creativity. This is apparent in Nietzsche's depiction of artistic creation in *The Twilight of the Idols*, which uses the familiar trope of the mirror to describe the role of the art object.

> In this state one enriches everything out of one's own fullness: whatever one sees, whatever one wills, is seen swelled, taut, strong, overloaded with strength. A man in this state transforms things until they mirror his power – until they are reflections of his perfection. This *having to* transform into perfection is – art.[71]

Woman's self-perfection marks her readiness for idealisation, a transformation that can only be completed by the true artist, the Dionysian genius, who will fashion her into a reflection of his values. Woman's construction as the degenerate also means that she acts as an inverse mirror; her hunger, impotence and dabbling in delicate handiwork all serve to sustain this vision of masculine genius and creativity.

I have demonstrated the ways in which aspects of Nietzsche's work can be seen to sediment particular imaginary pathways as well as opening up the roads not taken in order to trace some of the many different possibilities that emerge from his writings on art and truth. Importantly, Le Doeuff's approach can be seen to yield dividends when applied to Nietzsche's writing because of his overt reliance on gendered imagery as well as the use of specific figures and stories. Nietzsche offers two very different configurations of feminine modesty, which support and sustain two different theoretical objectives. Woman's closing her eyes to herself is an example of the reflexive movement of the degenerate, which serves to support the masculinist model of Dionysian creativity. Baubô's revelation of the surface beneath the surface baffles the philosophical quest for hidden truth and marks the joyful acceptance of life as illusion. I will trace the ways in which these two different configurations are taken up in the work of two key commentators: Derrida and Kofman respectively. This will involve noting how the images crystallise differently, sustaining different theoretical systems, once they are positioned within the commentaries.

3 Woman as *Différance*

This section will begin with an outline of one of the most famous commentaries on Nietzsche, Derrida's *Spurs*. His analysis of the configurations of woman and truth in Nietzsche's work has become one of the standard readings within Cultural Studies, so much so that the commentary is in danger of effacing the source material. The purpose of this section is to draw attention to the key differences between Nietzsche's deployment of the tropes of femininity and Derrida's utilisation of them. This will involve looking at the ways in which Derrida presents woman as a symbol of language itself and I will demonstrate that her new role as the figure of *différance* actually serves to sediment the familiar structures of chiasmic and binary logic.

In *Spurs*, Derrida offers an analysis of three different configurations of woman and truth in Nietzsche's work, which 'represent three positions of value'.[72] In the first configuration, woman operates as the figure of falsehood. As the epitome of mere appearance she is the opposite of the Platonic Forms: 'In the name of truth and metaphysics she is accused here by the credulous man who, in support of his testimony, offers truth and his phallus as his own proper credentials.'[73] For Derrida, Plato's metaphysics of presence positions woman as absence. She functions as the inverse of the phallocentric system and therefore represents castration or lack.[74]

Derrida's presentation of the second configuration of woman and truth is based on a line from 'How the "True World" Finally Became a Fable' in *The Twilight of the Idols*. Nietzsche suggests that the alteration of the Platonic conception of the world of Forms to the Christian understanding of an unreachable paradise marks the feminisation of the idea: '(Progress of the idea: it becomes more subtle, insidious, incomprehensible – *it becomes female*, it becomes Christian.)'[75] This transformation of the Platonic Forms is then paralleled with Kant's whose system is summed up as: 'the old sun . . . seen through *mist* and skepticism'.[76] The parallel suggests that feminisation can be seen as a mode of veiling over the sun. Importantly, this image uses the trope of the veil differently from the story of Isis that was discussed in Section 1. Nietzsche uses Isis to critique both Plato and Kant because their quests for truth are said to utilise sexualised images of penetrating the veil. In *The Twilight of the Idols*, the veil is not a covering to be pulled away, instead the critique of Kant uses the veil as a symbol of distance, emphasising the elusive and unattainable nature of the ideas. Derrida's commentary draws the two different images of the veil together.

> Now the stories start. Distance – woman – averts truth – the philosopher. She bestows the idea. And the idea withdraws, becomes transcendent, inaccessible, seductive. It beckons from afar … Its veils float in the distance. The dream of death begins. It is woman.[77]

In linking the imagery of distance to seduction, Derrida can be seen to draw on the trope of the veil as a sexual lure, which is its original function in the story of Isis. However, the emphasis is no longer on the body beyond the veil, the distant veils act as a promise that inspires pursuit rather than offering the possibility of an assignation.

The second configuration of woman is seen to differ from the first in that woman is no longer presented as a figure of falsehood but is instead 'debased and despised' as the 'potentate of truth'.[78] Woman represents the distance between the philosopher and the elusive Ideas as well as the unattainability of the Ideas. Derrida gives woman's association with distance a further twist in that it also symbolises her rational ability to manipulate truth. She 'either identifies with truth, or else she continues to play with it at a distance as if it were a fetish, manipulating it, even as she refuses to believe in it, to her own advantage'.[79] Derrida suggests that this construction of woman as truth is the inverse of the first stage. No longer characterised as castrated, woman has become castrating. Summarising both stages he comments 'woman, up to this point then, is twice castration: once as truth and once as nontruth [sic].'[80]

Both of the first two configurations of woman are said to position her within the phallocentric system. However, the third position is said to be 'beyond the double negation of the first two', in that 'woman is recognised and affirmed as an affirmative power, a dissimulatress, an artist, a dionysiac.'[81] No longer presented as either lacking or phallic, woman 'affirms herself, in and of herself, in man. Castration … does not take place.'[82] Having been both truth and non-truth woman is now famously constructed as the 'untruth of truth'.[83] Derrida charts this transformation by drawing on Nietzsche's version of Isis as a symbol of the 'indecent' truth that lies beyond the veil. This is then contrasted with an image of the third stage in which the veil hangs suspended in space, representing the impossibility of reaching beyond it.

> 'Truth' can only be a surface. But the blushing movement of that truth which is not suspended in quotation marks casts a modest veil over such a surface. And only

through such a veil which thus falls over it could 'truth' become truth, profound, indecent, desirable. But should that veil be suspended, or even fall a bit differently, there would no longer be any truth, only 'truth' written in quotation marks.[84]

The move away from the dialectical structure of phallic/castrated to a space where the dialectic itself is distanced and displaced is the move into the economy of the unde-cidable. Woman's knowledge of castration as a non-event is said to mark the beginning of a different model of signification. Derrida defines castration as 'a sort of syntax, which in its annulment and equalisation of any discourse in the mode of *pro et contra*, would have stabilised its undecidable.'[85] Structuralists are said to foreclose the play of *dif-férance* in language by presenting binary oppositions as foundational terms, for example Lacan's use of the binary having/lack as the basis of the Symbolic. In contrast, Derrida is interested in demonstrating the ways in which the unstable nature of language under-mines such oppositions. This involves the valorisation of terms that cannot be placed either side of a binary, such as the third woman's lack of castration, which is described as an 'undecidable mark, a non-mark'.[86] He also focuses on oppositions that appear to undermine themselves offering two dynamic constructions of this movement: the spur that tears through the veil revealing the absence of Isis and the reflexive movement of the folded veil: 'The stylate spur ... rips through the veil. It rents it in such a way that it ... undoes the sail's self-opposition, the opposition of veiled/unveiled (sailed/unsailed) which has folded over on itself.'[87]

The move into the economy of the undecidable has to be more than a reversal because that would simply sustain oppositional logic. The suspension of the dialectic of truth and falsity in the third stage is summed up in a line that draws on Nietzsche's image of feminine modesty as '[a] deliberate *closing of one's eyes to oneself* – '.[88] Rather than invert the system 'woman averts, she is averted of herself.'[89] Derrida can be seen to follow Nietzsche in his emphasis on the self-abnegation that sustains the circular reflexive movement of feminine modesty; 'averted of herself' his third woman becomes the vanishing point. While Nietzsche and Derrida can be seen to utilise the same trope, it crystallises differently in each theoretical system. For Nietzsche, the circular movement of modesty is the dynamic of the degenerate, which is the antithesis of Dionysian out-pouring. By contrast, Derrida presents the movement of turning away as a means of folding over oppositions, creating the economy of the undecidable, which, he argues, constitutes the Dionysian. Although Derrida's substantial reworking of the Dionysian might be seen to have a positive effect on the presentation of woman within the sys-tem, it is important to note that both theorists perpetuate the structure of denegation that underpins Roussel's work.

Derrida's third woman is linked to his version of the Dionysian in two ways. The movement of averting can be seen as the moment by which she is emptied of meaning, thus placing her beyond definition. Following Nietzsche, Derrida argues that feminist attempts to define the truth of woman are misguided imitations of masculinist logic.

> And in order to resemble the masculine dogmatic philosopher this woman lays claim –
> just as much claim as he – to truth, science and objectivity in all their castrated
> delusions of virility. Feminism too seeks to castrate. It wants a castrated woman. Gone
> the style.[90]

Any attempt to define woman is seen as a form of castration because it constitutes the stabilisation of the undecidable. As a result the third woman becomes an icon of *différance*, which serves to link her to a second dynamic that of the endless deferral of meaning within language. The exponential movement of meaning can be seen as a linguistic reworking of the Nietzschean model of Dionysian overflowing.[91]

Derrida's construction of his Dionysian woman as representative of two linguistic dynamics – folding over and overflowing – can be seen to position him as Roussel's successor. It constitutes a departure from the Nietzschean source material in which modesty and beauty are both said to have the same perverse reflexive movement. Derrida's analysis of averting and *différance* offers the same balance of centripetal and centrifugal movements as Roussel's account of feminine modesty and beauty. In this way, Derrida can be seen to perpetuate the dual structures of denegation and metonymic proliferation that constitute the basis of chiasmic logic. While the structures remain the same, Derrida makes some changes to the images that sustain them. Unlike Roussel and Nietzsche, he does not link modesty and beauty to altruism, but rather characterises his ideal woman in terms of playfulness.

The images of the third woman at play suggest that she enjoys a certain power.

> She who, unbelieving, still plays with castration, she is 'woman'. She takes aim and
> amuses herself (*en joue*) with it as she would with a new concept or structure of belief,
> but even as she plays she is gleefully anticipating her laughter, her mockery of man.[92]

The pun on woman playing with herself clearly emphasises her status as the icon of textual undecidability, acting as a demonstration of the way in which she eludes the logic of castration. However, her mocking laughter is directed at specific men, structuralist theorists, particularly Lacan, serving to undermine philosophical systems that are opposed to deconstruction. As a result, woman's mocking playfulness cannot be read as an indication of distance from the deconstructive model itself.[93] Moreover, her playfulness is limited by its positioning within the structure of chiasmic logic. Derrida presents woman's performance of the role of dissimulatress as a game: she '*plays at* dissimulation, at ornamentation, deceit, artifice'.[94] In playing at dissimulation woman destabilises language, in accordance with the structure of metonymic proliferation. However, the line also serves to distance her from the capacity to dissemble. Woman is unable to use the power of dissimulation for her own ends because she has no agenda of her own to dissimulate. The structure of denegation can therefore be seen to underpin and undercut her playfulness, containing any disruptive potential.

The chiasma that underpins the image of woman at play clearly draws on another logical structure, the gendered binary of subject/object. Derrida's ideal woman appears to offer the possibility of stabilising meaning, playing with castration, and thus drawing the eye in to the vanishing point. She also mocks the search for meaning and truth, her laughter denoting the moment at which the gaze is baffled and propelled outwards, negating the search. Doane argues that the third woman is presented as a lure that instigates an unending philosophical quest, thus functioning as the ultimate object of desire.[95] Derrida's commentary clearly positions him and other male readers as the subjects of the quest.

> One can no longer seek her, no more than one could search for woman's femininity or female sexuality. And she is certainly not to be found in any of the familiar modes of concept or knowledge. Yet *it is impossible to resist looking for her*.[96]

The familiar image of the philosophical quest perpetuates the very structures of desire that Nietzsche criticises in his analysis of Isis. It positions Derrida close to Nietzsche's version of Kant in that both utilise the image of the veil, while arguing that it is impossible to get beyond it, albeit for very different reasons. Derrida's use of familiar metaphors, such as the gesture of feminine modesty and the conception of philosophy as a quest, to augment his depiction of the playful dissimulatress, can thus be seen to ensure that he sediments the structures of chiasmic and binary logic.

4 Laughing with Baubô

This final section will take up Kofman's reading of the figure of Baubô in order to show how it could be used to form the basis of a different kind of theoretical system. Kofman links Baubô to Nietzsche's accounts of perspectivalism and the will-to-art, arguing that both can be seen to draw on the dynamic of the eternal return. I will demonstrate the ways in which her analysis sets up an alternative to the familiar structures of binary and chiasmic logic. I will show how Kofman's analysis of Baubô's encounter with Demeter replicates Nietzsche's sidelining of the female figures in favour of Dionysus; before drawing on aspects of her account to provide my own reading of the myth as a metaphor for the process of theorising itself.

I have already argued that Baubô can be linked to the figures of Helen, Maya and the sorceress in that she represents the joyful acceptance of life as illusion. Kofman also constructs Baubô as a figure that affirms appearances because of her association with laughter: '[t]o hold oneself in the camera obscura, not to refuse appearance but to affirm it and to laugh, for if life is ferocious and cruel, she is also fecundity and eternal return: her name is Baubô'.[97] This quote is interesting because it can be seen to invite the reader to take up Baubô's position and affirm illusion while presenting her as a figure of life, previously defined as 'feline, fierce, lying, and protean',[98] and thus connecting her to nature. This connection marks a key difference from the female figures of *The Birth of Tragedy* who were used to present affirmation as a recognition of the necessity of mere appearances and thus as a celebration of artifice. Kofman's analysis of Baubô uses the metaphors of the camera obscura and nature, both of which inform her account of Nietzsche's perspectivalism.

Kofman argues that '[t]he camera obscura was invented to give the most perfect imitation possible of nature.'[99] This is not achieved by attempting to create a perfect replica. Instead, the camera obscura is said to imitate nature's creative power in that it selects and foregrounds specific features while leaving others in relief. Importantly, this analysis of imitating nature means that she does not function as the object of the gaze, but instead is presented as a fellow subject. Kofman argues that the metaphor of the camera obscura is crucial to Nietzsche's account of perspectivalism as a process in which each subject generates their own point of view. 'The camera obscura of painters is immanent in the eye of each viewer and does not give a pre-existing reality. Rather it constitutes for each his or her own "reality", which is in fact one with "appearance".'[100] Perspectivalism is not about having a partial view of the entire field of vision defined as the real, instead reality is nothing over and above the ways in which it is constantly re/viewed. Kofman's analysis of perspectivalism can be seen to circumvent the binary of subject/object in two ways. First, the camera obscura imitates the creative power of nature as a fellow subject. Second, the process of gazing generates a series of perspectival appearances that, in turn, serve to construct and re/construct the viewing subject.

Kofman presents perspectivalism as a form of the Dionysian will-to-art in that it involves the creation of appearances. She constructs the will-to-art as a process of creation that is based on selective repetition: 'Art repeats nature . . . by placing certain forms in relief, by hiding others, and closing up gaps.'[101] This reading uses a key quotation from *The Twilight of the Idols* in which Nietzsche defends the Dionysian artist's preference for appearance over reality by arguing that 'appearance means reality repeated *once again*, as selection, redoubling, correction.'[102] All 'reality' has been 'repeated' in the sense of being re/viewed within the camera obscura of each viewer. As a result, Kofman argues that Dionysian art can be seen as a particular mode of affirmative repetition: 'appearance is willed and the world repeated . . . to enhance the creative capacity . . . of life. Thus *art wills for life yet again its eternal return in difference*, a dionysian mimetic power at one with creation and affirmation.'[103] It is this sense of the eternal return as a form of repetition in difference that affirms life, which I will utilise in later chapters.

Kofman's construction of the Dionysian will-to-art as a form of the eternal return is very different from the ejaculatory model of discharge outlined in Section 2. This reading of Nietzsche results in another version of the underlying dynamic of affirmation, thus re/working the opposition between the degenerate and the affirmative set out in Section 2. For Nietzsche, this opposition is expressed in directional terms, perversion is characterised by a centripetal inward movement and Dionysian outpouring by a centrifugal movement. Kofman alters the directional opposition, creating a new distinction between two different models of circularity. Following Nietzsche, she defines perversion as a centripetal movement in which the subject turns away from life and in on itself. Turning within this closed circle involves inversion and reversal in that it results in the promulgation of values, such as a world beyond, that are negative and destructive of life.[104] In contrast, affirmation returns to life, repeating it in a different form, thus creating values that sustain and celebrate life. This model of repetition is based on a circular movement that has a temporal aspect in that it is possible to loop back into the past and forwards into the future, selecting and foregrounding specific features in order to construct patterns of events across time. Importantly, the circle is open in that each return offers the possibility of tracing a different pattern.

Kofman's reading of the eternal return links Baubô to a circular structure, which is presented as the means to create something new. This constitutes a significant alternative from chiasmic logic, in which the centripetal movement of denegation and the centrifugal movement of metonymic proliferation combine to draw the eye in and out from a preset vanishing point. Chiasmic logic is structured around a centre that is a site of disappearance and thus traces out a circle that is ultimately a zero. Kofman's account of the eternal return enables a reconfiguration of the circle, via a temporal axis, that facilitates its reconstruction as a site of creativity. In visual terms this can be understood as a move away from the two-dimensional space that sets up a central vanishing point, to a three-dimensional space, in which each loop backwards, forwards and sideways constructs a pattern that may, or may not, have a symmetrical centre. The logic of the eternal return can be mapped as series of loops, each of which constitutes an emerging pattern, thus opening up the possibility of creating new relations between appearances.[105]

Kofman's presentation of the logical structure of the eternal return through the figure of Baubô is important because it provides a significant alternative to the images of women that compound the structures of chiasmic and binary logic, which dominate the philosophical imaginary. Kofman also analyses other aspects of the mythic material, linking the eternal return to female reproduction. She argues that Baubô can be read as a figure of life and nature because her very name is a slang term for the female reproductive organs: 'Baubô is the equivalent of koilia another of the "improper" words used in Greek to designate the female sex.'[106] In this way, she clearly represents female fertility and can therefore be read as an image of reproductive creativity. This is linked to the eternal return through the rites of the Eleusinian mysteries in which 'the female sexual organ [was] exalted as the symbol of fertility and a guarantee of . . . regeneration'.[107]

Kofman's reading of the encounter between Baubô and Demeter offers yet another representation of the eternal return. However, I shall argue that her focus on the image of Dionysus on Baubô's belly has the disappointing effect of displacing the two women. The representation of Dionysus is said to recall his status as 'twice born'. In the myth, Dionysus' mother, Semele, was tricked into asking to lie with Zeus in his natural form. He then appeared as a lightning bolt, killing her and causing the premature birth of Dionysus. Zeus took his embryonic son from Semele's body, sewing him into his thigh. Dionysus was later born again from the body of his father.[108] Kofman follows a cue from Nietzsche's *Fragments Posthumes*, presenting Demeter's recovery as a response to the revelation of the image of the 'twice-born' god: 'Demeter recovers joy in the thought that Dionysus will be reborn. This joy, which announces the birth of the genius, is Greek serenity.'[109]

The problem with this reading is that Kofman follows Nietzsche in making Dionysus emblematic of the eternal return and thus replicates his displacement of the two women who clearly symbolise cyclical fertility. While Baubô is less well known, having only appeared in six lines of orphic verse that was heavily censored,[110] the earth goddess Demeter is famously linked to the cycle of the changing seasons. The restoration of her daughter is said to mark the beginning of spring and the onset of winter occurs when Persephone returns to the underworld. The attempt to represent the dynamic of the eternal return through the image of the twice-born god and the later birth of the Dionysian artist/genius seems somewhat strained. This is because the analysis of Demeter's joy does not seem sufficient given the well-known mythological material. If the image of Dionysus on Baubô's belly represents the possibility of rebirth, then Demeter surely 'recovers joy' at the thought that Persephone will return.[111]

At stake here is Nietzsche's attempt to appropriate a cyclical dynamic that is traditionally expressed through images of female reproduction and creativity. This is clearly demonstrated in the song of the seven seals in which the female figure of the eternal return is serenaded by Zarathustra: 'Never yet have I found the woman from whom I wanted children, unless it be this woman whom I love: for I love you O eternity.'[112] While the song extolls Eternity as the only suitable mother for his children, the dynamic of fertility and birth is appropriated by the singer. Combining the power of Zeus and the affirmative values of Dionysus, Zarathustra characterises himself as a soothsayer who is 'pregnant with lightning bolts that say Yes and laugh Yes'.[113] The imagery attests to the strain of attempting to reconstruct the Dionysian as a cyclical dynamic in that the lightning bolts clearly exemplify the dynamic of discharge. Moreover, Zarathustra's song positions Eternity as the object of desire that sustains his creativity, thus undermining the egalitarian potential of the circular structure of the eternal return by positioning it within the hierarchical binary of subject/object.[114]

I want now to offer a different reading of the encounter between Baubô and Demeter, which both draws on and diverges from aspects of Kofman's analysis. Kofman reads

Baubô as a camera obscura, thus constructing her display as an imitation of the creative power of nature. In this way, Baubô's gesture of raising her skirts can be seen to stage her own body as one of a series of veils, presenting the image of Dionysus on her belly as confirmation that there is nothing outside the endless play and replay of appearances. Kofman argues that it is the accompaniment of Baubô's laughter that makes her display a moment of affirmation. 'It signifies ... that appearance should cause us neither pessimism nor skepticism, but rather the affirming laugh of a living being who knows that despite death, life can come back indefinitely'.[115]

Kofman's focus on Baubô's laughter leads her to overlook the crucial role played by Demeter in constructing the display as a moment of affirmation. In contrast, I want to suggest that it is through viewing Baubô's gesture that Demeter recovers, her mood changing from inconsolable desolation to joy, signified by her laughter. Baubô can thus be seen to function as a camera obscura, in that her gesture produces a shift of perspective that is evident from Demeter's change of mood. Rather than mourning Persephone's disappearance, Demeter resolves to look forward to her reappearance. This can be seen as a shift away from chiasmic logic, which is constructed around a central vanishing point, in this case the death of her daughter, to a model of looping back in which the centre of the chiasma is displaced and repositioned as a point on a circle, a disappearance that attests to the possibility of return. Demeter's laughter is followed by her acceptance of the drink that Baubô originally offered her, which can be read as the restoration of the cycle of fertility to the earth.[116] The change of perspective can therefore be seen to restore Demeter to herself.

In my reading of the myth, the figure of Baubô symbolises a reconfiguration of appearances that holds open the possibility of a perspectival shift. In terms of theorising, Baubô offers us the opportunity to review and thus to think again. She constitutes an image of the process of thinking that differs considerably from the more renowned construction of being provoked to thought, exemplified by Carroll's image of a courtroom debate between established rivals.[117] This model of thought revolves around a conception of progress, which can only be attained through arguments that successfully discredit the rival view. The encounter between Baubô and Demeter presents the opportunity for changing and developing a perspective as a moment that is facilitated by generosity in that it begins with the proffering of a gift and ends with its acceptance. The process of thinking again requires an acceptance of the images and arguments offered by others, building on their work to create new possibilities, which will, in turn, be taken up and changed in the future.

Notes

1. F. Nietzsche, 'On Truth and Lies in a Non-moral Sense', in *Philosophy and Truth: Selections from Nietzsche's Notebooks of the Early 1870s*, D. Breazeale (trans.) (Atlantic Highlands, NJ and London: Humanities Press International, 1979), p. 84.

2. I have chosen to follow Kaufmann's translation in rendering 'Apollinisch' as 'Apollinian' rather than 'Apollonian'. See W. Kaufmann, 'Translator's Introduction', F. Nietzsche, *The Birth of Tragedy* (New York: Vintage Books, 1967), p. 9, fn. 9.

3. W. Kaufmann, *Nietzsche, Philosopher, Psychologist, Anti-Christ* (Princeton, NJ: Princeton University Press, 1968), pp. 129–30. Kaufmann argues that the characterisation of the Dionysian changes radically in the later works, such as *The Twilight of the Idols*, where Dionysus is contrasted with Christ.

4. This section will focus on the chapter entitled 'The Will to Power as Art', in F. Nietzsche, *The Will to Power*, W. Kaufmann (trans.) (New York: Vintage Books, 1968), pp. 419–53.

5. F. Nietzsche, *The Birth of Tragedy*, W. Kaufmann (trans.) (New York: Vintage Books, 1967), p. 33.

6. Ibid., p. 35.

7. Ibid., p. 46.

8. M. S. Silk and J. P. Stern, *Nietzsche on Tragedy* (Cambridge: Cambridge University Press, 1981), p. 65.

9. Nietzsche, *The Birth of Tragedy*, p. 59.

10. Ibid., pp. 45, 143.

11. Ibid., pp. 35, 37.

12. Ibid., p. 45.

13. Ibid., p. 52.

14. Ibid., pp. 95, 97.

15. Nietzsche, *The Will to Power*, p. 451.

16. Nietzsche, *The Birth of Tragedy*, p. 45. Nietzsche also presents the Dionysian as the third stage of illusion on pp. 109–10.

17. Ibid., p. 143.

18. Ibid., p. 33.

19. See Section 2 of Chapter 2.

20. In this reading of the *Orestia*, patriarchal law is secured through the rejection of Clytemnestra's claims and the suppression of the Furies (chthonic female deities whose function was to pursue the murderers of blood kin). This forms the basis of Irigaray's critique of the law as the suppression of the maternal and the ties of 'red blood'. L. Irigaray, *Speculum of the Other Woman*, G. C. Gill (trans.) (Ithaca, NY: Cornell University Press, 1985), pp. 221–2.

21. Silk and Stern, *Nietzsche on Tragedy*, pp. 170–1.

22. Nietzsche, *The Birth of Tragedy*, pp. 35, 37.

23. Ibid., p. 41.

24. C. Marlowe, *Dr Faustus*, Michael Mangan (ed.) (London: Penguin, 1987), V, i, 97.

25. Nietzsche, *The Birth of Tragedy*, p. 143.

26. Ibid., p. 60.

27. Silk and Stern, *Nietzsche on Tragedy*, p. 181.

28. Ibid., p. 174. There is one reference to the bacchantes in *The Birth of Tragedy* on p. 63.

29. Nietzsche, *The Birth of Tragedy*, p. 64.

30. Ibid., p. 65.

31. E. Burke, *A Philosophical Enquiry into the Origin of our Ideas of the Sublime and the Beautiful*, J. Boulton (ed.) (Oxford: Oxford University Press, 1990), p. 53.

32. Ibid., p. 84.

33. Ibid., pp. 100–1.

34. I. Kant, *The Critique of Judgement*, W. Pluhar (trans.) (Indianapolis, IN and Cambridge: Hackett Publishing Company, 1987), p. 113.

35. Ibid., p. 115.

36. Ibid.

37. Nietzsche, *The Birth of Tragedy*, pp. 86–98.

38. Kant, *The Critique of Judgement*, p. 101.

39. For a more detailed account of the Isis myth and its take-up by Kant and others, please see C. Battersby, 'Stages on Kant's Way: Aesthetics, Morality and the Gendered Sublime', in P. Brand and C. Korsmeyer (eds), *Feminism and Tradition in Aesthetics* (University Park: Pennsylvania State University Press, 1995), pp. 100–2.

40. F. Nietzsche, *The Gay Science*, W. Kaufmann (trans.) (New York: Vintage Books, 1974), p. 38.

41. F. Nietzsche, *The Twilight of the Idols*, in *The Portable Nietzsche*, W. Kaufmann (ed. and trans.) (London: Chatto and Windus, 1971), p. 485.

42. Ibid., p. 484.

43. Nietzsche, *The Gay Science*, p. 38.

44. S. Kofman, 'Baubô: Theological Perversion and Fetishism', in M. A. Gillespie and T. B. Strong (eds), *Nietzsche's New Seas: Explorations in Philosophy, Aesthetics and Politics* (Chicago, IL and London: University of Chicago Press, 1988), p. 196.

45. M-A. Doane, *Femmes Fatales: Feminism, Film Theory, Psychoanalysis* (London: Routledge, 1991), pp. 65–6.

46. Kofman, 'Baubô', p. 197.

47. Nietzsche, *The Will to Power*, pp. 323–4.

48. Kofman, 'Baubô', p. 177.

49. Nietzsche, *The Will to Power*, p. 317.

50. Ibid., p. 445.

51. Ibid., p. 431.

52. Ibid., quotes from pp. 429 and 422 respectively.

53. Nietzsche, *The Twilight of the Idols*, p. 548.

54. Nietzsche, *The Will to Power*, p. 422.

55. Kofman, 'Baubô', p. 178. The first italics are mine.

56. Nietzsche, *The Will to Power*, p. 445.

57. Nietzsche, *The Twilight of the Idols*, p. 484.

58. Nietzsche, *The Will to Power*, p. 444.

59. Ibid.

60. F. Nietzsche, *Thus Spake Zarathustra*, in *The Portable Nietzsche*, W. Kaufmann (ed. and trans.) (London: Chatto and Windus, 1971), pp. 137–9.

61. Nietzsche, *The Will to Power*, p. 447.

62. Nietzsche, *The Twilight of the Idols*, p. 531. First set of italics is mine.

63. Nietzsche, *The Will to Power*, p. 433.

64. Ibid., p. 422.

65. Ibid., p. 424.

66. Ibid., p. 425.

67. See Chapter 2, Section 3.

68. Nietzsche, *The Will to Power*, pp. 432–3.

69. Kofman, 'Baubô', p. 201, fn. 14. Kofman also links Nietzsche and Rousseau, arguing that both set up modesty as the key feminine virtue.

70. Nietzsche, *The Will to Power*, pp. 424–5.

71. Nietzsche, *The Twilight of the Idols*, p. 518.

72. J. Derrida, *Spurs*, B. Harlow (trans.) (Chicago, IL and London: University of Chicago Press, 1978), p. 95.

73. Ibid., p. 97.

74. Ibid., p. 101.

75. Nietzsche, *The Twilight of the Idols*, p. 485.

76. Ibid. The image of the sun acts as reference to Plato's forms in that the sun is the Form of the Good. My italics.

77. Derrida, *Spurs*, pp. 87, 89.

78. Ibid., p. 97.

79. Ibid.

80. Ibid.

81. Ibid.

82. Ibid.

83. Ibid., p. 51.

84. Ibid., p. 59.

85. Ibid., p. 63.

86. Ibid., p. 61.

87. Ibid., p. 107.

88. Nietzsche, *The Will to Power*, p. 425.

89. Derrida, *Spurs*, p. 51.

90. Ibid., p. 65.

91. Given the substantial nature of Derrida's reworking of key Nietzschean terms, I will always indicate when I am referring to his versions of the Dionysian or affirmation.

92. Derrida, *Spurs*, p. 61.
93. Her laughter is quite unlike Wanda's mocking laughter, which reflects her positioning both inside and outside of the masochistic fantasy. See Chapter 3, Section 1.
94. Derrida *Spurs*, p. 67. My italics.
95. Doane, *Femmes Fatales*, p. 59.
96. Derrida, *Spurs*, p. 71. Doane uses the part of this quote that is given in italics.
97. Kofman, 'Baubô', p. 196.
98. Ibid., p. 191.
99. Ibid., p. 189.
100. Ibid.
101. Ibid.
102. Ibid. This is Kofman's translation of the end of section six of 'Reason in Philosophy' from *The Twilight of the Idols*.
103. Ibid., p. 181. My italics.
104. Ibid., pp. 180–1.
105. Le Doeuff's tracing of feedback loops, which result in the historicisation of philosophy, creating a new perspective on theory, can thus be read as another example of the logic of the eternal return.
106. Kofman, 'Baubô', p. 197.
107. Ibid.
108. This version of the myth is from E. Tripp, *Dictionary of Classical Mythology* (London and Glasgow: Collins, 1970), p. 203.
109. Kofman, 'Baubô', p. 197, quoting F. Nietzsche, in G. Colli and M. Montinari (eds), *Fragments Posthumes, Werke: Kritische Gesamtausgabe* (Berlin: de Gruyter, 1972), 9:261, 269.
110. Kofman, 'Baubô', p. 196.
111. I have to thank Rachel Jones for this suggestion.
112. Nietzsche, *Thus Spake Zarathustra*, p. 340.
113. Ibid.
114. Irigaray provides a critique of the way in which Nietzsche's conception of the eternal return is reliant on the appropriation of female reproduction in *Marine Lover of Friedrich Nietzsche*, G. C. Gill (trans.) (New York: Columbia University Press, 1991), pp. 31–5.
115. Kofman, 'Baubô', p. 197.
116. My reading of the drink is also enforced by Winkler's argument that barley and wheat had special significance at the annual festivals of Demeter because they were eight-month crops that symbolised a 'cycle of hard work'. J. J. Winkler, *The Constraints of Desire: An Anthology of Sex and Gender in Ancient Greece* (London, Routledge, 1990), p. 198.
117. N. Carroll, *Post-Theory*, p. 59.

5 | Woman as Caprice

The first section of this chapter will examine Mary-Ann Doane's take-up of Nietzsche and Derrida in order to analyse the gendered nature of cinematic representation.[1] It can therefore be seen to offer another perspective on these theorists, moving away from the dynamics of the theoretical models, which were discussed in the previous chapter, to focus on the issue of signification. I have chosen to address this approach to Nietzsche in a later chapter in order to present the reading that has gained ascendancy in Cultural Studies as one possible perspective on his work. This chapter begins with an analysis of Derrida's use of woman as the figure of *différance* before addressing aspects of Doane's critique of both Nietzsche and Derrida. I will argue that she concedes too much to their systems, ultimately perpetuating the tropes and structures that she wishes to undermine. I will demonstrate that the problem is the result of her methodology and will show the ways in which it serves to shut down the theoretical potential of the images.

The second section will show how Le Doeuff's methodology provides an escape from Doane's impasse through detailed textual analysis of *The Devil Is a Woman*. I will examine the ways in which the film deploys two specific tropes: the manipulative *femme fatale* and the changeable, capricious woman. This will involve comparing the film's presentation of woman as caprice to Nietzsche's figure of Life, who affirms the play of appearances in the same way as Helen, Maya and Baubô.[2] The two tropes can also be seen as variants of Derrida's definitions of woman as truth and the untruth of truth respectively. I will argue that the figures of the *femme fatale* and woman as caprice are used in very different ways across the film. This will involve drawing attention to the moments in which they serve to challenge the Derridean model; as well as tracing the ways in which they occasionally function in accordance with the model, thereby perpetuating the structures of chiasmic logic.

1 Woman as Figure

Derrida's analysis of three different configurations of woman in Nietzsche's work – untruth, truth and the untruth of truth – is explored in Section 3 of Chapter 4. I want now to consider some of the implications of presenting the third woman as a symbol of the movement of *différance* in language. Derrida raises the question of '*the woman's figure*' early on in *Spurs*.[3] The pun on 'figure' suggests that it can be viewed as both physical and linguistic, demonstrating the third woman's role of textual undecidability. The construction of woman as a symbol of language itself is also presented as a shift away from the ordinary use of woman as a trope within language. 'It is not the figure of the woman precisely because we shall bear witness here to her *abduction*, because the question of the figure is at once opened and closed by what is called woman. . . '.[4] The presentation of the transition from a specific figure to the figurative itself as a form of abduction constructs it in terms of absence.

The effects of this transition from one figure to the issue of the figurative can be demonstrated by focusing on a specific trope. I will therefore play out Derrida's scenario with reference to a famous abductee, Helen of Troy. In the myth, Helen is abducted by Paris and taken to Troy. Her husband, Menelaus, accompanied by her former suitors, who were bound by an oath to defend the marriage, set off in pursuit, beginning the Trojan War. The Euripides' play *Electra* adds a further twist in that the abduction is revealed to be a ruse designed by Zeus who wanted to provoke war. Hera was said to have provided Paris with a 'phantom Helen made of cloud', which was taken to Troy, thus instigating the war and fulfilling Zeus's plans.[5] At the level of the specific trope, Helen is associated with beauty and destruction, while her phantom is an instrument of the gods, which serves to reveal their callous inhumanity. However, the phantom Helen can also be read as representative of the process of language itself. Like Derrida's third woman, both figures are elusive, thus sustaining the endless search for truth and meaning.

I have juxtaposed the textual reading of the phantom of Helen with the linguistic reading of her as a figure of *différance* in order to show how the latter empties out the specific connotations of the trope. These connotations are effaced further because the Derridean model privileges the linguistic reading, ensuring that it becomes *the* reading of the figure of woman. This has a paradoxical effect in that the third woman symbolises textual undecidability, but her role as that symbol actually results in her being allocated a decided meaning. The conflict can be seen clearly in *Spurs*. Derrida famously extols textual plurality 'there is no such thing either as the truth of Nietzsche, or of Nietzsche's text.'[6] Yet on the previous page he asserts '[t]here is no such thing as a woman, as a truth in itself of woman in itself. That much, at least, Nietzsche has said.'[7] At this point then meaning is decided. Woman signifies meaning as deferral. Yet her own meaning is not deferred – she remains forever 'the untruth of truth'.[8]

The paradoxical presentation of woman as *différance*, in which she symbolises textual undecidability while simultaneously being allocated a decided meaning, can be read as another effect of the chiasmic structure that underpins the Derridean system. In this model of meaning, unending metonymic proliferation is ultimately reliant upon denegation. The third woman's role as *différance* is sustained by her construction as 'the untruth of truth' where she is entirely defined by negation, becoming a memorial to the loss of truth and meaning. The structure of denegation ensures that the search for meaning cannot end, thus the image of the phantom of Helen is appropriate in that her abduction instigates Menelaus's quest, yet she can never be found because as a phantom Helen is also, to paraphrase Derrida, abducted from herself.

Doane argues that the presentation of woman as 'averted of herself'[9] is a crucial moment in both Derrida's and Nietzsche's accounts of the reflexive gesture of feminine modesty. Averting her gaze, woman is said to become the ideal object of both philosophers' voyeurism in that she is unable to look back or to think for herself. In this way, woman's capacity to dissemble is contained. 'She does not *know* that she is deceiving or *plan* to deceive; conscious deception would be repellent to the man and quite dangerous ... Closing her eyes to herself she becomes the pure construct of a philosophical gaze.'[10] At one level this means that woman represents deception without being able to access its power. Doane also argues that the construction of woman as pure object presents her as the lure that instigates the subject's unending search for meaning. Importantly, her role as lure means that woman becomes a figure of the endless movement of desire in language that is the basis of the deconstructive project. Doane presents this as a crucial shift in that woman no longer acts as a figure of representation, but instead is said to form 'the substrate of representation itself'.[11]

Doane's shift towards a model of desire as textual depth can be seen to act as a freeze frame, in that the specific images of feminine modesty are caught and held to a single meaning, namely the structure of desire in language. The move to the linguistic level has the same effects as before in that it effaces the specific connotations of the figure of feminine modesty; for example, Nietzsche's use of the trope to indicate a reflexive movement of perversion which was the opposite of the Dionysian.[12] Importantly, it is also the moment at which the gendered binary of subject/object is perpetuated in its strongest form in that it is positioned as 'unconscious [textual] material' and thus designated as *the* construction of desire rather than one possible construction.[13] In this way, Doane's analysis of woman as 'the pure construct of a philosophical gaze' actually serves to strengthen the structures of the voyeurism that she criticises.

At stake here is the link between the images and their concomitant theoretical structures. Doane can be seen to offer a strong version of Le Doeuff's position, in that she argues for a necessary interrelation between Derrida's images of woman and his theoretical position.[14]

> Woman-truth, woman-lie, woman-affirmation – it is quite striking that the woman comes to represent all these things, as though affirmation, the most highly treasured category, *could somehow not be thought* except in and through the figure of the woman.[15]

However, this take-up of Le Doeuff also involves a lessening of the disruptive role of the imaginary, in that the images of woman are said to be entirely congruent with the system they create. In this way '[woman] enables the philosophical operation, becomes its *support*.'[16] What is lost here is the sense of the precarious nature of any philosophical system that is built up through such imagery and the ways in which specific images can have connotations that are not fully contained by the system.

Doane's commentary links the three figures of woman together, following Derrida's logic in which the third is seen to subsume and surpass the first two. However, the gesture of averting that she rightly picks out as the key to objectification is only characteristic of the third, Dionysian woman. This is important because the second and third figures are both credited with the capacity to dissemble. While the Dionysian dissimulatress is unable to utilise her powers of deception for herself, the second figure of woman does have the ability to manipulate truth 'to her own advantage'.[17] Her distance from the masculinist fetish of truth can thus be seen to provide her with critical power. This is immediately denigrated, in that it is defined as castrating, and therefore rejected. In this way, the smooth transition from the second to the third image of woman can be seen as a means of passing over the troublesome features of the former in order to promote the latter as the ideal. Interestingly, Derrida's schematic process of idealisation can be compared to Deleuze's selective reading of Sacher-Masoch in that both theorists' constructions of their ideal woman involve the elimination of the 'undesirable' feature of rational distance.

This awareness of the ways in which key images can be utilised to disrupt the system they are supposed to support is absolutely vital because it provides the means to think through the possibility of other structures. While the second figure of woman is presented as the 'veils [that] float in the distance',[18] indicating her function as an object of desire, her capacity for manipulation affects her positioning within the binary. While she is the object of the quest for truth and meaning, she also controls its results by revealing only what she wants to be seen, secure in the knowledge that the quest is in vain. This capacity to manipulate the results of the quest through staging her own appearances suggests that woman controls it as a game, thus presenting her as both object and subject, imploding the binary. Doane's argument that the images simply support the system closes down their potential meanings, ensuring that they can only be seen to perpetuate familiar logical structures. This is unfortunate because her careful tracing of the re-emergence of patriarchal binary logic within Derrida's work sustains a most convincing critique of his position. However, her methodology results in the sedimentation of the very structures that she wishes to undermine.

Doane's perpetuation of the very systems that she critiques leaves her unable to think through the implications of the figures that fall outside them. Her brief discussion of Baubô begins with an acknowledgment of her capacity to disrupt the 'phallocentric staging of truth', however, the analysis simply positions her at the margins of the system.[19] Doane summarises Wollen's reading of the laughter that Baubô provokes, suggesting that '[t]he laugh, outside the semantic and "on the edge of language," breaks the hold of a phallogocentric grammar.'[20] She then offers an account of Kofman's article, ending with a focus on the way in which the myth is censored as exemplary of 'the marginalisation of the woman's story . . . within a patriarchal discourse'.[21] Importantly, the commentary on both readings serves to position Baubô at the edge of discourse, which is then compared with Derrida's positioning of the affirming woman beyond the economy of castration and Lacan's version of feminine *jouissance* that lies outside the Symbolic. Doane argues that the presentation of woman as 'the very limit of what is theorizable' ultimately ensures that she supports the Derridean and Lacanian systems.[22] In this way, Baubô's laughter becomes a mode of disruption that is always already recuperated.

Positioning woman at the edge of discourse means that her capacities are constantly viewed in relation to the system rather than forming the basis of other potential structures or systems. In this way, Doane's analysis means that she cannot begin to see how Baubô might open up other possible structures such as that of the eternal return. In circumventing this possibility, Doane replicates aspects of the Lacanian model in which the very thought of woman being used to create new structures is explicitly prohibited. Woman's *jouissance* is said to set up a mirage of a 'beyond' because there is nothing outside the Symbolic.[23] Importantly, Le Doeuff provides the means to challenge the construction of woman as a figure that symbolises the edge of language or language itself. Her methodology enables a charting of the transition from the specific figure to the figurative itself as the moment in which one reading of woman crystallises into *the* reading because it is the only one that the system will permit. This tracing of the transition as an attempt to secure specific tropes can thus be seen to open up the possibility of using the imagery in different ways.

This move is important because it enables the charting of a variety of possible roads not taken. Otherwise the only conceivable way out is a reversal in which woman takes up the masculine subject position. Doane begins to make this move in her final analysis of two images of Catherine from *The Scarlet Empress*. 'It might be useful to imagine what Dietrich's return look might be, from behind the veil.'[24] However, the acceptance of the philosophical constructions of the veiled woman as pure object ensures that Doane lacks the means to think through this possibility. 'But how can we imagine, conceive her look back? Everything would become woven, narrativized, dissimulation ... It would be preferable to disentangle the woman and the veil, to tell another story.'[25] Finding a way out is thus seen to require the complete rejection of the 'worn' tropes of femininity. In contrast, I will focus on the presentation of such tropes throughout *The Devil Is a Woman* in order to demonstrate the ways in which the variety of images of woman in the film serve to hold open a multiplicity of imaginary pathways.

2 Caprice Espagnol

The Devil Is a Woman can be seen to utilise two different tropes of femininity that were common in nineteenth-century literature: the manipulative *femme fatale* and the changeable, capricious woman. These tropes can be seen to offer contradictory constructions of woman: the first constructs her as a figure of rationality; while the second presents her as a creature of whims, whose continual changes of mind suggest that she does not have a mind to change. Both can be seen to present the conjunction of femininity and rationality as aberrant, constructing it as a locus of danger and an unnatural combination respectively. I will argue that *The Devil Is a Woman* utilises these tropes in a complex way by presenting them as points of intersection, which opens up their range of potential meanings and theorisations. However, these possibilities are not sustained consistently across the film. I will demonstrate that some of the changes in the presentation of the female protagonist, Concha Perez, who begins the film as an exuberant figure of life and ends as a harbinger of death, serve to mark a return to some familiar imaginary pathways. The vilification of Concha is also the result of the presentation of the male protagonist, Don Pasqual, and I will trace the ways in which the privileging of his perspective affects her characterisation.

The nineteenth-century literary sources of *The Devil Is a Woman* become clear when tracing the genealogy of the film's title. I will look at each of the three proposed titles in turn, sketching out their use of cultural imagery and will then briefly outline the take-up of the images within philosophy. The first, *The Woman and the Puppet*, was a translation of the title of a novella by Pierre Louys, which was published in France in 1898. The original French title, *La Femme et le Pantin*, is clearly gendered, showing the *femme fatale*'s manipulative power over her male victims. The novella formed the basis of the screenplay, and supplies a key motif of the *mise en scène* in which the primary contenders for Concha's affections are presented alongside or holding puppets, clearly indicating her power over them. Dijkstra comments that the representation of the *femme fatale* in *fin-de-siècle* art emphasises her power by showing her ability to gaze back while also demarcating the limitations of the desire for manipulation:

> In a visual world populated by images of woman with faintly flickering or already extinguished eyes, the sexual woman, with her malevolent but spirited glance actually comes as a relief, a sign that woman still existed as a thinking entity – even if all she could think about . . . was the destruction of man . . .[26]

The cultural imagery of the *femme fatale* can be seen to re-emerge in Derrida's reconstruction of the figure of Isis in *Spurs*. In a departure from the Nietzschean and Kantian source material, Derrida represents Isis as a manipulative figure, who is able to turn the truth to her advantage. The second woman's link to rationality is presented through her construction as the 'veils [that] float in the distance' and this is immediately given a fatal aspect in that she becomes a 'dream of death'.[27] I have already argued that the definition of the second woman as 'castrating' is an attempt to denigrate her relation to rational distance. However, tracing the cultural basis of the philosophical image draws attention to Derrida's take-up of an established mode of denigration. The key assumption Dijkstra notes, that any woman who has rational power will invariably use it to destroy man, can thus be seen to pass from the cultural to the philosophical imaginary.

The second title proposed for the film was *Caprice Espagnol*, which was suggested by Sternberg because he had used Rimsky-Korsakov's *Capriccio Espagnol* in the score.[28] A capriccio is an 'unbridled musical composition' which does not follow formal rules and the choice of title can be seen to draw attention to the carnival setting of the film as well as the capricious nature of the female protagonist.[29] The final change to *The Devil Is a Woman*[30] derives from an early collection of plays by Mérimée, *Théâtre de Clara Gazul*, which were published in 1825. The female protagonist was a Spanish actress and playwright whose first publication was a work entitled *Une Femme est un diable*.[31] While the final choice clearly draws on a traditional Christian construction of femininity as a locus of temptation and evil, the reference to Mérimée also invites a parallel with his most famous work, *Carmen*, thus linking the second and third titles. Carmen can be seen as an exemplary instance of woman as caprice in that the novella presents her as a creature of whim: exciting, exotic and unpredictable. She is also described as 'a strange and wild beauty' and her eyes are compared to those of a wolf, emphasising her link to nature and thus to sexual instincts.[32]

Nietzsche takes up the cultural construction of woman as an unpredictable force of nature in his presentation of the figure of Life in Zarathustra's first dancing song.

Into your eyes I looked recently, O life! And into the unfathomable I then seemed to be sinking. But you pulled me out with a golden fishing rod; and you laughed mockingly when I called you unfathomable.

'Thus runs the speech of all fish', you said; 'what *they* do not fathom is unfathomable. But I am merely changeable and wild and a woman in every way ...'

Thus she laughed, the incredible one ...[33]

Zarathustra also characterises woman as a 'mobile, stormy film over shallow water', suggesting that Life's laughter at being called unfathomable is the mockery of the fathomless, stormy surface.[34] Her unpredictable changeability is the result of her vitality, which is also signalled by her continual movement. Life is a dancer and her additional qualities of lightness and laughter serve to construct her as a key trope of the Dionysian. Life's continual changes of mood resemble Baubô's display of a series of veils in that both affirm the play of appearances. Both figures are linked to nature in different ways: Baubô symbolises the creative power of nature conceptualised as repetition, the eternal return in difference, whereas Life represents the unpredictable power of nature, which takes the form of continual change.

The image of Life in *Thus Spake Zarathustra* can be linked to Derrida's construction of the third woman in that both are presented as figures of changeability albeit in very different ways. Life describes herself as 'changeable and wild', thus stressing her link to nature, whereas the third woman represents the continual changes of meaning wrought by the movement of *différance* in language. Both figures are associated with a mocking laughter that is directed at specific men.[35] They are also sites of non-knowledge in that they represent two very different constructions of the Dionysian without being able to access its power. Life learns the secret of what she represents from Zarathustra who whispers it in her ear, 'through her tangled yellow foolish tresses'; while Derrida's third woman is unaware of her power of dissimulation, contenting herself with playing at deception.[36] However, Life's response to being called 'unfathomable' is interesting: 'Thus runs the speech of all fish . . . what *they* do not fathom is unfathomable.' This suggests that her construction is the result of the limits of the frame through which she is viewed, a possibility that I will explore later in relation to the presentation of Concha in *The Devil Is a Woman*.

I have sketched out some of the constructions of the tropes of the *femme fatale* and woman as caprice in cultural discourses as well as philosophy in order to consider the ways in which *The Devil Is a Woman* both borrows from and alters the established cultural and philosophical imagery. I will begin my examination of the film's unusual presentation of these two incompatible tropes of woman in combination by focusing on the initial representation of Concha in the carnival sequence. This will involve placing her alongside Nietzsche's figures of Baubô and Life. I will then consider the way in which the imagery can be seen to challenge familiar theoretical structures by examining Concha's presentation as an unattainable object of desire in the chase sequence that follows the carnival. My analysis of the challenge that the images pose to the Derridean model will culminate with a reading of Concha's performance of the musical number, 'Three Sweethearts', in the theatre. This reading will draw on Florence Jacobowitz's analysis of the number as crucial to the construction of the female protagonist's narrative voice.[37] I will then go on to discuss the effects that the presentation of Don Pasqual's perspective has on the characterisation of Concha.

The carnival sequence introduces two of the three main characters: Antonio and Concha. Antonio's first appearance is immediately preceded by a medium shot of a reveller dressed as a rooster chasing the women who crowd around him, which Gaylyn Studlar reads as symbolic of the male protagonist's sexual quest.[38] Antonio's appearance is followed by a long shot of a pantomime bull chasing a matador while the crowd cheers them on. He is thus linked to an iconography of machismo, which is repeatedly presented as a cultural construction, given the emphasis on costume and performance. The first images of the carnival also emphasise the ways in which it undermines masculine power structures. Contrary to Don Paquito's instructions, the police officers are not controlling the crowd by force, but instead are themselves contained by two circles of dancing revellers, who are moving in opposite directions, entangling them in a giant web of streamers. Jacobowitz draws attention to the gendered aspects of the traditional inversion of the law wrought by the carnival in that the police are 'encircled and overpowered by a crowd prominently peopled with women'.[39] This adds an element of the bacchanalia to the lawless and transgressive space of the carnival in that the chief celebrants of Dionysian rites were women who were thus able to gain temporary access to the public space.

Concha's elaborately staged entrance occurs a few moments later in the sequence. The sound of a fanfare of trumpets heralds the appearance of a horse and carriage, which is liberally decorated with balloons. The carriage moves across the screen to the right and the camera pans slowly with it, as the occupant throws flowers into the crowd. Her actions are partially obscured by a procession of two carriages in the foreground, which move in the opposite direction and the camera then pans slightly to the left, following them. The last camera movement acts as a visual bluff, tantalising the viewer and frustrating the desire to see the character whose arrival has been heralded by the music. There is a cut to a medium close-up of Antonio standing transfixed, his smile fading as he gazes steadily off screen to the left. He pulls away the streamers entwined in his clothes and there is a cut to a close-up of Concha. The teasing movement of the camera and the medium close-up of Antonio's gaze clearly set up the point-of-view shot as the first full appearance of a supreme object of desire. Antonio's quest has found its focus.

The close-up of Concha shows she is costumed in layers of veils. She is wearing a dark, filigree mask over her eyes as well as a dark loose-weave mantilla, liberally decorated with pom-poms, which hangs down over her mask. Her hair is parted and a single kiss curl is visible beneath the mantilla in the centre of her forehead. Her mouth is unveiled and her dark lipstick draws attention to her wide smile. The layers of veiling have the same effect as Baubô's display of the painting of Dionysus on her belly in that both characters can be seen to present themselves as art. The double veiling over Concha's eyes draws attention to her mouth, which is also veiled by lipstick. The forehead that can be glimpsed through the veil is decorated by a kiss-curl. Like Baubô's belly, Concha's face is presented as yet another veil, yet another surface. The play of surfaces acts as an affirmation of appearances in that Concha is associated with festive music and dancing movement. Her eyes scan rapidly over the crowd as she continues to throw the white flowers to them, swinging her shoulders from side to side, conveying her excitement. These continual movements create the impression of festive exuberance.

Antonio gains Concha's attention by using a catapult to burst the balloons decorating her coach. Having identified the perpetrator, her response is a seamless play of expressions, which construct her as an icon of feminine changeability and caprice. She responds to the bursting of the second balloon by putting her index finger to her lips and kissing it. She moves her finger slightly from her mouth as if to blow Antonio a kiss, and then waves her finger at him in a gesture of admonishment. There is a cut to a close-up of Antonio who responds enthusiastically to Concha's display of diverse reactions. This is followed by a return to the medium close-up of Concha who sits wide-eyed looking up and left, turning her face away from Antonio. The movement suggests both indignation and indifference. Her eyes then move back to the right and she drops her eyelids and looks provocatively at him from beneath her eyelashes. She then begins to swing her shoulders from side to side. The rapid transition from indifference to seductiveness means that Concha's fleeting facial expressions resemble her dancing shoulder movements in that both represent her capacity for continual movement.

Nietzsche's portrayal of Life sets up a similar parallel between emotional changeability and physical exuberance. Zarathustra's second dancing song characterises Life's multiform zest:

> Into your eyes I looked recently, O life: I saw gold blinking in your night-eye; my heart stopped in delight: a golden boat I saw blinking on nocturnal waters, a golden rocking boat, sinking, drinking, and winking again. At my foot, frantic to dance, you cast a glance, a laughing, questioning, melting rocking-glance: twice only you stirred your rattle with your small hands, and my foot was already rocking with dancing frenzy.[40]

In the original German the word for rocking-boat is *Schaukel-Kahn*. The prefix '*Schaukel*' can mean rocking or swinging, it suggests a movement to and fro.[41] Life's rocking glance, *Schaukel-Blick*, is unstable, moving from quizzical laughter to love. In the same way, Concha's expressions change from flirtation to admonition and indifference to seduction. The *Schaukel-Blick* of both female figures is manifested in physical movement. Life stirs her rattle, an invitation to dance, and Concha swings her shoulders as the carnival music plays on.

Nietzsche's representation of woman as caprice differs from *The Devil Is a Woman* in one key respect. In line with nineteenth-century constructions of the trope, Life's 'natural' sexuality is conveyed through a series of animal metaphors. Life is described as a 'temptress' who displays a 'serpent's ire' and a 'wildcat' with a 'mane' of hair as well as a hunting 'hound', clearly conveying her role as a sexual predator.[42] The film does not follow in this tradition of representing female sexuality as an animalistic, natural force, thus ensuring that the Dionysian aspect of the carnival is presented as a cultural construction. Indeed, the emphasis on artifice evident in the *mise en scène*, as well as the use of costume and performance throughout the carnival, can be said to foreground the constructed nature of all the gender roles that are played out in this sequence.

The carnival sequence also demonstrates that cultural constructions of gender are multiple and malleable by offering an immediate inversion of its initial scenario in which the male protagonist pursued an ideal object. The change is demarcated by a shift to Concha's point of view presented through a high-angle medium shot of Antonio, showing the moment at which his pursuit founders.[43] Buffeted by the crowd, he staggers into the bottom lefthand corner of the screen and is then pushed back into the centre, entirely off course. His discomfiture is apparent from two further shots in which he is progressively entangled in streamers, finally becoming entrapped in a paper web spun by a circle of female revellers. The image marks the reversal of Antonio's initial presentation as the hunter, symbolised by the rooster and the matador; he is now the hunted, a fly caught in a paper web. The inversion is completed by the arrival of a carnival puppet resembling a man's head on an elongated neck, which bobs into view suggesting that Antonio has been 'caught like a puppet on a string'.[44]

Concha's response to the sight of Antonio's predicament is presented by two medium close-ups, which serve to emphasise her power in a variety of ways. Looking off-screen right, towards him, she lifts her eyes, throws her head back and laughs, mocking his unsuccessful efforts to reach her. She is presented in a space of her own and is thus entirely unaffected by the other revellers. The rapidly falling streamers do not impede her dancing shoulder movements, they simply lie across her mantilla and flowers, embellishing the decorative layers of her costume. Her freedom of movement within the paper web constructs her as a spider that entangles her prey.[45] The inversion of the power relations between the hunter and the hunted is thus partly effected by a change in Concha's presentation: from caprice to *femme fatale*. The second role is indicated by the use of the traditional metaphor of the spider to suggest a sexual predator who succeeds by manipulation. The emphasis on Concha's rational control of the entire quest and thus the game of desire is consolidated by the use of the puppet to form the final image of the sequence.

The intersection of the two different sets of tropes in a single character has some very interesting effects. The introduction of the motifs of the spider and the puppeteer give Concha a rational power that she had not previously possessed. In turn, her festive changeability affects the manipulative power of the *femme fatale*, giving her interests beyond the destruction of man. Concha can thus be seen to move beyond Derrida's construction of the second woman who simply plays with the logic of male desire to form a fatal endgame. The way in which the conjunction of the two tropes serves to create a different mode of characterisation can be seen in the moments of her laughter. The two reaction shots show her facing in Antonio's direction, mocking his efforts to reach her. However, her laughter is also an expression of the festive exuberance that has characterised her dancing movements throughout the sequence. Like Life, Concha throws back her head and laughs. The fulsome gesture constructs her as the spirit of carnival itself, its mocking inflections a byproduct of her exuberant enjoyment.

The carnival sequence can be seen to present a quest model of desire and its inversion, only to offer an alternative to both structures. This succession of moves is immediately repeated in the chase sequence, which makes extensive use of visual patterns, providing a series of images that sustain a detailed Derridean reading. I will trace the way in which the images can be seen to sustain three rather different constructions of desire and will argue that the third highlights the limitations of the Derridean model.

In my analysis of the carnival sequence, I read Concha's dancing movements as indicative of her emotional changeability, positioning her alongside Nietzsche's figure of Life.

In the chase sequence, her rapid movements are continually presented within the context of an overall pattern, expanding the play of veils across the *mise en scène*. In the establishing shot Concha is seen running down the stairs, occasionally looking back over her shoulder. The dark pom-poms decorating her high mantilla and wide, hooped skirt are mirrored by a string of dark, spherical decorations hanging over the stairway. In her second appearance, Concha peers through the latticework of the gate, looking excitedly from side to side, the wrought ironwork providing a third layer of dark veiling for her face. Concha's physical elusiveness is thus conveyed by her presentation within a series of patterns. Like Derrida's third woman, 'it is impossible to resist looking for her' because the play of the veils is beautiful and bewitching.[46] Concha's gradual subsumption within the décor of the festival decorations and the latticework of the gate reaches its climax in her final appearance at the window.

The medium close-up of Concha at the window can be seen to consolidate her presentation as a play of veils. She is framed in two glass panes: her masked face with its covering mantilla and the fingertips of one hand in the right pane; while her other hand in its black lace glove is pressed against the left. Concha is doubly framed by a rolled-up bamboo screen which runs across the top edge of the window, creating a series of parallel lines that contrast with the swirling details of the white lace curtains which hang down on either side of her. There is a proliferation of pattern, the white lace curtains setting off the darker filigree lace, covering Concha's face and hands. As she moves away from the window, she brushes against the curtains, which sway slightly in her absence. Within the Derridean framework, her 'disappearance' can be seen as the moment in which the third woman diffuses into the play of veils. It marks the absence of the body behind the veil and its reconstruction as a series of surfaces. In this reading, Concha's 'disappearance' represents the self-abnegation of the third woman, marking the moment in which she becomes the ultimate unattainable object of desire.

I have already argued that Derrida's construction of the third woman as the veils that 'fall a bit differently', revealing that there is nothing behind them, sustains a traditional quest model of desire.[47] This structure is briefly presented by Antonio's search for Concha. However, Antonio's positioning as the subject in pursuit of an elusive object is swiftly reversed in that he is being pursued by the police. Their entrance is marked by a change in the background music: from the rapid theme of the capriccio to the deeper sound of rumbling drums, suggesting the danger they present to him. Antonio's take-up of the role of object is complete when he seeks refuge in a gateway. His presentation mirrors Concha's final appearance at the window, in that both characters are clearly positioned within a frame, although each is constructed differently. Antonio hides in the indented framing of the gateway, using the depth of the three-dimensional frame as a space of shelter, while Concha is displayed as part of the proliferation of surfaces in the window. Antonio's transition from hunter to hunted is conveyed by his cowering within the frame. His loss of control over the situation is further indicated by his starts of surprise at the gift of a jack-in-the-box and the revelation of the accompanying note. The gift doubles the previous reversal in that the repetition of the motif of the male puppet clearly presents Antonio as the object of the *femme fatale*'s machinations.

The transition from the traditional quest for an unattainable object to a quest that is ultimately controlled by a female subject acting as object, can be seen to correspond to a shift back from Derrida's idealised third woman to the far from ideal figure of the castrating woman. Indeed, it suggests that the double bluff practised by the woman who controls the play of the veils, staging her disappearance only to fool man into thinking that he is in control, constitutes the most damnable wile of all. Within the Derridean model, this change to the structure of desire is a fatal inversion, a return to the 'dream of death'.[48] This reading is upheld by Don Pasqual's later warning that dalliance with Concha could cost Antonio his life. However, the film may also be said to draw attention to the limits of this perspective in that Don Pasqual clearly has his own reasons for wishing to remove a prospective lover from the scene.

Importantly, the sequence consolidates Concha's presentation as the spirit of carnival: she becomes an expression of its décor as well as being associated with its theme music: the bubbling, exuberant capriccio. This has the effect of presenting her pursuit of the pleasures of dalliance with Antonio as a further expression of her vitality and zest. He corresponds to the physical type that she is seen to find attractive throughout the film, being tall and dark like the 'cousin' waiting in her mother's flat and the matador at the theatre. The latter's poverty clearly presents Concha's liaison with him as a source of pleasure rather than income. The motif of the jack-in-the-box conveys both Concha's power and her sense of the game of desire as a joke, a source of surprises and humour. This presentation foregrounds the limits of the Derridean model in that the quest of desire can only be playful and pleasurable if woman takes up her proper role of pure object. Concha's pursuit of the prospect of an amusing, pleasurable dalliance can therefore be seen to offer an alternative construction of female desire.

The productive intersection of the film's presentation of the tropes of woman as caprice and the *femme fatale* is not sustained. Once Don Pasqual takes over the narration, telling Antonio the story of his long association with Concha, the tropes are often shown separately and their negative aspects are usually foregrounded. The narrative unfolds in a series of flashbacks, which are punctuated by returns to the conversation in the gentlemen's club. The second flashback reconstructs Concha's capriciousness as a series of inexplicable changes of mood: she bestows a kiss on Don Pasqual, initiating their physical contact, only to struggle and move away from him, placing her hands on her hips and telling him not to touch her, as though he had made unwanted advances. This is followed by a display of petulant anger in which she does not dismiss him but instead shouts at him for not loving her. Don Pasqual's attempt to reassure her in the midst of these abrupt changes involves him referring to Concha as 'my child', an assessment that becomes increasingly apt in that her sudden display of anger resembles a childish temper tantrum. The scene demonstrates the problematic infantilisation of woman that is often part of her depiction as caprice.[49]

The third flashback presents Concha as cold and manipulative through the complete variance between the description she dictates to the scribe: 'As I write this my heart is bleeding and my eyes are filled with tears' and her current situation, sitting utterly dry-eyed while primping her coiffure in an unconcerned fashion. Wilson comments that the scribe's repetition of Concha's words 'intones the positive nonemotion [sic] of her speech'.[50] However, the negative construction of Concha in this flashback is also problematised, given that Don Pasqual is claiming to remember a scene at which he was not present.

Don Pasqual's 'memories' and his commentary to Antonio create a complex perspective in that they offer contradictory material. His comments repeatedly present the encounters with Concha as the result of fate but it is clear from the content of the flashbacks that he actively pursues her.[51] The change of narrative form that delineates Don Pasqual's perspective also has the effect of privileging the initial presentation of Concha in that it gains an objective status by comparison. The fifth flashback to the theatre in which Concha performs the musical number 'Three Sweethearts' is closest to her initial

Concha delights in her catch. Still from *The Devil Is a Woman*

appearances as the spirit of carnival. It can be given a privileged status on two grounds: first, it corresponds to a presentation that falls outside Don Pasqual's narration; second, the performance of the number is clearly consistent with Dietrich's star persona and utilises aspects of her star style.

The fifth flashback presents Concha's manipulative power through the repeated presentation of Don Pasqual in medium shot, sitting alone in a box at the theatre, framed by a ship in the bottom lefthand corner of the screen and a swathe of netting across the top righthand corner. The netting constructs him as a 'catch', continuing a motif that begins in the second flashback: Concha enters her flat carrying a goldfish in a small bowl on a long string handle, announcing: 'Look Mama, I've got a fish!' as Don Pasqual trails in behind her.[52] This use of fishing motifs to designate the capture of male prey contrasts with Nietzsche's description of Life in which she uses a golden fishing rod to rescue Zarathustra by preventing him from drowning in her eyes.[53]

The musical number recalls Concha's presentation at the carnival through her use of swinging movement, fleeting facial expressions and mocking laughter. Her costume resembles a Spanish flamenco dress, the hemline of the long dark skirt rises at the front and is trimmed with ruffles, which are liberally sequined, catching the light. The light shawl she wears over her shoulders is also sequined, drawing attention to her dancing shoulder movements. The high combs in her hair sparkle, highlighting her face. Positioned alongside her three drab suitors, Concha seems to emanate light. Her rapid movements and changes of facial expression are demonstrated during the first lines of the song: 'I'm romantic, so romantic, that I often wish I had a more discreet heart. But believe me, please believe me, when I tell you that I haven't got a sweetheart.' Concha shrugs her shoulders upwards on each utterance of the word 'believe' while playing with the carnation that she holds in her hands. The apparent assertion of her solo status is accompanied by a fleeting expression of wide-eyed innocence that rapidly dissolves into laughter as she listens to the chorus' question: 'Do you mean to say that you have none?' Her answer finishes with the line: 'No, I only said I haven't *one*!'

The musical number provides a star moment in that Dietrich takes on the role of cabaret performer in three previous films of the cycle: *The Blue Angel*, *Morocco* and *Blonde Venus*. The joke line from the song is not particularly good and Concha's dissolution into laughter also suggests her sense of the sheer silliness of the number itself, allowing a mocking inflection of the whole scenario that is typical of Dietrich.[54] The number also showcases Dietrich's distinctive intonation patterns. Concha's description of what the first lover, the son of the gardener, offers her: 'he gives me daisies and roses and orchids, regardless of the price' demonstrates Dietrich's familiar drawled delivery on the 'r' of 'roses'. The next line: 'And other things that are so nice', has a rising inflection on 'things' and a lengthening of 'are' to form a positive purr that suggests sexual pleasure. The innu-

Concha's sparkling flamenco-style dress. Publicity still for *The Devil Is a Woman*

endo is visually sustained by the lover's phallic false nose. The song's final line: 'To all three I'm true and I could be as true to you' also displays Dietrich's distinctive drawl on the repetition of 'true'. This coupled with Concha's wink, sustains the impression of a doubled level of mockery of the courtship rituals presented in the number.

The number offers a series of reversals. The first is familiar in that the suitors are presented as a trio of exaggeratedly bashful grotesques who appear overwhelmed by the attentions of their desired object, thus inverting the quest model of desire. The inversion applies to Don Pasqual's pursuit of Concha in that he is visually aligned with the trio of suitors. As Concha sings the line 'Three sweethearts have I' for the first time, the camera tracks from the medium shot of her with the first suitor, passing the other two in turn, and this is followed by a cut to the medium shot of Don Pasqual, clearly presenting him as fourth in line. The false nose worn by the first suitor is the same as that worn by the pimp who offers to show Antonio where the pretty girls are in the carnival sequence. The scenario of courtship reverses the pimp's exploitation of women for his own economic gain in that the woman clearly has power over her suitors. However, Concha's market price is indicated by the gifts she is offered, equating prostitution and matrimony by demonstrating that the commodification of women clearly underpins both systems of exchange.

Florence Jacobowitz argues that Concha's song is a parody of courtship that shows her refusal of commodification. Within the number, her acceptance of gifts from three sweethearts and her appeal for more is said to demonstrate her 'transgression of the patriarchal rules of ownership and monogamy'.[55] It also provides a different way of looking at her response to Don Pasqual's repeated attempts to buy her: initially with groceries (like the suitors in the song) and cash, later with offers of 'protection' and finally marriage. Don Pasqual denounces her acceptance of his material gifts without providing the required reciprocation, saying: 'What I gave gladly you took like a thief.' The alliteration on the repeated 'g' offers a disingenuous construction of his gifts as largesse in that generosity should not really require a response. Importantly, what Don Pasqual takes as Concha's 'inability to learn the rules of sexual commodification', can be seen as her refusal to subscribe to this economy of exchange.[56] Her response is 'unfathomable' to him in two ways: first, she has been offered everything that she should want, including matrimony, and second, it falls outside the accepted logic of exchange.

In reading the number as a parody which indicates a rejection of the laws of exchange, Jacobowitz provides a means of tracing Concha's reasons for constructing herself as an unattainable object of desire. I have already argued that Concha's liaisons with her other lovers offer a different scenario of female desire. She can therefore be seen to construct herself as unattainable in relation to Don Pasqual in order to undermine his social and economic power over her. In this way, she poses a challenge to the Derridean model in which the question: what might woman gain from her reconstruction as the object of an unending quest, simply cannot be asked. Concha's response to Don Pasqual can also be seen to utilise the contradictions generated by different discursive constructions of femininity. She mobilises the definition of woman as an unattainable phantom in order to challenge her construction as an object of possession, playing one off against the other, for her own ends.

The exchange between Don Pasqual and Concha after her number highlights another aspect of their clash of perspectives. Her visit to his box suggests that she believes he will be pleased to renew their acquaintance, an assumption he attempts to dispel by saying: 'My emotions appear to make little impression on you. Aren't you afraid of anything Concha? Have you no fear of death?' She replies in joking tones: 'No, not today – I feel too happy!', her delivery slowing and becoming more thoughtful as she adds: 'Why do you ask? Are you going to kill me?' The second question parallels her with Carmen, another figure of woman as caprice who is finally killed for her 'infidelity'. However, the factual way in which Concha poses the second question suggests that she does not fear the same fate. The exchange sets up an opposition between Concha as the dancing, joking figure of Life and Don Pasqual's death-driven perspective. His relation to death shifts across the film: from threats, which culminate in his violent beating of Concha, to his own embrace of the prospect of death in the duel with Antonio.[57] I want to focus on the way in which the film's complex presentation of Don Pasqual's perspective results in a reconstruction of Concha from the figure of Life to the harbinger of death.

George Wilson's detailed reading of *The Devil Is a Woman* focuses on the ways in which Don Pasqual's perspective, particularly his emotions, is expressed through the details of the *mise en scène*. This sustains his overall argument that 'Don Pasqual's sensibility has a privileged position within the film.'[58] However, I would suggest that this claim needs to be tempered in that the use of the music and *mise en scène* to present Concha's vitality, changeability and rationality in the carnival and chase sequences present the shift to Don Pasqual's perspective as one of many structures of inversion that are played out across the text. I want to focus on the ways in which the externalisation of his emotions affects the presentation of Concha, reconstructing her capriciousness in an entirely negative light.[59] This will involve a detailed reading of the scene in which she visits Don Pasqual the morning after he has beaten her.

The scene begins with a long shot of ships swaying gently in the fog. The haphazard arrangement of the masts and rigging coupled with the spectral quality of the mist gives the impression of a collection of shipwrecks rather than an active port. The sense of desolation is compounded by the background music. The eerie sounds of the muted brass instruments repeat a refrain that is built around several discords. Concha rattles at the lattice of the door and then opens it, trilling a cheerful 'Good morning'. The tonal quality of her greeting is completely at odds with the minor key of the music, thus sounding literally off-key. The long shot of her taking a seat shows Don Pasqual for the first time.

He is standing with his back to her on the balcony and the faint outline of a ship's rigging can be seen in the background on the lefthand side of the screen. The long shot contextualises the opening shot of the ships in that they constitute Don Pasqual's view from his balcony. He can thus be seen to contemplate the prospect of his ruin at the hands of a woman, like ships wrecked by the Sirens, and the bleakness of the view symbolises his sense of desolation.[60]

Wilson comments that the contrast between Don Pasqual's desolation and Concha's vivacity is striking because 'the morning-after condition of each member of the pair is the reverse of what was to be expected.'[61] Concha's costume presents her as a *femme fatale*. She is dressed in black, immaculately coiffured and wearing a necklace of dark hearts around her throat, which suggest her numerous victims. This is sustained by her announcement of the purpose of her visit: 'I came to see if you were dead! If you had loved me enough you would have killed yourself last night!' Wilson reads her meeting with Don Pasqual as a post-coital encounter. Don Pasqual's trance-like immersion in the view, coupled with his ravaged expression, is said to suggest that he has been drained of his life's blood, constructing Concha as a vampiric *femme fatale*.[62] Wilson connects the vampire to the figure of Life: 'the fatal woman . . . is . . . as vital, as desirable, and as arbitrarily uncontrollable as life itself . . . to gain possession of such a force of life is intolerably dangerous and destructive. Possession is the ruin of the possessor.'[63] His comment fuses the two tropes so far explored, subordinating the figure of woman as caprice by presenting her as an aspect of the *femme fatale*.

In contrast, I would suggest that the scene presents Concha as both *femme fatale* and caprice. While the negative aspects of the latter are highlighted, Concha's startling ability to regenerate herself after the beating that was intended to control and subdue her, suggests that she has evaded Don Pasqual once again. His haunted desolation would therefore be the result of his continual failure to possess her. Her macabre comment initiates a conversation, which displays her usual changeability of expression. Once seated, she taunts Don Pasqual and then glances up at him flirtatiously from beneath her lashes as she pours herself a cup of chocolate. On tasting it, her conversation veers abruptly from the prospect of his imminent suicide to the poor quality of the chocolate. The bizarre juxtaposition can be seen to present her capriciousness as utter callousness. Don Pasqual responds by angrily announcing that he is finished with her and walking back onto the balcony.

Concha's callousness is presented as a complete inability to comprehend Don Pasqual's pain through her positioning in the medium shot in which she joins him on the balcony. She stands in front of him, to his left, her face full on to the camera, with her back to the ships whose rigging and masts can be seen silhouetted in the background. Given that the view operates as an externalisation of Don Pasqual's mood, her placing implies that she is ignoring his feelings, although she is facing him. She asks Don Pasqual to look at her and he turns his head to the right. She then moves to the right, repeating her request, but Don Pasqual has already turned to the left. Concha's playful endeavours to gain his attention are unsuccessful and she then alters her tone saying plaintively, 'Look at me Pasqualito – I'm black and blue.' This exchange constitutes a reversal of Concha's previous presentation as an object who commands the gaze, in that Don Pasqual has found it impossible to continue to look away from her on previous occasions, such as her number at the theatre. The medium shot that presents him as the fourth suitor, shows him turning away from the spectacle in a huff, only to turn back as if irresistibly compelled to gaze at her. Her insistent demands for attention thus show a diminishment of her power. The ghostly ships form an odd backdrop to Concha's dancing counterpoint, presenting her customary changeability: from playful to plaintive cajoling, as a superficial display of emotion in that it is contrasted with the insistent bleakness of the view.

Concha's changeability is reconstructed as duplicity, traditionally exhibited by the *femme fatale*, as the scene progresses. Her purring tones change the moment Don Pasqual succumbs to her overtures, suggesting that they leave together. She immediately draws back from him, plaintively explaining that she cannot leave because of her contract with the theatre. Her immediate withdrawal once he responds to her closeness, suggests that she is not interested in leaving with him, preparing the way for her eventual exit with the matador. Their departure in a later scene is followed by a return to the medium shot of Don Pasqual on the balcony gazing out at the ships. In the previous images the fog acted as a filter, softening the outline of the ships and creating an impression of distance. The fog has now lifted and the haphazard lines of the shipwrecks seem oppressively close. It is as if Don Pasqual's previous vision of his desolate future has been actively realised. He turns and walks towards the camera, his dark shape finally filling the entire frame. His proximity to the camera can be seen to express his emotional state, as the screen goes black so he is engulfed by despair. Wilson reads Don Pasqual's transformation into 'a hulking shadow' as a moment of death.[64]

The externalisation of Don Pasqual's despair has a significant effect on the presentation of Concha in that her changeability becomes a callous duplicity that displays her lack of any deep emotion. She is positioned within a gendered binary of surface/depth in which her playful superficiality becomes an inhuman absence of depth. The mismatch between Concha's vivacity and the desolate setting can thus be seen to operate to her disadvantage and the two scenes described here constitute key instances of her presentation as demonic within the film. These scenes are the culmination of Don Pasqual's flashback narration and Antonio's response to his story summarises their significance in one line: 'What a devil of a woman!' The partial nature of Don Pasqual's perspective is suggested shortly afterwards when he interrupts Antonio's liaison with Concha, abruptly admitting that 'reading the cards is one of her virtues I forgot to tell you about.' The comment indicates that his presentation of her as demonic has involved the elimination of her virtues. The ultimate reconstruction of Concha from the figure of Life to the harbinger of death takes place in her final encounter with Don Pasqual.

The short scene is set in a hospital where Concha visits Don Pasqual after he has been badly injured in the duel with Antonio. She is dressed entirely in black, wearing a black hat with a large brim that is angled down on the left of her face. The hat is covered by a black mantilla, which falls to her shoulders veiling her face and neck. The black lace shawl that drapes over her shoulders and hangs down her arms shrouds Concha further. The overly funereal nature of her costuming suggests that she has become Don Pasqual's angel of death. The considerable use of veiling is reminiscent of the first sequences in the film and I will go on to argue that this scene plays out a second disappearance, which differs from the first in that it conforms to key aspects of the Derridean model.

The scene displays Concha's customary changeability in that her first exchange with Don Pasqual includes a somewhat macabre joke: 'Getting yourself shot for me – you might have been killed!' However, Don Pasqual's response shows the diminishment of her power over him in that he turns away from her, and she does not succeed in engaging his gaze throughout the scene. Concha goes on to admit that she's always done everything wrong and to request Don Pasqual's forgiveness, delivering both comments in a light tone that suggests that she is far from guilt-ridden. The positioning of both characters in the medium shot emphasises the lack of impact of Concha's words in that she is positioned slightly behind Don Pasqual on the left and he does not respond, simply staring straight ahead. She then turns towards him, her hat entirely obscuring her face, extending her right hand in a gesture of reconciliation that is unexpected given her previous levity. He ignores her proffered hand, continuing to look straight ahead and telling her to get out.

Concha's exit marks the end of her power over Don Pasqual. It offers another reversal of the carnival sequence in which the presentation of Concha's point of view showed her power over Antonio who was being buffeted by the crowd and entangled in streamers in his attempt to pursue her. Concha pauses by the door, turning back to look at Don Pasqual. The movement means that the downturned brim of her hat completely covers her face, presenting her as a column of veils. She looks back at the door and opens and shuts it swiftly, faking an exit. She turns rapidly to gauge Don Pasqual's reaction, her hat covering her face once again. There is a cut to a point-of-view shot of Don Pasqual who turns his head to the left, where she had been standing, for the first time. He sighs and sinks back down into his pillows as if welcoming oblivion. He appears to be unaware of Concha's efforts to get his attention, suggesting he is finally free of the need to pursue her.[65] The scene plays out Concha's disappearance in that she becomes nothing more than a column of veils. It differs from her first disappearance in the window because the play of the veils is no longer presented as bewitching, instead it marks the moment at which Don Pasqual ceases to look for her.

The final shot of the hospital scene is a close-up of Concha's face as she pauses before exiting the room. Her elaborate coiffure and dark lipsticked mouth are visible beneath her dark lace mantilla and the shot resembles the close-ups in the carnival sequence, which also drew attention to the layers of veiling presented by her make-up, mask and mantilla, constructing her face as yet another veil. I compared her initial presentation to Baubô because Concha's wide smile and association with festive music meant that she could be seen to affirm the play of appearances. Her exuberant changeability and dancing movements were also said to link her to Nietzsche's figure of Life. Concha's construction as an affirming figure is reliant on her congruence with the *mise en scène* of the carnival and the bubbling refrain of the capriccio. The film may be said to stage two very different forms of disappearance. The first, Concha's subsumption into pattern during the chase sequence, consolidates her presentation as Life by constructing her as the spirit of carnival, offering a scenario of female desire that differs from those sustained by Derrida's figures of woman. The second disappearance inverts the first in that Concha becomes a figure of Death. I will trace the ways in which her reconstruction as a play of dark veils corresponds to the structures of denegation and metonymic proliferation, thus linking her to Derrida's third woman.

Concha's presentation as Death can be seen as her final appearance as the *femme fatale* in the film and clearly indicates what she has meant to Don Pasqual. However, the control over the game of desire that Derrida ascribes to his second, fatal woman is absent here, as Don Pasqual simply refuses to play any longer. Importantly, his lack of response means that the purpose of her visit becomes very difficult to assess. Her duplicity is previously indicated by her withdrawal from Don Pasqual once he succumbs to her charms. However, this scene does not provide the means to judge whether her endeavours to get his attention are part of a strategy of manipulation. In addition, her transformation into a column of veils is played out against a setting that does not augment her characterisation. Her reconstruction as the play of dark veils can therefore be seen to mark a moment of disappearance in that it empties out the details of her previous characterisation and presents her in a way that makes her impossible to read, forming a double structure of denegation.

This construction of Concha as averted of herself is also part of her later presentation as caprice, foregrounding the problematic aspects of the trope. The final close-up presents a moment of contemplation and decision. Concha takes sidelong glances to the right from under her lashes as if making sure that Don Pasqual has not moved. In between these glances her eyes flick upwards, suggesting thoughtful indecision, which ends abruptly as she whirls around and exits through the door. Her sudden departure appears to mark her decision to leave with Antonio but she changes her mind again at the station and the announcement that she is leaving him for Don Pasqual is also unconvincing. The final scenes present Concha's repeated changes of mind in a way that suggests she does not have a mind to change. Her continual changeability can be seen to correspond to the structure of metonymic proliferation. This is underpinned by absence, conforming to the structure of denegation, thus reinforcing the doubled logic of denegation set up by the use of the trope of the *femme fatale*.

The presentation of Concha in the hospital scene corresponds to Derrida's third woman in that the specific presentation of the two key tropes results in a return to the familiar structures of chiasmic logic. Concha becomes the vanishing point, making her impossible to read and this, in turn, sustains an endless proliferation of critical interpretations. Oms reads her visit to Don Pasqual as evidence of remorse for her previous behaviour.[66] Green argues that the visit displays a sadistic side to Concha that 'springs from class vindictiveness'.[67] Studlar comments:

> whatever process of thought is mirrored in Concha's face is open to interpretation – so open that her motivation for returning [to Don Pasqual] has been variously described as the desire to murder him, the wish to keep torturing him, and even gratitude.[68]

While the multiplicity of conflicting interpretations attests to Concha's suitability for the role of *différance*, I do not wish to read her as a symbol of language itself. Instead, I want to argue that it is the specificity of her representation at this moment in the film, the particular intersection of the key tropes that permits the emergence of the structures of chiasmic logic at this point.

This is important because it means that the ending of the film cannot be regarded as a negation of all that has gone before, in that the image of Concha as vanishing point is one that is created by a very specific intersection of tropes. This particular image therefore cannot be positioned as the truth of the text. I have used Le Doeuff's methodology to trace the ways in which key images of Concha go beyond the Derridean model, offering another construction of female desire. The different constructions of the intersecting tropes of the *femme fatale* and woman as caprice across the text can thus be seen to sustain different theorisations; rendering the structure of the chiasma one among many and opening up ways of rethinking female desire within philosophy.

Notes

1. M-A. Doane, *Femmes Fatales: Feminism, Film Theory, Psychoanalysis* (New York and London: Routledge, 1991), pp. 44–75. While Doane also uses Lacan in this chapter, I will focus on her reading of Nietzsche and Derrida.
2. See the end of Section 1 in Chapter 4.
3. J. Derrida, *Spurs*, B. Harlow (trans.), S. Agosti (intro) (Chicago, IL and London: University of Chicago Press, 1978), p. 41.
4. Ibid.
5. E. Tripp, *Dictionary of Classical Mythology* (London and Glasgow: Collins, 1970), p. 266.
6. Derrida, *Spurs*, p. 103.
7. Ibid., p. 101.
8. Ibid., p. 51. Kelly Oliver also argues that Derrida goes against his own claims of textual

undecidability by insisting that woman in Nietzsche's work has a decidable meaning. K. Oliver, *Womanising Nietzsche: Philosophy's Relation to the Feminine* (New York and London: Routledge, 1995), p. 61.

9. Derrida, *Spurs*, p. 51.

10. Doane, *Femmes Fatales*, p. 59.

11. Ibid.

12. See Section 2 of Chapter 4.

13. Doane, *Femmes Fatales*, p. 59.

14. Ibid., p. 278, fn. 38. There is a single reference to Le Doeuff in the footnotes for Doane's chapter.

15. Ibid., p. 62. The word 'thought' is italicised in the original, the additional italics are mine.

16. Ibid. My italics.

17. Derrida, *Spurs*, p. 97.

18. Ibid., p. 89.

19. Doane, *Femmes Fatales*, p. 65.

20. Ibid., p. 66.

21. Ibid.

22. Ibid., p. 69.

23. Žižek explains this aspect of the Lacanian system most clearly in *The Fright of Real Tears: Krzysztof Kieślowski between Theory and Post-Theory* (London: BFI, 2001), p. 91.

24. Doane, *Femmes Fatales*, p.75.

25. Ibid.

26. B. Dijkstra, *Idols of Perversity: Fantasies of Feminine Evil in Fin-de-Siècle Culture* (Oxford: Oxford University Press, 1986), p. 251.

27. Derrida, *Spurs*, p. 89.

28. M. Oms, 'Josef von Sternberg', in P. Baxter (ed.), *Sternberg* (London: BFI, 1980), p. 73.

29. Ibid.

30. The final choice of title was made by Lubitsch who insisted that 'no-one would pay to see a picture with a title they couldn't understand.' M. Riva, *Marlene Dietrich* (London: Coronet Books, 1994), p. 344.

31. N. Segal, *Narcissus and Echo: Women in the French Récit* (Manchester: Manchester University Press, 1988), p. 35.

32. P. Mérimée, *Carmen* (Paris: Bordas, 1966), pp. 55–6. The novella was first published in 1845. I must thank Adrian Armstrong for translating the key passages for me. For more details of the construction of woman as nature in art through her representation with or as a wild animal see 'connoisseurs of bestiality' in Chapter 9 of Dijkstra, *Idols of Perversity*, pp. 291–301.

33. F. Nietzsche, *Thus Spake Zarathustra*, in *The Portable Nietzsche*, W. Kaufmann (ed. and trans.) (London: Chatto and Windus, 1971), p. 220.

34. Ibid., p. 179.
35. For more details of Derrida's construction of the third woman please see Section 3 of Chapter 4.
36. Nietzsche, *Zarathustra*, p. 339.
37. F. Jacobowitz, 'Power and the Masquerade: *The Devil Is a Woman*', *CineAction!*, Spring 1987, pp. 33–4, 39.
38. G. Studlar, *In the Realm of Pleasure: Von Sternberg, Dietrich and the Masochistic Aesthetic* (Urbana and Chicago: University of Illinois Press, 1988), p. 167.
39. Jacobowitz, 'Power and the Masquerade', p. 36. Her reading differs from mine in that she argues that Antonio's links to machismo are compromised from the moment he first appears.
40. Nietzsche, *Zarathustra*, p. 336.
41. I must thank Rachel Jones for her translation.
42. Nietzsche, *Zarathustra*, pp. 336–7.
43. Jacobowitz, 'Power and the Masquerade', p. 36.
44. Ibid.
45. Oms, 'Josef von Sternberg', p. 73.
46. Derrida, *Spurs*, p. 71.
47. Ibid., p. 59.
48. Ibid., p. 89.
49. Mérimée's first description of Carmen emphasises her youth. See *Carmen*, p. 55.
50. G. Wilson, *Narration in Light: Studies in Cinematic Point of View* (Baltimore, MD and London: Johns Hopkins University Press, 1986), p. 148.
51. Studlar argues that Don Pasqual is a typical masochistic male protagonist in that he repeatedly blames fate and chooses misery. Studlar, *In the Realm of Pleasure*, p. 117.
52. Jacobowitz, 'Power and the Masquerade', p. 38.
53. Nietzsche, *Zarathustra*, p. 220.
54. Maria Riva records that Dietrich was unable to perform the whole of this number without laughing because she thought the lyrics were so silly. M. Riva, *Marlene Dietrich*, pp. 360–1.
55. Jacobowitz, 'Power and the Masquerade', p. 34.
56. Ibid., p. 39.
57. Studlar reads Don Pasqual's desire for death as an exemplification of a masochistic logic of desire in which consummation is always deferred until its fantasy fulfilment in death. Studlar, *In the Realm of Pleasure*, pp. 26, 73–4, 126–9.
58. Wilson, *Narration in Light*, pp. 158–9. He goes on to argue that this means that Don Pasqual can be read as von Sternberg's surrogate, a problematic move, which always sustains highly negative analyses of Concha/Dietrich as utterly destructive.

59. Ibid., p. 153. Wilson offers a more detailed reading of the 'meteorological sympathy' displayed by the storms that accompany Don Pasqual's discovery of Concha's affair with the matador and his duel with Antonio.

60. Ibid., p. 159. Wilson argues that Don Pasqual contemplates the prospect of his own death.

61. Ibid., p. 158.

62. Ibid., pp. 154, 158.

63. Ibid., p. 158.

64. Ibid., p. 159.

65. On Studlar's model, the masochistic protagonist desires death as the ultimate fantasy of reunion with the desired object. While Concha represents death to Don Pasqual and thus might seem to personify the masochistic ideal at this moment, his lack of response to her would seem to indicate that his acceptance of death marks his freedom from the cycle of pursuit that is desire. Studlar, *In the Realm of Pleasure*, p. 26.

66. Oms, 'Josef von Sternberg', p. 72.

67. O. O. Green, 'Six Films of Joseph von Sternberg', *Movie* vol. 13, Summer 1965, p. 30.

68. Studlar, *In the Realm of Pleasure*, p. 163.

6 | The Seductress

This chapter will address a third commentary on Nietzsche, Baudrillard's *Seduction*, in which he offers another account of the relation between the loss of absolute truth and the creation of meaning. I will trace the ways in which it both resembles and differs from the Derridean model explored in Chapters 4 and 5. I am concerned to emphasise those aspects of the Baudrillardian account that move beyond the perpetuation of the structures of chiasmic logic, particularly his endeavour to link signification with the eternal return. His presentation of the eternal return will then be related to elements of my analysis of Kofman from Chapter 4. Like Derrida, Baudrillard links his account of meaning to the figure of woman. I will argue in favour of viewing the seductress as a figure that affirms the play of appearances as a site of authenticity, positioning her alongside Baubô.

Baudrillard's account of the loss of absolute truth and meaning has a doubled aspect that is typical of its Nietzschean source material. Nietzsche presents the move into perspectivalism as a nihilistic loss of truth and the beginning of the creation of a range of possible truths. In *The Will to Power*, he characterises a world of appearances in terms of falsity: 'If the character of existence should be false – which would be possible – what would truth, all our truth, be then? – An unconscionable falsification of the false? The false raised to a higher power? – '[1] Given that conscience was the repository of absolute value in the individual, the 'unconscionable' character of the false indicates its status as the negation of all such values. In contrast, the final sentence constructs the play of appearances as a mode of affirmation that transforms the false into a higher power. Baudrillard's account of the reconstruction of the sign as pure surface in *Seduction* displays the same doubleness. This feminisation of language, which is created by the loss of the signified, is presented in two ways: as the end of all signification and the beginning of a new economy of signification.[2] Importantly, Nietzsche stresses the productive possibilities of a world of mere appearance, while Baudrillard offers a predominantly nihilistic account of becoming the surface. My reading of Baudrillard will emphasise the constructive potential of his analysis, thus positioning him closer to the model of affirmation offered by his source material.

This chapter will begin with an analysis of Baudrillard's definitions of seduction, which will involve focusing on the different structures that underpin his two different models of circularity. I will argue that the construction of seduction as an endgame follows Derrida's system; while aspects of its presentation as the eternal return can be linked to Kofman. The two models of signification can be seen to construct specific and different roles for the seductress and I will trace the ways in which the second can be seen to construct her as a figure of affirmation. Baudrillard's second conception of the seductress as a parodic, artificial figure who opens up a space of critique will be used to form a detailed reading of *Shanghai Express* in Section 2. This will involve taking issue with Carole Zucker's reading of Dietrich's performance as Shanghai Lily as a series of acts that are all seen to be equally inauthentic. In contrast, I will draw attention to the ways in which Lily's acts serve to set up different constructions of authenticity. I will demonstrate that *Shanghai Express* presents a sophisticated construction of appearance as truth and will show how the character of Lily expands Baudrillard's conception of the seductress.

1 Seduction and the Eternal Return

Baudrillard begins by defining seduction in opposition to production: both are said to form two distinct orders.[3] Production is the 'natural' order; it encompasses the discourses of psychoanalysis and commerce. In contrast, seduction is an artificial order consisting of signs and rituals. Production is based on the conception of a real, such as the anatomical body, which functions as the ground of language. The sign is therefore said to correspond to these fundamental truths: 'In order for sex to exist, signs must reduplicate biological being.'[4] Seduction, however, occurs at the level of the sign. It 'breaks the referentiality of sex'[5] by destroying the notion of a body outside language. 'It knows (this is its secret) that *there is no anatomy*'.[6] Baudrillard argues that production fetishises the nude body as a mode of objective truth. Like Nietzsche's story of Isis,[7] the discourses of production set up the veil as a covering that must be torn away in order to reveal the truth. In seduction, there is nothing beyond the veil. The body '*cannot* be seen nude' for nudity is just another form of veiling 'and it is by way of this play of veils, which, literally, abolishes the body "as such", that seduction occurs.'[8]

The doubleness with which Baudrillard characterises seduction itself can be seen in his reading of the Narcissus myth. In standard versions of the myth, the beautiful youth Narcissus spurns all his suitors and falls in love with his own reflection. The Freudian reading constructs the reflection as Narcissus's own ego-ideal. In traditional psychoanalysis, narcissism is 'the attraction of like to like, in a mimetic exaltation of one's own image, or an ideal mirage of resemblance'.[9] For Baudrillard, this psychoanalytic reading contains the signifying potential of the image within an account of identity. Instead, he chooses to follow Pausanias's version of the myth in which Narcissus is said to have had a beloved twin sister who died. Narcissus therefore constructs his reflection as the face of his lost sister. He is able to keep her alive by gazing into the woodland pool.[10]

For Baudrillard, the woodland pool is 'a surface that absorbs and seduces' Narcissus.[11] This is the primary version of seduction in which the image is a site of self-absorption and death. The image functions as the signifier alone, a surface that 'shines as nonsense' because depth in the form of the signified has been taken away.[12] This form of 'linguistic seduction' is said to be 'a radically different operation that absorbs rather than

produces meaning.'[13] The signifier alone therefore constitutes the end of all signification. However, Baudrillard also offers another reading of Narcissus's reflection. The
surface of the pool becomes a space in which Narcissus can re/construct himself as illusion: 'Narcissus ... loses himself in his own illusory image; that is why he turns from his
truth, and by his example turns others from their truth – and so becomes a model of
love.'[14] The image in the pool is constructed as a realm of illusion that is outside the
reach of the 'truth'. By re/constructing himself as deception, Narcissus becomes his sister and turns away from the truth of her death.

The different readings of the image in the pool as a site of absorption and a space of
deception can be linked to two different models of circularity. I will set out each in turn,
examining the ways in which they draw on and differ from the Derridean model. The
first definition of the image arises from Baudrillard's analysis of the relationship between
seduction and production. Seduction is presented as an 'inverse power', which reacts
against the processes of production.[15] 'In itself it is nul [sic], seduction has no power of
its own, only that of annulling the power of production. But it always annuls the latter.'[16] Seduction is a process of reactive reversibility that results in the annulment of all
meaning. 'For we grant meaning only to what is irreversible: accumulation, progress,
growth, production.'[17] In this first account, the movement of seduction is said to fold
the discourses of production over on themselves, creating a circle that conforms to the
logic of a duel: 'a circular, reversible process of challenges, oneupmanship and death.'[18]
This circularity is said to undo the logic of opposition that sustains the system of production, rendering opposites equal partners in an agonistic game. This undoing of the
hierarchical positioning of master/slave is evident from Baudrillard's analysis of the classic
scenario of seduction in which he argues that the male seducer and female seducee are
equally complicit.[19]

The circular movement of folding over that implodes the logic of opposition clearly
resembles Derrida's account of the reflexive movement of the folded veil, which is said
to undo the binaries of veiled/unveiled and sailed/unsailed.[20] For Derrida, this movement
causes an interpenetration of oppositional terms resulting in a con/fusion of meanings,
initiating the economy of the undecidable. The structure of denegation indicated by the
reflexive movement of folding over is thus linked to the proliferation of meaning, conforming to both aspects of the chiasma.[21] The Baudrillardian model presents the process
of folding over as an endgame. Seduction constitutes the end of meaning in that it is a
'null signifier or empty term'.[22] Baudrillard's presentation of the undoing of the logic of
opposition as a relentless process of nullification can therefore be seen to conform to
the structure of denegation alone.

The second image of the pool as a space of deception presents seduction as the
'ability to turn appearances *in on themselves*', creating a space of pure illusion.[23] The
second form of seduction turns away from all modes of production: 'the manifest discourse ... turns back on the deeper order ... in order to invalidate it, substituting the

charm and illusion of appearances.'[24] The rejection of both aspects of the binaries of true/false and surface/depth means that the new order of appearance is not presented as fake or superficial: '[t]hese appearances are not in the least frivolous, but occasions for a game and its stakes, and a passion for deviation'.[25] In this way, Narcissus can be seen to move beyond truth to a creative space of illusion that enables him to reconstruct his reflection as his sister. This is the moment at which the realm of pure appearances clearly becomes '[t]he false raised to a higher power'.[26]

The self-reflexive, circular movement that creates the new realm of pure illusion can be seen to resemble the centripetal movement of the structure of denegation. However, in the Baudrillardian model, the gesture of turning in on itself constitutes a moment of transition to the realm of games and rituals, which serves to create the possibility of new meanings. This is very different from Derrida's presentation of the gesture of averting as a form of self-abnegation, which constructs woman as the vanishing point, thus marking the destruction of meaning and truth. The second version of seduction differs from the first in that the realm of games and rituals is conceptualised as more than an endgame; exemplified by the duel to the death, it becomes a space of play which accords to formal rules. This sustains the creation of new meanings that are defined as 'more adventurous and seductive than the directive line of meaning.'[27] The realm of pure appearances is said to divert meaning, thus creating a multidirectional model of signification. This model differs from Derrida's in two ways: first, the emphasis on the rule-governed nature of games presents the creation of meaning as a controlled series of new combinations and patterns rather than an unending, inevitable slide; and second, the multidirectional quality of meaning goes beyond the structure of *différance*, which is simply envisaged as a flowing outwards, conforming to the structure of metonymic proliferation.

The multidirectional nature of the model of meaning presented by the second version of seduction can be seen to indicate its reliance on the dynamic of the eternal return. Nietzsche's model conjoins temporality and meaning in that the creation of the perspective that forms the subject is reliant on a non-linear tracing of patterns of repetition set up by past, present and future actions. The past becomes integral to the present moment in that each action gains significance from its relation to those that have been performed previously. In Nietzsche's model, the future is not determined by the past. While future acts have to have a relation to previous patterns, they may also be seen fundamentally to rework the terms of repetition. The future emerges in relation to the past and the present and is thus neither determined nor a limitless free play. The future is a set of contingent possibilities, which become 'necessary' once an action is positioned in relation to others and judged in retrospect.

Baudrillard does not trace the considerable resemblance between his second version of seduction and the eternal return. Instead, he presents the eternal return as a form of exact repetition in that games are said to 'reproduce a given arbitrary constellation in the same terms an indefinite number of times'.[28] This repetition is said to result in an emptying out of meaning, thus conforming to the first mode of seduction.[29] He also argues that games present a tragic form of the eternal return in which signification itself becomes a deterministic process: 'each sign seeks out the next relentlessly'.[30] Games and rituals are said to offer a world 'built of networks of symbolic relations – not contingent connections, but webs of obligation, webs of seduction.'[31] The move from production to seduction is presented as the transition from a world of chance to a web of necessity. This clearly constitutes a considerable departure from the non-deterministic nature of the Nietzschean model in which it is the subject's recognition and affirmation of a particular patterning of events that transforms the contingent into the necessary.

Baudrillard explicitly defines the eternal return as a nullifying form of repetition and a deterministic ludic system. However, I want to relate his model of multidirectional signification to Kofman's analysis of the eternal return as a repetition in difference that creates meaning, which was explored in Chapter 4. This will involve re/reading Baudrillard's account of the transition from the order of production to the order of games and rituals, which constitute the realm of illusion per se, as a mode of differential repetition. Within the realm of production, Narcissus's reflection in the woodland pool is a form of duplication that entraps him in a circle of self-absorption. The order of seduction begins once the water image is read as the face of his sister, a mode of repetition in difference that exceeds mere duplication, creating something new. In this way, Narcissus's use of his reflection can be seen as more than a turning away from his sister's death, his reflection becomes the means by which she is restored to life, thus providing an example of affirmative repetition in which 'art wills for life yet again its eternal return in difference'.[32]

I want now to explore the way in which both forms of seduction construct different roles for the seductress. She is typically presented as the personification of the first form of seduction and thus constructed as the point where meaning empties out. 'Eyes that seduce have no meaning, their meaning being exhausted in the gaze, as a face with makeup is exhausted in its appearance, in the formal rigour of a senseless labour.'[33] Baudrillard presents the application of cosmetics as an erasure, which creates 'a pure appearance denuded of meaning.'[34] The attraction of pure appearance is that of the void: 'the woman with makeup, who is absent to herself, an absence of a focussed look, the absence of a face – how can one not be swallowed up in it?'[35] The red-lipsticked seductress signifies the absence of a face and thus the lack of an objective truth below the surface. Baudrillard can thus be seen to draw on Derrida's prototype of the ideal woman, the untruth of truth, who is also defined in terms of absence. Both theorists construct woman as the vanishing point, presenting a structure of denegation that is also a moment of self-abnegation. For Baudrillard, the seductress is an utterly empty term, 'she is a blank, with neither age nor history.'[36]

Importantly, it is this first version of the seductive fascination of the void that Baudrillard positions as the basis of the power of cinema. The modern seductress is said to construct herself as cinematographic image, becoming a celluloid surface.

> The star is by no means an ideal or sublime being: she is artificial. She need not be an actress in the psychological sense; her face is not the reflection of a soul or sensitivity which she does not have. On the contrary, her presence serves to submerge all sensibility and expression beneath a ritual fascination with the void, beneath the ecstasy of her gaze and the nullity of her smile.[37]

The star as image is the glossy surface of non-sense. Although Baudrillard's account of cinema is hugely reductive, his comments draw attention to a commonly held equation of artifice with a lack of psychological depth. This link can be seen to underpin key aspects of Zucker's analysis of performance style in *Shanghai Express*, in which she argues that the 'acting is so stylized, exaggerated and controlled' that the dramatis personae do not have the status of characters.[38] I will examine her reading of Dietrich's performance as Shanghai Lily in some detail in order to show how Zucker's analysis repeatedly presents artifice as a null term. In contrast, I will argue that the character of Shanghai Lily offers a complex play of illusions that cannot be understood as a simple lack of depth.

The second version of seduction offers a different role for the seductress to play. Rather than constructing the seductress's makeup as an emptying out of her significance, Baudrillard presents it as 'a solution by excess':[39]

> How can one mistake this 'exceeding of nature' for a vulgar camouflaging of truth? Only falsehoods can alienate the truth, but makeup is not false, or else ... it is falser than falsehood and *so recovers a kind of superior innocence* or transparency.[40]

The construction of the seductress as excessive, more false than false, enables her to regain a superior innocence because it breaks the traditional dichotomy of truth versus falsehood. This argument can be seen to draw on a Nietzschean move in which the false is no longer seen to be the opposite of the truth, but instead becomes the site of many truths. In this way, the seductress' foregrounding of her status as illusion can be seen to construct her as a pure play of appearances that is not deceptive, but rather possesses a particular authenticity. As a result, she can be seen to affirm the play of appearances, like Baubô, however; the seductress's specific quality is to represent that play as a site of truth.

Baudrillard presents the seductress herself as a repetition in difference. She is said to be a parodic hypersimulation of the role of sex object.[41] This repetition of the object as pure artifice has the effect of removing her from the discourses of sexuality, providing her with an ironic distance that enables her to critique the structures of objectification.

She embodies the second mode of seduction, which is defined as 'an ironic, alternative form, one that breaks the referentiality of sex and provides a space, not of desire, but of *play and defiance*.'[42] This distinction between the discourses of sexuality and the discourses of artifice, such as glamour, provides a means of assessing the ways in which the latter can function as a space of critique. In this way, Concha's performance of the 'Three Sweethearts' number in *The Devil Is a Woman* can be seen as a moment in which she takes up the role of seductress. Dietrich's exaggerated expressions of wide-eyed innocence and mocking laughter present the number as a parodic hypersimulation of courtship rituals, creating an ironic distance that functions as a critique of the system of commodification that underpins them.

2 *Shanghai Express*

My reading of *Shanghai Express* will focus on Dietrich's character, Shanghai Lily, and the ways in which the film's presentation of her persona foregrounds its status as a role. Moreover, Dietrich's character can be seen to have a doubled aspect in that she is identified as both the notorious Shanghai Lily and Madelaine, Doc's respectable fiancée. I will trace the ways in which the film sets up a complex relation between the two different roles and will demonstrate that both are presented as authentic at different moments in the text. This will involve arguing against Zucker's reading of Dietrich's performance in which her highly theatrical acting style is seen to undercut any attempt at genuine emotion.[43] For Zucker,

Dietrich in the black feather-trimmed costume of Shanghai Lily. Publicity still for *Shanghai Express*

the film's foregrounding of theatricality and artifice coupled with the proliferation of Dietrich's contradictory roles serves to render Lily/Madelaine completely inauthentic.

I will trace the ways in which the role of Shanghai Lily both instantiates and develops Baudrillard's concept of the seductress. This will involve showing how Lily's first presentation at the station constructs her as an exaggerated image of indecency, which is then played to the hilt during her first meeting with Doc. These initial presentations intersect with Lily's other appearances, such as her meeting with Mrs Haggerty, reconstructing the role as both authentic and a site of critique. I will argue that Lily can be seen to expand Baudrillard's model of the seductress, giving it a more Nietzschean inflection. This will involve tracing the ways in which Lily's play of appearances moves beyond deconstructive critique, allowing her to convey her own perspective. In this way, I will demonstrate that the film's presentation of Shanghai Lily offers a complex vision of '[t]he false raised to a higher power'.[44]

Shanghai Lily's notoriety is clearly indicated through the use of costume in her first presentation at the station. She is wearing a black dress that is lavishly trimmed with dark feathers around her neck and wrists. The first close-up of Lily as she hands over her ticket serves to show off her close-fitting black cloche hat constructed of glossy cock feathers, which has a deeply banded black veil that slants across her face, revealing her mouth and left cheek. The profusion of glossy surfaces and the deeply banded veil serves to proclaim her profession in an unequivocal way. Verbal confirmation of her notoriety is immediately provided by the officers who are seeing Doc off onto the train. Their definition of her as 'a woman who lives by her wits along the China coast' forms a sound bridge to a medium shot of Lily joining Hui Fei in her compartment and thus acts as an introduction to them both. The comment consolidates Mr Carmichael's previous denunciation of Hui Fei, presented in his refusal to travel in the same compartment as her, constructing them both as 'fallen women'.

The intersection of the officers' gossip with Mr Carmichael's comments can be seen to provide a doubled context that emphasises Lily's indecency. The officers' discussion of her reputation also constructs her as larger than life. Shanghai Lily can thus be seen as a public construction, an exaggerated image of indecency that is created by social networks such as the officers' club and the church. Indeed, her status as a locus of gossip and speculation is seen in the other passengers' numerous discussions about her behaviour during the course of the train journey. This presentation of Lily's continual reconstruction as the notorious Shanghai Lily foregrounds the fictional nature of her public persona, drawing attention to its status as a role. Lily's costuming and actions in the initial sequence clearly consolidate her reputation, emphasising her status as the epitome of sexual notoriety.

The first encounter with Doc consolidates the presentation of Shanghai Lily as a role in that it contains two key moments in which Lily can be seen to play up to her reputation. At these moments the take-up of her public persona is presented as a role that is played to the hilt. The first exchange between Doc and Lily begins with a medium shot of them leaning out of two adjoining train windows. They turn their heads towards each other and Doc greets her saying, 'Madelaine'. Their positioning within the different windows visually represents their separation and the film cuts between shots of each in their own window as they discuss how long it has been since their break-up. Lily's reaction to Doc's protestation that he has thought of nothing else but her for five years and four weeks is disbelieving, she snaps out the line: 'You were always polite, Doc. You haven't changed a bit.' There is a cut back to the original medium shot as both withdraw from their windows, turning in unison to face each other in the corridor. Doc comments that she has changed a lot, taking up a position at the lefthand side of the window, furthest from Lily, while she occupies the symmetrical space at the righthand window. Lily asks if she has lost her looks and after being told she is more beautiful than ever suddenly moves into the central space between the windows. This foray into Doc's space is clearly confrontational and it is accompanied by Lily's demanding to know how she has changed. Her posture supplies an unequivocal answer. Her left hand is placed on her hip in a provocative stance, which draws attention to the black feathers that form a lavish trimming to the sleeves of her costume, clearly presenting her as a prostitute. Lily's confrontational behaviour towards Doc shows a certain delight in playing up to her reputation. Her question coupled with her stance in the corridor, positively dares him to state what she has become. Doc's polite response – that he cannot describe how she's changed – is clearly a failure to pick up the gauntlet.

Lily says that she has changed her name and Doc asks if she is married. She laughs and replies in the negative while moving back to the window. There is a cut to a close-up of Lily, who has leaned her head out of the window. She utters the film's most famous line: 'It took more than one man to change my name to – Shanghai Lily', while turning her head towards Doc. The use of the significant pause before she drawls her new name heightens the theatrical effect. Her movement positions the unveiled part of her face in the light, presenting her announcement as a moment of revelation. However, the gesture of turning towards Doc means that this is a revelation for a specific audience. She confronts him with her new name just as she had confronted him with her stance, forcing him to view her new persona. Doc's reaction is studiously devoid of emotion. The film cuts back to the close-up of Lily who moves so that her face is in shadow, emphasising her status as mysterious, as she describes herself as 'the notorious white flower of China'. The line shows that she is fully aware of her public construction as an icon of indecency. She continues to address Doc quietly, saying 'You heard of me – and you always believed what you heard.' The soft intonation of her final words to him contrasts with her previous behaviour and compounds the impression that she has been playing up her public persona.

I have discussed the beginning of the film in some detail in order to show the ways in which Lily is presented as a complex play of appearances. The brief scene between the ex-lovers shows her playing up to her notorious reputation and the sense in which this is an act is heightened by the revelation of her respectable past. The exchange with Doc sets up a somewhat incongruous contrast between the past persona of Madelaine, the fiancée of Dr Harvey, Captain of the British army, and the present persona of the notorious Shanghai Lily. Gaylyn Studlar comments that Madelaine's transformation into 'the most flagrantly faithless and promiscuous of women' is positively dream-like.[45] Indeed, Lily can be seen as Doc's nightmare in that she is clearly the antithesis of his conceptions of politeness and propriety. However, it is important to note that playing up the role of Shanghai Lily enables Lily to confront Doc and to criticise his system of values. She is dismissive of his politeness and her endeavour to force him to say exactly how she has changed makes his tactful refusal to pick up the gauntlet look evasive. The construction of Doc's acceptable behaviour as a means of avoiding unpleasantness or confrontation has resonances across the film in that it also applies to the way he ended the relationship, leaving Lily 'without a word'. In this way, Lily's hypersimulation of her public role as an image of indecency can be seen to open up a space for her to critique Doc's values, constructing her as a Baudrillardian seductress.

My reading of Shanghai Lily draws attention to the ways in which the overt fictionality of the role is linked to the presentation of specific systems of value, allowing her acts of provocation to begin to form a space of critique. Importantly, this linking of artifice and value means that Lily cannot be read as an empty surface. I now want to examine Zucker's reading of Dietrich's performance as Shanghai Lily, which also highlights the theatricality of the role. However, I will show that Zucker's analysis of the overt artificiality of Dietrich's acting style relies on a familiar conceptual framework in which the surface is defined in terms of absence. This will involve examining Zucker's detailed analyses of two key scenes, the confrontation with Mrs Haggerty and the meeting with Doc on the observation platform of the train, in order to show how she ultimately comes to construct Dietrich/Lily as a null point.

Zucker argues that Dietrich's performance style distinguishes her from any other actress of the 1930s because of its 'extraordinary rhythm, deployment of artifice and confrontation of acting as acting'.[46] Dietrich's technique is said to consist of the use of tone, rhythm and gesture, all of which serve to emphasise the exterior features of a performance. 'The emotional content of a scene is displaced from the interior processes of the actor and brought to the surface of Dietrich's performance by choreographed gesture and movement.'[47] The choreographed quality of the actions is said to foreground their status as acting, constructing the performance as a play of surfaces.[48] Importantly, on this model, all the lines, gestures and actions performed by the Dietrich character are read as 'acts', which draw attention to their own artifice, and are therefore constructed as equally inauthentic. Zucker does not address the way in which an exterior performance style might construct authenticity differently.

Zucker continually contrasts this exterior performance style with true characterisation, which is based on a model of psychological depth. She comments 'the acting is so stylised, exaggerated and controlled, we may wonder if what is created *is* a character or a performance.'[49] The overt artificiality of the style means that the actors are said to be 'withdrawn from anything resembling "real-life" behaviour'.[50] Moreover, this lack of realism is said to have a considerable effect on the positioning of the spectator. 'There is no call for the spectator's belief, involvement or identification.'[51] Importantly, these comments simply position the exterior style within the binary hierarchies of surface/depth and absence/presence, defining it as a lack of characterisation, realism, depth and emotion.

The strength of Zucker's readings lies in her attention to textual detail and I want to demonstrate the ways in which her overarching theoretical model of artifice as absence prevents her from capitalising on her many penetrating observations. I will look at the scene in which Mrs Haggerty introduces herself to Hui Fei and Lily, incorporating a number of Zucker's comments. I will then indicate the ways in which my reading of the spectacle of Lily playing up to her reputation differs significantly from Zucker's analysis of Lily as a product of Dietrich's performance style.

The establishing shot of Mrs Haggerty entering the compartment positions the gramophone in the foreground of the frame. The loud, squawking jazz music emanating from it clearly serves to present both young women as disreputable, suggesting that Mrs Haggerty's search for respectable customers for her boarding house is not going to go well! Hui Fei continues her game of solitaire, scarcely glancing at Mrs Haggerty's proffered card before putting it to one side. Her dismissive attitude contrasts with the confrontational nature of Lily's exchange.

Mrs Haggerty hands her card to Lily, saying that she only accepts 'the most respectable people' as lodgers. There is a cut to a medium shot of Lily, who has untied the black feather trim that formed the neckline of her costume. The feathers now hang in a boa around her neck. A brief expression of amusement flickers across Lily's face as she accepts the card. She flips it over dismissively while smiling and says, 'Don't you find respectable people terribly – dull?' She pauses before the word 'dull', looking up at Mrs Haggerty and winking at her. The suggestive line coupled with her expression indicates that Lily is deriving mischievous pleasure from playing up to her reputation. The film cuts back to the medium shot of Mrs Haggerty, who exclaims that she has only known respectable people because she keeps a boarding house. This is followed by a close-up of Lily, who is examining the card closely. She then looks up wide-eyed and asks innocently, 'What kind of a house did you say?' Zucker comments that 'Dietrich phrases the question with a rising inflection that suggests both astonishment and ingenuous curiosity.'[52] Lily is clearly implying that Mrs Haggerty runs a bawdy house.

The scene cuts to a medium close-up of Mrs Haggerty who repeats the words 'a boarding house' slowly and with disfavour. There is a cut back to the close-up of Lily, who is looking down at the card. She looks up and says 'Oh!', her lips forming a perfect pout in an exaggerated expression of understanding. She then lowers her eyelids slowly. Zucker reads Lily's expression as a parody of dismay. 'The extended pause and final lowering of her eyes is a parody of embarrassment and shame, at the base of which is an infinite contempt for bourgeois respectability.'[53] Indeed, Zucker goes on to suggest that the scene shows Dietrich playing up the role of Shanghai Lily in order to shock Mrs Haggerty, whose rigid moral code makes her a stand-in for Doc.[54]

While I agree with Zucker's reading of the details of the scene, problems arise from her decision to analyse the spectacle of Lily playing up to her reputation as proof of Dietrich's virtuosity. Dietrich's performance as Shanghai Lily in this scene is said to constitute her '"profane" act', and is thus positioned as one role among the many she takes up during the course of the film.[55] For Zucker, it is Dietrich's seamless movement between the different roles that commands attention: 'Dietrich performs her "acts" so skilfully that it becomes impossible to define her "real" character.'[56] Importantly, this focus on the diversity of acts renders them all equally inauthentic. The range of inauthentic roles is multiplied further by Zucker's reading of the mocking questions that Lily poses to Mrs Haggerty as an act within an act: '[Dietrich] can even play Shanghai Lily *playing* someone else'.[57] This focus on performance can be seen to empty out the significance of the diegetic spectacle. Dietrich is simply seen to perform a series of acts, both profane and innocent, which are all equal as 'acts'. However, I would argue that the text invites us to privilege particular aspects of Lily's role-play, thus ensuring that some acts are more equal than others.

In contrast to Zucker's reading of the scene as a series of inauthentic acts that make it impossible to define the Dietrich character, I want to argue that it constitutes a crucial moment of repetition, which serves to delineate a key aspect of Lily. The confrontation with Mrs Haggerty can be regarded as a repetition in difference in that it is a comic version of the previous encounter with Doc. Importantly, Lily plays up to her reputation on both occasions in order to confront her fellow passengers' standards of propriety and morality. Thus, her '"profane" act' of playing Shanghai Lily to the hilt has a serious purpose. Her flagrant performance of immorality serves to send up the very systems of morality that would condemn her, creating a space whereby such values are parodied and critiqued. Playing up to her reputation foregrounds the ways in which the role of Shanghai Lily is an act that Lily can assume at will. However, the repetition of this act serves to create the truth of the character, conveying Lily's rejection of bourgeois morality. It thus constitutes the moment whereby the false becomes the true, consolidating Lily's status as the seductress.

Zucker's analysis of the Dietrich character as a series of inauthentic acts feeds into her conception of stardom as a pure image that transcends all roles.[58] I will demonstrate that this definition of stardom serves to construct Dietrich as a null point. Zucker's analyses of characterisation and stardom in *Shanghai Express* can therefore be seen to conform to the structures of metonymic proliferation and denegation. The structures re-emerge because Zucker defines the exterior performance style as utterly inauthentic, leading her to overlook the ways in which it can be used to set up privileged private moments. I will examine Zucker's arguments by looking at the way she reads the first part of the exchange between Doc and Lily on the observation platform of the train.

Lily joins Doc, who is sitting alone on the observation platform, staring out into the darkness. The literal presentation of the pair of them looking back sets up their discussion of the past. Lily is wearing a long coat with an upstanding fur collar that frames her face. She takes the seat on Doc's left, which is angled towards him and asks the time. She leans towards him, reaching for his watch with her right hand while her left arm steals around his shoulders. Doc responds to her embrace by turning his face away from her and staring out into the night. There is a cut to a close-up of the watch, showing the portrait of Madelaine on the lid. Her face is tilted upwards so that it appears rounder and her hair is tied back. The film cuts to a medium shot of the pair, Doc positioned in the foreground, sitting bolt upright, while Lily is still draped over him. Lily notes that he has kept the watch that she gave him and adds 'I had long hair then.' Her comment draws attention to the contrast between the past and present images; Madelaine's face is fuller and her hair appears darker, suggesting health and innocence. The high key light in the medium shot adds a blonde glow to Lily's bobbed hair, emphasising her hollow cheekbones, and giving her a fashionable, sexy appearance. Lily continues to attempt to engage Doc in conversation. He answers briefly, still facing straight ahead and she responds to his unyielding stiffness by withdrawing to her chair.

The next part of the sequence takes the form of a series of ten close-ups, alternating from Lily to Doc, as she quizzes him about the recent past. Her intonation patterns are rapid and light, rising at the end of each question. The last two questions are accompanied by her turning her head towards Doc as if to gauge his reaction to their increasing intimacy. The cutting sets up a contrast between Lily's overt movements and light, bantering tone and Doc's mask-like lack of expression and even intonation. The pattern of shots is broken by a cut to a medium shot of Lily who draws away from Doc, leaning forward to face the receding view as she accuses him of selfishness. The shot marks the transition from her quizzing Doc to offering her own memories of their break-up.

The sequence reverts to the pattern of alternating close-ups. Lily's change of position in her chair means that the upstanding collar of her coat forms a wall of rippling fur around her face, cocooning her within her own private space. Her head barely moves, drawing attention to the detail of her eye movements. She faces right and her eyes flick upwards and towards the left as she begins her description of their break-up. 'You left me without a word, purely because I indulged in a woman's trick to make you – jealous.' The tone of her voice has dropped and the line is delivered slowly. Lily's eyelids drop as she pauses and there is a cut to a close-up of Doc as she drawls the word 'jealous'. He turns his head to the left fully, looking at her properly for the first time. The sequence cuts back to the close-up of Lily, who is still glancing downwards, and she continues, 'I wanted to be certain that you loved me –'. Her eyes flick upwards as she says, 'Instead I lost you –'. She looks downwards again and from beneath lowered lids says, 'I suffered quite a bit –'. Her eyes flick back up and to the right, towards Doc, as she adds, 'And I probably deserved it.'

The contrasting use of gesture and intonation in the shots in which Lily quizzes Doc and the two close-ups in which she tells her story has the effect of constructing the latter as a privileged private moment. Lily's movements towards Doc cease and she barely moves her head, indicating that his reaction is no longer her primary concern. Her bantering lightness of tone is replaced by a deeper pitch and slower pace, suggesting that the words are being dragged out of her. The lowering of her eyelids before she makes the key admissions of her need for reassurance and her suffering consolidate this presentation of a glimpse into Lily's private thoughts. Zucker comments that 'the ... angst-filled poses – eyes downcast' seem credible.[59] However, she argues that the dialogue is highly stylised: 'the tempo is so regular it gives the speech a rehearsed effect', thus reading it as a strategy to get Doc to capitulate.[60] Importantly, Zucker reads Lily's transition from playful banter to confession as a series of acts: 'the character is merely discarding one role and adopting another. She discontinues the sophisticated and detached façade, seizing on a character who is insecure, vulnerable, and contrite; she gets the desired result – capitulation – from Brook.'[61]

Zucker's contention that Lily's confession is a performance of penitence rather than a moment of private disclosure leads her to argue that it constitutes yet another role in the series that Dietrich plays across the film.[62] However, she also argues that the sequence contains a key moment in which the series of inauthentic roles is suspended, offering a glimpse of Dietrich as star. This occurs after Doc admits that he was a fool to let Lily go and she reaches towards him, pulling him down onto the arm of her chair. There is a cut to a closer medium shot of Lily in the lower part of the frame with Doc leaning over her as she reaches up to remove his army cap. This is followed by a high-angle medium close-up of Lily's face taken from over Doc's shoulder as he is slowly pulled down into an embrace.[63] Zucker argues that 'for the duration of the fifteen-frame shot ... the face of Dietrich becomes disengaged from all specific roles.'[64] The momentary suspension of the acts that have constituted the character of Lily is said to reveal the star. 'Dietrich relinquishes her roles; she does not *need* to act. She is revealed as a "pure" image, independent of the fiction that envelops her.'[65]

Zucker's analysis of stardom defines it in terms of absence. The suspension of roles in the medium close-up serves to highlight their status as a series of acts. 'The absence of an act evokes the presence of the acts that enfold this shot.' This can be seen to conform to chiasmic logic in that the structural absence, the void at the centre, underpins the endless play of surfaces, the metonymic proliferation of inauthentic roles. Zucker's reading of Dietrich's face does not address the details of her expression. Indeed, her account of Dietrich's disengagement from all roles suggests that her face is devoid of expression. This combination of absence with overt artifice – the shot reveals Dietrich to be nothing but pure image – is very similar to Baudrillard's analysis of the female star. For Baudrillard, the attraction of the celluloid seductress is that of the void. The 'nullity of her smile' is said to reveal the absence of psychological or soulful depths, drawing attention to the star's status as a purely artificial construct.[66]

Zucker's reading of the medium close-up of Dietrich's face as a star moment does not address the content of the shot. This is unfortunate because the lighting set-up might be seen to support her argument. The placing of a key light in line with Dietrich's forehead as she gazes upwards etches out her prominent cheekbones, sculpting her face into the familiar contours of her star image. However, the expression on her face does not conform to the sculpted beauty of a star moment. Indeed, the intensity with which Lily gazes up at Doc has the effect of making her look somewhat haggard. Thus, in contrast to Zucker, I would argue that this shot can only be understood within the context of the sequence. It uses the same vocabulary of gesture as the confessional moment and the minimal movements serve, once again, as the means of revealing Lily's private emotions. The slow pace of her verbal admissions is echoed by Doc's gradual descent into the embrace. The prolonging of the prelude to the kiss helps to convey the intensity of Lily's desire for him. In this way, the shot can be seen to offer a key moment of disclosure, showing the truth of Lily's feelings for Doc.

Importantly, this presentation of a privileged private moment does not negate the previous truth set up about Lily's character. This is because the construction of interiority is effected through performance and thus does not stand in opposition to Lily's earlier, exteriorised theatricality. Instead, each of the character's moments of truth can be seen to use performance in a different way. In the first, the performance style is overtly artificial and it is the repetition of Lily's overplayed profane act to Mrs Haggerty that consolidates the presentation of her disdain for bourgeois morality. In the second, the range of actions, gestures and intonations sets up a contrast between Lily's light-hearted quizzing of Doc and her later confession, constructing the latter as a moment of private disclosure. Both scenes offer an insight into the truth of Lily's character, formulating a key tension that propels the plot. Lily's marked disdain for bourgeois morality is matched only by her love for a man who epitomises that morality, and thus it is clear that someone will have to give!

The rest of the sequence on the observation platform may be said to mark the return of Shanghai Lily. I will show that the transition from a private moment of disclosure to a public role does not invalidate the latter. This will involve demonstrating the ways in which Lily's public persona is presented as authentic. The lovers' embrace ends as Doc pulls away from Lily, perching on the arm of her chair, saying 'I wish you could tell me there'd been no other men.' Lily rises, moving right and turning her back to the camera, putting on his military cap, which she had removed prior to the embrace. There is a cut to a medium close-up of Lily who turns around to face the camera while adjusting the cap to a jaunty angle. The theatricality of the turn coupled with her new costume constructs the return of Shanghai Lily as the resumption of an act. Her eyes narrow as she focuses on Doc while drawling her response: 'I wish I could. But five years in China is a long time.' The last two words are dragged out as if to suggest the numerous liaisons she has had during this period and the delivery shows Lily playing the role to the hilt.

Doc perches on the arm of his chair, his arms stretched straight out as he leans on the railing. He looks back into the night as he wishes he could relive the last five years. Lily comes up behind him, leaning her right arm across his shoulders, suggesting that they might have parted anyway. Doc replies vehemently, 'We wouldn't have parted, Madelaine – ' and Lily glances downward at him, her lips briefly compressing as if to stifle laughter. He continues, 'We'd have gone back to England – married – and been very happy.' It is notable that Doc does not look at Lily while offering his romantic version of what might have been. He continues to stare into space, suggesting he is conjuring up a vision of a perfect past with an ideal woman. Lily's stifled laughter and increasingly incredulous expressions convey her doubts about his vision of wedded bliss and her suitability for the role of Madelaine, Doc's perfect wife. Doc continues to regret the past as she walks around him, exiting the frame to the left.

This movement away from Doc marks the beginning of Lily's humorous response to his romantic regrets. There is a cut to a medium close-up of Lily who jauntily announces that there is only one thing she would not have done. The scene cuts to a medium close-up of Doc, who smiles at her and asks what that was. Lily's movement away from Doc thus forces him to turn and face her, rather than constructing visions of the past. There is a cut back to the medium close-up of Lily, which can thus be read as a point-of-view shot. She answers smiling: 'I wouldn't have bobbed my hair!' flicking his cap back with the forefinger of her right hand. The reference to her current hairstyle recalls the portrait in the watch. Madelaine's long hair conveyed her innocence and the portrait can be seen as part of Doc's idealised vision of the past. Lily is therefore mocking his regrets for her apparent loss of innocence and faithfulness, by merely questioning her choice of hairstyle. Importantly, Lily confronts Doc with a display of vivacious humour during the point-of-view shot, her mockery coupled with her flippant gesture can be seen as the means by which she forces him to view her as Shanghai Lily. The medium shot of the pair that follows shows Doc's face in profile. He is still perched on the arm of the chair, facing Lily who is opposite him. The smile has been completely wiped off his face. The hardening of his expression into one of schooled impassivity conveys his shock and displeasure at the sight of Lily. It is as if he has been forced to acknowledge the gulf between his idealised dream of Madelaine and the woman who faces him.

This particular repetition of Lily's profane act recalls other moments in the Dietrich/Sternberg cycle. Dietrich frequently appears in men's clothing: from the hats and military-style jackets of The Scarlet Empress to the evening wear of Morocco and Blonde Venus. The repetition of these images is vital to the star's construction as sexually ambiguous.[67] In Shanghai Express the adoption of male attire is used to indicate

Doc's expression of displeasure on turning to view Shanghai Lily. Still from *Shanghai Express*

sexual experience. Indeed, the first medium close-up of Lily in the cap coincides with her drawling acknowledgment of her many other lovers, suggesting that she has taken up the traditionally male privilege of having numerous sexual partners. This use of the motif also occurs in *Blonde Venus*. Helen's appearance in a white tuxedo in the last musical number is a visual representation of her take-up of a masculine 'love them and leave them' ethos, which has enabled her to get to the top of the cabaret circuit in Paris. Moreover, the lyrics of the song: 'If the moon began to waltz/Or the sun turned summersaults/Do you think I'd care/Or stop and stare/I couldn't be annoyed', encapsulate Dietrich's particular form of studied insouciance.

These intertextual references have the effect of constructing Lily's display of jaunty vitality as a star moment. The second medium close-up in which she flicks the visor of Doc's cap can thus be seen as an image of mocking humour that instantiates and reinforces the Dietrich persona. Importantly, the use of intertextual repetition can be seen to offer another instance of the false become the true. While the repetition of Lily's profane act within the diegesis sets up a key 'moment of truth', providing insight into the character; the repetition of key aspects of Dietrich's star persona serves to reinforce Lily's use of mocking humour, thus authenticating her profane act as a pleasurable moment of 'pure' Dietrich.

The sequence on the observation platform also expands on the moral conflict between Doc and Lily, reworking it as a clash about the past. Lily plays up to he reputation in order to challenge Doc's idealised vision of the past, rudely awakening him from his dreams of a perfect marriage with Madelaine. Lily's parody of Doc's nostalgia for the past also serves to open up a space of critique in that it shows the futility of such regrets. In addition, the parody allows for the expression of Lily's own perspective on the past, which she refuses to view as a perfect space. The ending of the sequence clearly shows that Lily views her past relationship with Doc as imperfect. Their argument over the telegram she receives contains another moment of parody in which Lily assumes an expression of mock innocence when refuting Doc's suggestion that the letter is from one of her lovers. Her response on handing him the telegram: 'Will you never learn to believe without proof?' raises the key issue of his lack of faith in her.

Importantly, the observation sequence marks a crucial shift in Shanghai Lily's use of parodic theatricality across the film. It begins as a deconstructive critique of bourgeois morality, conforming to Baudrillard's vision of the critical distance created by the seductress's hypersimulation of other roles. However, Lily's send-up of Doc's nostalgia is also the means by which she presents her own perspective on the past. This shift can be seen to alter the Baudrillardian definition, offering a more Nietzschean presentation of the seductress as a play of appearances, which serves to create and sustain her own particular perspective.

I have suggested that the character of Lily is built up through the presentation of a number of 'moments of truth' that take different forms. She is constructed through a series of playful 'acts' and privileged private moments that combine to work together. I want to use this insight to examine the way the character is developed in the second half of the film, focusing on the presentation of Lily's reformation, which I will argue shows her transformation into Madelaine, and the final re-emergence of Shanghai Lily. The reformation is normally said to show Lily's oscillation between conflicting roles, constructing her as contradictory and inauthentic.[68] In contrast, I will argue that Lily's transformation into Madelaine is presented as genuine and will go on to trace the ways in which the return of Shanghai Lily marks the final development in the construction of the seductress's own perspective.

Lily's reformation occurs after the train has been captured by the rebels. Doc risks his life to save Lily from Chang's advances and is subsequently taken hostage and tied up while she is returned to the train. Lily has an angry confrontation with the missionary Mr Carmichael, on the platform, during which he advises her to get down on her knees and pray. She disappears into her compartment, turning off the light. There is a cut to a medium shot of Mr Carmichael and the camera pans left with him as he moves towards the train, stopping at the window of Lily's compartment and peering in.[69] This is followed by a point-of-view shot of Lily, making him a key witness to her spiritual struggle. The frame of the compartment door forms a dark bar across the upper half of the screen, hiding Lily's face. Its darkness draws attention to the whiteness of Lily's hands, which are positioned below it. The spiritual conflict suggested by the division between darkness and light within the frame is echoed in her hand gestures. She clasps and unclasps her fingers as if contemplating whether or not to pray.

There is a cut back to the medium shot of Mr Carmichael who looks away from the window and back again as if to be sure of what he has seen. This is followed by a second point-of-view shot, a close-up of Lily's hands and wrists. Her hands are pressed together touching along the length of the finger in the classic position of prayer. The close-up is swiftly superimposed with an image of steam rising from a train chimney in the centre and a ringing bell on the righthand side. Both images serve to emphasise the speed of the locomotive. Lily's hands gradually relax, her fingers interlacing as the close-up fades. The superimposed image presents Lily's prayer as effective in that it hastens the arrival of the train with the prisoner who will be exchanged for Doc. The technique also emphasises the passing of time, to which Mr Carmichael later bears witness, informing Doc that Lily prayed for his safety all night.

The sequence may be said to show the transformation of Lily into Madelaine as the name also has Biblical connotations. Mary Magdelene was a prostitute who repented of her sinful life to become one of Christ's most faithful followers. This sequence charts a similar transformation in that the flagrantly faithless Lily becomes the faithful Madelaine. The immediate answer to Madelaine's prayer presents Lily's repentance as genuine. Moreover, like Magdelene, her repentance is seen to result in a faith that is stronger than those who have never strayed. Madelaine prays successfully for Doc's safe release while Mr Carmichael can only look on. The punning of Madelaine/Magdelene means that the role takes on broader connotations than that of Doc's ideal wife. However, the theme of faithfulness, be it sexual or religious, acts as a thread of continuity within the role.

Within the diegesis Lily's reformation is clearly presented as genuine. Mr Carmichael's profession makes him the ideal witness and his complete change of attitude towards Lily, clearly shows that he believes she has reformed. Mr Carmichael's new-found faith in Lily is paralleled with Doc's new-found cynicism. Having rescued Lily from Chang he reveals that he has lost the watch that contained her portrait 'along with a few ideals'. Doc's rejection of Lily results in her deciding to resume the role of Shanghai Lily. Her resumption of the role is shown in a short scene in her compartment. It begins with a close-up of the gramophone playing squawking jazz music, which is positioned alongside one of Lily's fluffy-slippered feet. There is a cut to a medium shot of Lily who is dressed in a brightly patterned kimono, its oriental design recalling the description of her as the 'white flower of China'. She is presented en déshabillée, her black-stockinged leg visible between the folds of her kimono and she drags on her cigarette before stretching out her arms, revealing the low neckline of her costume. The details of her dress coupled with her smoking and the accompanying music clearly indicate that Shanghai Lily is back with a vengeance.

Lily's brazen behaviour is a topic of discussion among the passengers. Mr Carmichael's defence of her when the other passengers express their disgust at her decision to leave with Chang, results in his completely swapping roles with Doc. Having defended Lily from the missionary's accusations of immorality at the beginning of the journey, Doc refuses to countenance the suggestion that she prayed for his safety. His scepticism provokes Mr Carmichael to find out the truth. The scene that follows can be said to constitute a second confrontation between Mr Carmichael and Lily. However, unlike the first in which Lily acceded to his suggestions, praying and reforming, the second shows her developing her own perspective on the issue of faith.

Mr Carmichael's initial request for a conversation with Lily is denied but he persists and Hui Fei exits, leaving them alone together. Lily rises to close the compartment door, pausing in the doorway with her right hand on her hip. She is still wearing the kimono and her provocative posture recalls her first confrontation with Doc. Undeterred, Mr Carmichael sits down facing her. He points out the inconsistency between her prayers the night before and her decision to leave with Chang in the morning, concluding exasperatedly, 'You can't tell me that a human being can do two things like that within six hours!' Lily offers to explain on condition that he does not repeat it and tells him of Chang's plans to blind Doc. There is a cut to a medium shot of the pair as Mr Carmichael rises, clearly wishing to leave and inform Doc, but Lily stops him and sits down.

The medium shot serves to preface a series of three close-ups of Lily, which are presented as moments of private disclosure. In the first, she turns to face Mr Carmichael, saying: 'It may sound odd for me to use your language but it's purely a question of – faith.' Her eyes flick up and down five times during this short sentence, her gaze narrowing and becoming steady as she pauses and delivers the word 'faith'. Her low, steady intonation and use of the pause recall the sequence on the observation platform in which she paused

Lily in conversation with Dr Carmichael. Publicity still for *Shanghai Express*

before the delivery of the word 'jealous'. In the second close-up, Lily turns away from Mr Carmichael, exhaling cigarette smoke as she talks about her past with Doc. The smoke temporarily hides her face but, as it fades, she turns back towards the missionary to explain that she 'didn't care to bargain for love with words.' The vaporisation of the smoke means that this line is presented as a key moment of disclosure. There is a cut to a close-up of Mr Carmichael, who asks if Lily still loves Doc. The third close-up of Lily is slightly tighter than the first two. Her eyes are downcast as she utters the word 'Yes.' The change of inflection as she speaks the word means that the admission seems to be forced out of her. Her low-pitched delivery and facial expression recall the confession of her suffering to Doc, giving her admission the status of the truth.

Lily's comments also recall the sequence on the observation platform in that they build on her criticism of Doc's inability to believe without proof. In this scene, her refusal to explain her behaviour to Doc, thus providing him with proof, is entirely supported by Mr Carmichael who comments: 'You're right, love without faith is like religion without faith. It isn't worth very much.' The reaffirmation of the strength of Lily's feelings for Doc also recalls the key conundrum of her position: the critic of bourgeois morality in love with its chief exponent. This can be seen to facilitate a more complex appreciation of the roles of the faithful Madelaine versus the flagrantly faithless Shanghai Lily in that both can be seen to offer different solutions to the problem.

Becoming Madelaine involves giving up the role of critic and conforming to the standards of bourgeois morality. Madelaine/Magdelene's repentance of her former life shows that she accepts the evaluation of her lifestyle as sinful and unsuitable. Her transformation from the faithless to the faithful means that she can be mapped onto the lowest and the highest points of the Christian scale. Redemption through love transforms Lily into Madelaine, the ideal woman that Doc deems worthy of his affections, allowing them to be together on his terms. In contrast, Lily's refusal to bargain for love with words means that she will not be held accountable to Doc. This can be seen to expand her role of critic in that she takes up a position outside the system of bourgeois morality. Mr Carmichael's parallel between the faiths required by love and religion effectively places Lily outside the moral system that would simply condemn her as faithless. His comment can be seen to reconstruct her as a goddess in that she is regarded as the rightful recipient of Doc's faith rather than being the object of his judgment. The return of Shanghai Lily can thus be seen to mark the further delineation of Lily's own perspective, providing the means whereby she sets up her terms for any future relationship with Doc.

The presentation of Lily's perspective is consolidated by the moment of mocking humour that marks the end of her encounter with Mr Carmichael. The missionary leaves, saying that he is unable to help her, and she replies 'No', while turning her head slightly towards him and giving a little half smile. The rising inflection of her intonation and the smile turns her reply into a mockery of surprise, suggesting that she knew he would not be able to help. She will have to convert Doc herself. The return to the mocking humour that has characterised her previous encounters with Doc and Mrs Haggerty recalls her use of it to ridicule their standards of respectability. In this scene, her mockery becomes the laughter of a goddess who is outside the moral system. It also suggests her confidence in her ability to convert Doc to her way of thinking.

The narrative trajectory of *Shanghai Express* may be said to explore both of the solutions to Lily's conundrum. While Lily's reformation is clearly presented as genuine, Doc's refusal to believe the key witness effectively suspends the narrative trajectory of becoming Madelaine. The return of Shanghai Lily is also the moment at which the narrative diverges sharply from the conventional morality tales of the fallen woman promulgated by Hollywood in the 1930s. In *Shanghai Express*, the reformation of the fallen woman and her subsumption within the system of moral values does not constitute the denouement. The final presentation of Shanghai Lily's return can thus be seen to affirm the development of her own perspective and to uphold her refusal to conform to the moral system.

The last sequence may be said to show Shanghai Lily's successful imposition of her terms for the relationship onto Doc. Lily emerges from the train in the black cock-feather costume that she wore at the beginning of the film, clearly indicating her refusal to conform to Doc's standards of respectability. She sashays out of the station and buys Doc another watch. On returning, she says goodbye to some of the other passengers, including Mr Carmichael, who wishes her luck. Doc comes over to Lily who presents him with his new watch before bidding him goodbye. He moves rapidly towards her, preventing her from leaving. There is a cut to a medium close-up of their faces. Doc is wearing a pith helmet and is positioned with his face in profile. Lily is centre screen, facing the camera, and she glances briefly towards Doc as he promises to be different in the future. Her expression is impassive but positive – a slight smile can be seen below her veil. Doc leans down towards her, the brim of his hat covering his eyes and casting his face into shadow, granting him a little privacy in his moment of utter capitulation as he says, 'Please forgive me for my lack of faith, please do.' His movement towards Lily shows that it is he who has to bend to her expectations.

The next shot is a close-up of the pair in which the profile of Doc's face is just visible in the upper lefthand corner of the screen. This second close-up is Lily's confessional moment. She turns her head to the left, looking over her shoulder towards Doc, as she tells him that she has always loved him and always will. Doc admits that he has behaved badly and she responds saying, 'Perhaps it was my fault. I should have told you everything.' However, the line does not act as a preface to Lily's account of events; it is as close as she gets to an apology or an explanation. As a result, Lily can be seen to remain steadfast in her refusal to be held accountable to Doc. Her continued status as Shanghai Lily is clearly indicated by the profusion of black feathers framing her face within the shot. The balance of power indicated in the two close-ups is summarised in the final shot of the pair embracing. Doc is positioned with his back to the camera and Lily's feathered sleeves are clearly visible as she clasps him. She is holding Doc's riding crop in her left hand and passes it over to the right, across his back, before dropping it onto her pile of luggage. The gesture makes it very clear that Lily has retained the whip hand.

Andrew Sarris argues that the end of *Shanghai Express* clearly shows Doc's capitulation to Lily. 'Her face merely taunts him with a myriad of mirrors until he surrenders to the illusion that she represents, but on her terms rather than his.'[70] I have traced the ways in which the text presents a complex series of playful acts and privileged private moments combining to create a sense of Lily's terms. Doc's final capitulation resolves the conundrum created by Shanghai Lily's love for him, upholding her perspective on their past and future together.

Lily's flagrant acts of provocation set up a key aspect of her character, creating the terms in which she must be understood. In this way, the false operates as a site of authenticity, offering a critique of bourgeois values as well as becoming the means whereby Lily defines her own terms. This move beyond critique to the presentation of her own perspective is the moment at which Lily expands Baudrillard's conception of the seductress, providing a Nietzschean instance of the false raised to a higher power. I will show how this reworked figure of the seductress can provide us with a way of mapping the positive potential of the cinematic presentation of woman as illusion in Chapter 7.

Notes

1. F. Nietzsche, *The Will to Power*, W. Kaufmann (ed. and trans.) (New York: Vintage Books, 1968), p. 292.
2. J. Baudrillard, *Seduction*, B. Singer (trans.) (London: Macmillan, 1990). This was originally published in French in 1979, a year after Derrida's *Spurs*. Baudrillard sets up a distinction between hot and cool seduction in that the latter is said to be more extreme than the former. My distinction between viewing the surface as the end of signification or a site for signifying differently *cannot* be mapped onto his distinction between hot and cold.
3. Baudrillard, *Seduction*, pp. 1–2.
4. Ibid., p. 12.
5. Ibid., p. 21.
6. Ibid., p. 10.
7. See Section 1 of Chapter 4.
8. Baudrillard, *Seduction*, p. 33.
9. Ibid., p. 68.
10. Ibid., pp. 69, 70.
11. Ibid., p. 67.
12. Ibid., p. 70.
13. Ibid., p. 57.

14. Ibid., p. 69.
15. Ibid., p. 15.
16. Ibid.
17. Ibid., p. 47.
18. Ibid.
19. Ibid., p. 113.
20. Derrida, *Spurs*, p. 107.
21. See Chapter 4, Section 3 for more details.
22. Baudrillard, *Seduction*, p. 75.
23. Ibid., p. 8. My italics.
24. Ibid., p. 53.
25. Ibid.
26. Nietzsche, *The Will to Power*, p. 292.
27. Baudrillard, *Seduction*, p. 54.
28. Ibid., p. 146.
29. Ibid., p. 75.
30. Ibid., p. 147.
31. Ibid., p. 144.
32. S. Kofman, 'Baubô: Theological Perversion and Fetishism', in M. A. Gillespie and T. B. Strong (eds), *Nietzsche's New Seas: Explorations in Philosophy, Aesthetics and Politics* (Chicago, IL and London: University of Chicago Press, 1988), p. 181.
33. Baudrillard, *Seduction*, p. 76.
34. Ibid., p. 94.
35. Ibid., p. 77.
36. Ibid., p. 87.
37. Ibid., p. 95.
38. C. Zucker, *The Idea of the Image: Josef von Sternberg's Dietrich Films* (London and Toronto: Associated University Presses, 1988), p. 114.
39. Baudrillard, *Seduction*, p. 15.
40. Ibid., p. 94. My italics.
41. Ibid., p. 15.
42. Ibid., p. 21. My italics.
43. Zucker, *The Idea of the Image*, p. 109.
44. Nietzsche, *The Will to Power*, p. 292.
45. G. Studlar, *In the Realm of Pleasure: Von Sternberg, Dietrich and the Masochistic Aesthetic* (Urbana and Chicago: University of Illinois Press, 1988), p. 160.
46. C. Zucker, 'I Am Dietrich and Dietrich Is Me: An Investigation of Performance Style in *Morocco* and *Shanghai Express*', in C. Zucker (ed.), *Making Visible the Invisible: An Anthology of Original Essays in Film Acting* (Metuchen, NJ and London: Scarecrow Press, 1990), p. 255.

47. C. Zucker, 'Some Observations on von Sternberg and Dietrich', *The Cinema Journal* vol. 19 no. 2, Spring 1980, p. 22.

48. Zucker also reads the choreographed quality of the performances as proof of Sternberg's directorial control. Her analysis of the director as choreographer constructs him as the substance behind Dietrich's play of appearances, containing her within the familiar gendered dichotomy of subject/object. Zucker, *The Idea of the Image*, pp. 86, 94, 116.

49. Zucker, *The Idea of the Image*, p. 114.

50. Ibid.

51. Ibid.

52. Ibid., p. 105.

53. Ibid.

54. Ibid., p. 106.

55. Ibid.

56. Ibid.

57. Ibid.

58. Ibid., p. 115.

59. Ibid., p. 109.

60. Ibid.

61. Ibid.

62. Ibid., p. 115.

63. Zucker describes this shot as a reverse-angle medium close-up. Unfortunately the shot is misnumbered in the written analysis as Figure 132 when the description clearly applies to the still designated Figure 133. Ibid., pp. 108–10.

64. Ibid., p. 110.

65. Ibid., p. 115.

66. Baudrillard, *Seduction*, p. 95.

67. For a discussion of the lesbian take-up of Dietrich's image see: M. Citron *et al.* 'Woman and Film: A Discussion of Feminist Aesthetics', *New German Critique*, Winter (1978), pp. 90–1.

68. Zucker, *The Idea of the Image*, p. 115; Studlar, *In the Realm of Pleasure*, p. 171.

69. This is a multiple point-of-view shot because it is shared by the Chinese attendant who is also staring in through the window. However, I have focused on Mr Carmichael because he goes on to bear witness to the reformation.

70. A. Sarris, *The Films of Joseph von Sternberg* (New York: Museum of Modern Art, 1966), p. 35.

7 | Conclusion

I have demonstrated that the take-up of Le Doeuff's and Irigaray's methodology can be tremendously useful for Film Studies because it enables a fundamental rethinking of the relations between philosophy, film theory and textual analysis. Following their methodology ensures that theory no longer has the status of a privileged discourse. Instead, it is redefined as provisional and precarious because it is intrinsically reliant on imagery. This model of theory provides new roles for literary, artistic and filmic images as they constitute the means through which any theoretical system is created, as well as forming its points of possible destabilisation. While this book demonstrates the disruptive potential of specific images, I have also been concerned to move beyond a deconstructive model of critique in which the image is seen simply to undermine its concomitant theoretical system. Combining Le Doeuff and Irigaray has allowed me to draw attention to the ways in which specific philosophical, literary and filmic images constitute imaginary resources that hold open the possibility of other theorisations, thus providing the means to map the roads not yet taken.

I have traced the ways in which a number of key images disrupt and challenge the theoretical frames through which they have typically been viewed. Chapter 3 demonstrates that Catherine's increasing stillness in *The Scarlet Empress* can be read as emblematic of her increasing power, focusing on the scene in which she becomes stone, thus evading Alexei's embraces and thwarting his ambitions. This reading challenges the standard equation of stillness and objectification by expanding on an aspect of Sacher-Masoch's work that is not crystallised into theory, namely, the torturess's capacity to turn back into stone. Chapter 5 explores the ways in which Concha's exuberant entanglement of Antonio at the beginning of *The Devil Is a Woman* challenges the Derridean model in which any scenario of desire controlled by woman is conceptualised as a fatal endgame. Both films present an image of a woman who stages her appearances for her own ends: either to gain political power or to control the game of desire, thus fundamentally reworking the binary of subject/object.

While Chapter 4 charts the re-emergence of the structures of chiasmic and binary logic in the work of key theorists such as Nietzsche and Derrida, it also focuses on the possibility of other logical structures such as the model of repetition in difference offered by the eternal return. This can be seen to offer an alternative form of visual logic from the chiasma, in which the balance of centripetal and centrifugal movements ultimately forms a zero, positioning woman as the vanishing point. By contrast, the eternal return offers a temporal representation of circularity as a potentially infinite series of three-dimensional loops, reconstructing it as a site of creativity and change. This recon-figuration of the circle utilises Kofman's reworking of the eternal return, which is explicitly linked to the myth of Baubô. My re/reading of the encounter between Baubô and Demeter as emblematic of a perspectival shift crystallises the myth into a particular form, which in turn, reconstructs the eternal return as a mode of affirmative repetition that also symbolises the process of thinking again.

Importantly, these alternative theorisations are created and expressed through dif-ferent figures of woman. It is clear that the move away from the construction of woman as the vanishing point, which presents her as pure object, to the affirmative perspectival shift represented by Demeter's breaking into laughter at the sight of Baubô's belly, an exchange which constructs both women as subjects, constitutes a significant change to the representation of woman within philosophy. Moreover, this book offers a range of theorisations of woman as appearance that are much more positive than the famous constructions of her as an absence of depth, truth and/or meaning. Helen, Maya and the sorceress confirm the necessity of 'mere' appearances; Baubô presents the recognition that there is nothing beyond appearance as a joyful moment of affirmation; and the seductress reconfigures the play of appearances as a site of authenticity and truth. It is absolutely vital that these theoretical moves are expressed through these figures of woman because '[w]ho gets to represent what to whom and why; what image, icon or person shall stand for what to whom are ques-tions . . . that . . . tie into issues of social and political consequence.'[1] My representation and re/working of these figures of woman in philosophy creates a range of alternative theorisations, which draw on the social and cultural discourses of film and literature, providing conceptual models that can, in turn, be used to map the field of the social in different ways.

I have used these alternative theorisations of woman as appearance as a means of re/viewing the highly glamorised presentation of Dietrich in two key films from the Stern-berg cycle. I have taken up Demeter's use of Baubô as a camera obscura, presenting her as a lens through which to view the character of Concha in *The Devil Is a Woman*. This enables us to view Concha in a different way from previous readings in which her play of veils is seen as a classic instance of the 'dangerous deception or duplicity attached to the feminine'.[2] Viewing Concha through Baubô foregrounds the key aspect of affirma-tion: she affirms the play of appearances through her laughter and her presentation as the spirit of carnival. In the same way, the figure of the seductress enables us to map the character of Shanghai Lily differently from her previous construction as a series of inauthentic acts.[3] However, the film reading also contributes to the development of the seductress as a lens, expanding the re/reading of Baudrillard by combining it with the complexities of Shanghai Lily's characterisation. As a result, the seductress's play of appearances comes to constitute more than a deconstructive critique of patriarchal values; it becomes the means by which she presents her own perspective.

The figures of Baubô and the seductress should *not* be regarded as templates for reading, stamping their replica onto every film to which they are applied. Instead, each constitutes a lens that foregrounds different aspects of the play of appearances, thus providing a means of tracing the ways in which that play is represented differently in each film. The process of differential repetition that is expressed through the figures of Baubô and the seductress thus informs the way in which they themselves are reworked by being applied to particular film texts. I want now to provide a demonstration of this type of differential reading by using the figure of the seductress as a lens through which to view *Gilda*,[4] noting the similarities and differences between the representations of the titular character and Shanghai Lily. I will then explore the contemporary presentation of woman as appearance by analysing two films starring Nicole Kidman: *Eyes Wide Shut* and *Moulin Rouge*.[5]

1 Rita Hayworth as Gilda

My reading of *Gilda* will focus on the ways in which the title character plays up an image of flagrant faithlessness, which is clearly designated as an act within the text, in order to provoke a response from Johnny. This foregrounding of the role of the seductress as a performance is the same as Shanghai Lily's profane act, which she uses to disconcert and thwart Doc, among others. In each case the role of seductress intersects with the actress's star persona, providing an intertextual reinforcement that constructs the role as a site of authenticity. While the presentation of Shanghai Lily as Dietrich is momentary, the gesture with which she flicks back Doc's cap and refuses to be regretful displays her characteristic mockery and insouciance; the role of Gilda is seen as an exemplary instance of Hayworth's construction as a 'love goddess'.[6] I will argue that Hayworth plays a double role throughout *Gilda*, and that both serve to reinforce or recreate elements of her star persona. However, her performance as the seductress differs from her other role in that it is clearly designated as an act; as a result its take-up as a 'natural' expression of her star persona conflicts with its presentation within the film's narrative.[7]

The doubling of roles that make up Gilda's character is evident from her first appearance. The first medium close-up of her is a multiple point-of-view shot, which shows the sight that greets Ballin and Johnny. She appears to rise up into the frame, throwing back her hair in a gesture of abandon. The ruffled edge of her white negligee, which has fallen off both shoulders, is just visible so that she resembles Venus rising from the foam. Ballin's question: 'Are you decent?' is answered with a smiling response of mock surprise: 'Me?' The laughter in her voice and the visual impact of her presentation as a goddess clearly suggest that she belongs outside such moral codes. Gilda's presentation in this shot accords with the way in which Hayworth is often seen to express a '*healthy sexuality*', in that it offers an image of a woman who expresses and enjoys her own sensuality free from moral criteria, such as shame.[8]

This justifiably famous shot is followed by a point-of-view shot of Johnny, and the film cuts back to the medium close-up of Gilda, giving her reaction on seeing him. She pulls up one shoulder of her fallen negligee, her smile fading and her chin tilting up slightly as if preparing for battle, drawling the line: 'Sure – I'm decent.' Her intonation of the words suggests precisely the reverse. Her gesture of partially covering herself has the effect of making her state of undress seem indecent, asserting the moral codes that are jokingly suspended in the first shot. The two shots can thus be seen to present two roles: the first offers an image of sensual enjoyment that is often associated with Hayworth, while the second is an exaggerated image of indecency that is clearly performed for Johnny alone. The status of the second as an act and therefore a pure play of appearances means that it corresponds to the role of seductress.

The presentation of Gilda's performance of indecency as a role that is played up for Johnny is signalled through the use of point-of-view shots across the film. He takes up the position of ideal audience in Gilda's first dance at the nightclub. Their relative spatial positions are indicated by an establishing shot over Johnny's shoulder, which shows Gilda dancing with Captain Delgado in the mid-ground. The dance is presented through a series of point-of-view shots that are intercut with medium shots of Johnny's reaction, clearly indicating his displeasure at the sight of them. Moreover, his refusal of Delgado's initial invitation to dance on Gilda's behalf means that the sight of the couple empha-

Gilda moves closer to Delgado, while staring at Johnny. Still from *Gilda*

sises his lack of power over her, reversing the power structure of the gaze. Delgado responds to Gilda's comment that she used to be a professional dancer by immediately pulling her into a close embrace, indicating his understanding of her profession. She adroitly out-manoeuvres him by using the hand that holds hers to push him away, while saying lightly 'That's against our union rules.' Her awareness of Johnny's gaze is shown by her change of expression when she turns to face him while encircling her partner: her eyes narrow, mocking his inability to control her actions.

This reversal of the power structure of the gaze reaches a climax when the pair virtually come to a halt on the dance floor, subjecting Johnny to their combined look as Delgado suggests that Johnny wishes he were her young man. Gilda responds by moving closer to Delgado, sliding her hand around his neck in a close embrace while staring directly at Johnny. The film cuts back to the medium shot of Johnny showing that her performance has had the effect of discomfiting him still further, provoking his departure shortly afterwards. The dance continues and the use of a medium close-up of the pair emphasises the intimacy of Gilda's position in Delgado's arms.[9] She looks over his shoulder, registering Johnny's exit, and immediately becomes aware of the inappropriate nature of their closeness, sliding away from Delgado and reminding him of the Union rules. He responds, commenting: 'Your rules are very changeable my lady' and she replies, somewhat disingenuously: 'They change with the weather.'

Delgado's comment positions Gilda as the familiar figure of woman as caprice, a changeable series of surfaces, and she does not choose to disabuse him by explaining her motives for changing her mind. However, her repeated glances towards Johnny mean that her motivation is obvious and she pulls away the moment that he is no longer around to appreciate her performance. Delgado's view of Gilda echoes Johnny's, which is expressed earlier in the same scene. Johnny compares her to Ballin's 'little friend', by defining the swordstick as feminine: 'It looks like one thing and right in front of your eyes it becomes another thing.' Ballin's reply that Johnny does not have faith in the stability of women, presents this play of appearances as pure caprice. However, the comparison also suggests that Gilda is both duplicitous and deadly, showing that Johnny views her as a *femme fatale*.

This view of Gilda needs to be treated with caution given that the limitations of Johnny's 'cockeyed' perspective are signalled throughout the film. Importantly, his view is based on an uncritical acceptance of an image that is clearly played to the hilt in order to provoke him. The film provides a key scene in which Gilda attempts to relate to him in a more straightforward way. This occurs after her first performance of 'Put the Blame on Mame', which Richard Dyer reads as a privileged private moment. This is partly because it is sung to Uncle Pio who is associated with a 'down to earth' truthfulness that is expressed through his use of proverbial folk wisdom throughout the film.[10] Dyer argues that the song clearly undermines Gilda's construction as a deadly force because it demonstrates the ways in which men always blame natural disasters on Mame – that is, women. The song states the case against the way film noir characteristically constructs women ... point[ing] to the illegitimacy of men blaming women, where film noir generally is concerned to assert just that.[11]

The song can therefore be read as a commentary on Johnny's perspective, suggesting that his view of Gilda as a *femme fatale* is maintained by an illegitimate shifting of responsibility, which requires a level of self-deception.

The exchange that follows the song continues to confirm Gilda's truthfulness through her relation to Uncle Pio in that she admonishes Johnny's rudeness to him by offering a piece of proverbial wisdom: 'Put a beggar on horseback – huh Uncle Pio.' On his exit, her tone changes back to its customary lightness as she banters with Johnny. This is particularly noticeable in her deliberately shocking offer to show him her swimsuit under her dress, ostensibly to substantiate the flimsy excuse for her presence in the nightclub in the early hours of the morning. However, the banter is momentary and her quips fail, giving Johnny the upper hand verbally for the first time. The reversal occurs after she asks why he will not allow Ballin to find out about her antics, ending with: 'Or are you

Gilda singing to Uncle Pio. Still from *Gilda*

afraid of what he might do to me?' He responds by turning to leave but Gilda regains his attention, offering a confession of her own feelings: 'because I am – afraid'. Her pause is filled by an exasperated: 'What?' from Johnny, indicating that he is treating the conversation as yet another ploy to get his attention. However, the low pitch and slower pace with which she delivers the line form a clear contrast to her previous bantering tones, suggesting that she is being entirely truthful. Johnny's incredulous response to her admissions of fear and foolishness, in that she regrets marrying someone else, clearly shows that he views her confession as yet another lie.

Gilda responds to his outright rejection of her confession by attempting to resume her bantering style. She reverts to her customary lightness of tone saying: 'Would it interest you to know how much I hate you, Johnny?' The delivery of the line is undercut by the defensive way in which she holds the guitar in front of herself like a shield. She adds: 'I hate you so much that – I would destroy myself to take you down with me.' The first part of the line is delivered at speed, continuing her light tone, however, the pause prefaces a change of pitch and pace that gives her warning complete credibility. The line reconstructs her acts of flagrant faithlessness as a mode of revenge, in which she provokes Ballin's wrath, regardless of the consequences to herself, in order to bring Johnny down. While the remark clearly presents her as a locus of destruction, her direct assertion of her intentions in the form of a 'fair warning' and her willingness to sacrifice herself in the process means that she clearly lacks the qualities of duplicity and manipulation that characterise the *femme fatale*.

The scene constructs the relation between Gilda's roles in two different ways. First, the presentation of a privileged private moment has the effect of constructing her innuendo-laden banter as a mask that conceals her true face, glimpsed in her confession of her fears and regrets. However, Johnny's rejection of her gives rise to a second construction in which both roles become authentic. Gilda's resumption of her 'indecent' act after her warning can be seen as a repetition in difference that authenticates the mask. It constitutes the only available expression of her desire for Johnny because it is the only one that he will accept. Her desire takes on the twisted form of hatred and revenge, just as her fidelity to him is expressed through her acts of faithlessness. This reconstruction of Gilda's play of appearances as a site of authenticity also illustrates the way in which she fundamentally differs from the figure of the seductress. The twisted logic displayed by Gilda's 'indecent' act takes the perverse form of negation, a turning away from life and willing for death, which therefore constitutes a form of degeneracy rather than affirmation.[12]

Importantly, it is Johnny's refusal to accept Gilda's confession because it would undermine his loyalty to Ballin, whom he clearly views as more than a benefactor,[13] which results in this reconstruction of desire as an endgame.[14] The nihilistic trajectory of Gilda's play of appearances is clearly indicated in the scene where she dresses for the carnival festivities, which also utilises her connection with folk traditions in order to emphasise her truthfulness. The maid's definition of carnival conjoins the feasting with the Lenten fasting that follows it. Gilda responds by paralleling her current circumstances with this duality: '– three days of sowing wild oats and then comes the harvest.' Her fearfulness throughout the scene, arising from the superstitious feeling that: 'This is it', emphasises the sense that her 'indecent' act can only result in dire consequences for herself. Her expectations gain intertextual reinforcement from the genre codes of film noir in which highly sexualised female figures are usually contained through their destruction.[15] The culmination of Gilda's acts of flagrant faithlessness is presented in her last number. I will demonstrate the ways in which it is clearly signalled as her final act, by contrasting it with the earlier number, 'Amado Mio'.

'Amado Mio' can be seen as a showcase for Rita Hayworth. The number is in the Latin-American style, which was particularly associated with Hayworth because she had started dancing for her parents' Spanish troupe. A general slippage in the 'Latin' as a category can therefore be seen to underpin this key aspect of her star persona.[16] The number offers a virtuoso display of intricate footwork and movement that is performed through numerous changes of tempo. It takes place after Gilda has temporarily escaped from the confinement of marriage to Johnny by running away to Montevideo. The sense of her escape is heightened by the decrease in point-of-view shots, which are far fewer than in the dance with Delgado. The effect sustains the sense that Gilda is performing to enjoy herself rather than putting on an act for anyone's benefit, consolidating this feature of Hayworth's star persona.[17] The number contains one cut to a medium shot of Tom that occurs between two long shots of Gilda, which are taken from over his shoulder, positioning him within the frame. However, his importance to her is almost immediately undermined in that she directs some of the lines of her song to him and then looks elsewhere, moving on to address the rest of the crowd.

The entire number comprises nine shots including five long shots, which also constitute the lengthiest takes. The cutting to medium shots of Gilda occurs when the tempo of the music slows, the first as she sings the line: 'But now when I whisper Amado Mio', the tune lengthening the last two words as she also becomes virtually stationary. Importantly, the predominance of the long shots showcases Hayworth's dancing, enabling an appreciation of the complexity of her movements. The lack of emphasis on bodily fragmentation means that the number cannot be read in terms of simple objectification.[18] Hayworth is dressed in a long sarong skirt, which allows her to perform particular steps and jumps easily, and a cropped, long-sleeved top, leaving her midriff bare. The entire outfit is patterned with sequins that create a delicate floral design, darker bands picking out the neckline and waistline. The costume sparkles whenever she moves. Her range of movement varies from a hip-swaying sashay as she performs small steps while extending her arms outwards, tracing small circles with her hands, to a final series of three rapid turns. These occur after she lifts the edge of her sarong, revealing her legs and

Gilda dancing 'Amado Mio'. Still from *Gilda*

tossing her hair back in familiar fashion, recalling her first appearance in the film and consolidating the presentation of the dance as an effortless and therefore 'natural' expression of her own sensuality.

While the 'Amado Mio' number showcases Hayworth's virtuosity, the final reprise of 'Put the Blame on Mame' demonstrates her ability to use dance as a means of expressing her character's emotions. The close juxtaposition of both dances at the end of the film invites comparisons and the repertoire of movement used in each is very different. The first number makes use of highly controlled small movements, such as the circular tracing of Hayworth's softly extended arms and the intricate steps that sustain her sashaying from side to side. The second begins with an exaggerated movement as Hayworth flings both her arms out wide, singing the opening line. This gesture is repeated throughout and combined with great swinging hip movements, which are also occasionally emphasised by the drum accompaniment. The contrast suggests that Gilda is spiralling out of control and moreover that she has lost the ability to control herself. This means that the highly exaggerated, emphatic movements of the second dance can be viewed in two slightly different ways. The dance is an expression of Gilda's utter desperation and thus the culmination of her attempts to provoke Johnny, regardless of the consequences for herself. It is also the grand finale of her 'indecent' act, the exaggerated style drawing attention to its status as a performance. I will trace both these trajectories in turn.

The dance is presented as the culmination of the nihilistic trajectory of Gilda's endeavour to take Johnny down because he is set up as its ideal spectator. He wakes to her first rendition of 'Put the Blame on Mame' believing that he is dreaming and the reprise represents his nightmares. The high-angle long shot that begins the number is clearly demarcated as his point of view and his reaction to the spectacle is given as the number progresses in a medium shot, in which his grim expression contrasts with the enthralled enjoyment of the surrounding crowd. The film cuts back to him again immediately after the number reaches the heights of indecency. Gilda makes her most provocative remark: 'I'm not very good with zippers', inviting the men in the audience to undress her. The following medium shot of Johnny shows his horrified expression, continuing his position as her ideal audience while also forming a contrast with the two later reaction shots of men falling over themselves to take her up on the offer.

The sense in which the nihilistic trajectory of Gilda's plan must result in her destruction is highlighted after the dance. The loss of control conveyed through her exaggerated hip and arm movements is compounded by her performance of the striptease that follows. The great swinging movement with which she hurls her necklace into the crowd has the effect of throwing her off-balance. This is repeated when she is buffeted by the two men trying to undo her zip. Her performance provokes a reaction that she is quite unable to control, given her own desperation, leaving her hugely vulnerable. The spiral towards violence is presented when the minder finally succeeds in pulling her off the dance floor, only for her to be so buffeted by the crowd that she falls backwards into his arms. Gilda's laughter at being forced to leave has the ring of hysteria and Johnny's violent response, grabbing her by the elbow and throwing her into a corner, before finally hitting her, suggests that her desire to provoke him has been fulfilled, resulting in her own destruction.

While the slap constitutes the most extreme expression of the nihilistic aspect of Johnny's and Gilda's relationship within the film, their reactions to it form a key moment in that they both draw back from their spiral of destruction. Gilda's response is a sharp gasp, suggesting her surprise. This is followed by a medium close-up of Johnny, taken over Gilda's shoulder, showing that she views his reaction, in which his grim expression is seen to falter before he makes a swift exit. Gilda then buries her face in her hands and begins to cry. Both responses are unexpected: Gilda's surprise and Johnny's withdrawal attest to their refusal to follow through the consequences of their mutually destructive model of desire. Their withdrawal from the model is possible because it is reliant on an image of indecency that is seen to be both true and false. This doubled aspect becomes apparent if the dance is viewed as a grand finale, an act that draws attention to its status as a performance.

While the number presents Gilda as Johnny's nightmare, it is also played to the hilt. Her use of exaggerated and emphatic movements foregrounds its status as a performance, which both deconstructs the role and reconstructs it as a space of defiance. This is particularly noticeable in the two moments when she marches back and forth. The first occurs after she has removed her glove, which she swings round in her right hand while marching. She then holds the glove over her head, stretched out like a banner, as she swings her hips from side to side singing: 'Mame did a dance called the hitchie coo', before turning to face the band, her back to camera as she repeats the gesture, waving her black 'banner', the movement of her bottom humorously emphasised by the accompanying drum beat. She then turns back to face the camera, singing the next line: 'That's the thing that slew McGrew.' The presentation of her 'shakin' her booty' between the two lines of the verse constructs her as Mame. The exaggeration and humour with which she performs the dance can thus be seen to offer a critique of the patriarchal view of Mame as nothing more than a locus of destruction. These aspects of the performance sustain Dyer's reading of the final number as: 'a song of defiance, not just of a trapped wife against her husband, but of a woman against a male system.'[19]

By playing up the role of Mame, Gilda recreates the image of indecency that is imposed on her by Johnny. This repetition in difference changes the act in that it becomes more than an expression of nihilistic logic. This reconstructs Gilda as the seductress because her performance opens up a space of play and defiance, becoming a mode of affirmation. She confronts Johnny with his own nightmare, recreating and parodying the image in order to make him see the limits of his perspective. The slap is a shock to them both. It shows Gilda that Johnny has simply read her performance as further proof of her indecency, thus demonstrating how little he understands her or himself. Her

reaction to the slap has the effect of awakening Johnny in that it provokes a dawning awareness that his response is entirely inappropriate.

Gilda's final performance can be compared with Shanghai Lily's profane act in that both mobilise images of indecency as a means of critiquing a particular set of values. Each also offers a different configuration of the seductress. Shanghai Lily uses her image to force Doc to see the ways in which she does not conform to his idealised image of Madelaine, thus sustaining the sense in which her profane act is her true self. By contrast, Gilda plays up an image of indecency that is defined by Johnny in order to show him that his view of her is false. This suggests that Gilda's performance as Mame is an illusion that is both true and false. It is authenticated as an act of utter desperation and a statement of defiance. However, the role is also presented as an act designed to provoke Johnny and therefore as something that is not really her – it is all she has been allowed to be.

My reading of Gilda differs from other feminist readings, which have sought to separate her from the criteria of 'indecency' and the concomitant evaluations of promiscuity and guilt that are imposed upon her by Johnny.[20] I have traced the ways in which her 'indecent' act does subject her to these criteria, moreover, her acceptance of them can be seen in her willingness to embrace the probable consequence of her self-destruction. However, Gilda's final number jams the machinery of this logic by revealing its power structures, while simultaneously creating a space in which she parodies and defies them. The recuperation of the iconography of the dance as the encapsulation of Hayworth's image as a 'love goddess' therefore conflicts with the complexity of the narrative in which this particular image is presented as both true and false. Viewing Gilda through the figure of the seductress can thus be seen to enable an appreciation of the play of appearances that she presents across the text and the complex ways in which she engages with the discourses of morality.

2 Femininity and Duplicity in *Eyes Wide Shut*

I have chosen to focus on *Eyes Wide Shut* because it constitutes a contemporary presentation of the nineteenth-century tropes of woman and the veil that inform the work of Nietzsche and Derrida, previously addressed in Chapter 4. The film is based on Arthur Schnitzler's *Traumnovelle*, first published in 1925.[21] Schnitzler is said to have anticipated Freud and the psychoanalytic framework that informs the novel, specifically the sense of the 'primacy of the erotic' and its expression in dreams and dream-like scenarios, is an important aspect of the film.[22] I will argue that the film presents a series of familiar psychoanalytic reversals, indeed, the title indicates that waking life is an unreality, positioning the dream as the truth. The inversion of reality/dream, true/false intersects with the presentation of woman as a play of veils that reveals the absence of truth, altering the trope.

Gilda waves her glove/banner in 'Put the Blame on Mame'. Still from *Gilda*

Larry Gross argues that the film offers two levels of narrative, tracing Bill Harwood's trajectory through the text. He argues that Bill shifts 'from erotic confusion about what he does and doesn't desire to epistemological confusion about what he does and doesn't know', concluding: 'It's a tribute to . . . Kubrick's design that we can't fully articulate when or how the shift from one level of narrative concern to the other occurred, though obviously both levels have anxiety as their shared motive and result.'[23] I would suggest that the conjunction of erotic and epistemological confusion is present from the beginning and that it takes the familiar form of woman as an unknowable, duplicitous play of veils.

The characterisation of woman as duplicity is clear from the extract used in the film's marketing, forming the trailer and later merchandising, such as the front cover of the DVD.[24] The scene from which it is taken occurs early in the film and is the first sexual encounter between Bill and Alice. The short scene is composed of a single take, which begins as a medium shot of Alice standing naked in front of a mirror, removing her earrings while swaying from side to side as if she can hear the extra-diegetic music. She is joined by Bill, who starts to kiss her, and the camera turns away from the mirror, suggesting a movement into an 'authentic' private space, presenting a medium close-up of the pair in profile as they embrace. Bill's eyes shut as he begins to kiss Alice's neck, while she stares off-screen right, her steady gaze suggesting her detachment. The camera slowly zooms into close-up, suggesting further intimacy as they kiss passionately. The implications of the camera movement are immediately undercut by the repetition of Alice's expression. She stares steadily off-screen right while her head is jolted slightly by

Alice gazes off-screen while Bill kisses her. Still from *Eyes Wide Shut*

Bill's increasingly urgent embraces, and the scene fades to black as the extra-diegetic music intones the key line from the chorus: 'Baby do bad bad thing'.

The first presentation of Alice frames her frontal nudity in the mirror, suggesting an awareness and enjoyment of herself as image that is shared by Bill, who instigates their embraces while staring into the mirror space. The camera's transition into an 'authentic' private space reflects Bill's movement out of the mirror in that he shuts his eyes as he kisses her. Importantly, Alice's two long looks off-screen, back towards the mirror space, are not visible to Bill. She appears to be returning his embraces in a satisfactory fashion, thus providing an iconic image of woman as duplicity. In *The Gay Science*, Nietzsche reworks the figure of Isis, whose body represented the truth beyond the veil, to argue that it is impossible to view any woman naked because they are perpetually 'veiled' in that they are always acting.

> Finally, *women*. Reflect on the whole history of women: do they not *have* to be first of all and above all else actresses? Listen to physicians who have hypnotized women; finally, love them – let yourself be 'hypnotized by them'! What is always the end result? That they 'put on something' even when they take off everything.[25]

The original German is even more explicit: '[d]*ass sie "sich geben," selbst noch, wenn sie – sich geben.* Literally: that they "give themselves" (that is, act or play a part) even when they – give themselves.'[26] This ability to use nakedness and sexual intimacy as a mode of dissimulation utterly undermines the logic of penetrating the veil in which the body represents truth and sexual relations are constructed as a form of knowledge.

Alice's role of dissimulatress is initially presented to the audience alone. Bill does not become aware of it until a later scene in which she confesses to having desired another man, giving form to the 'bad thing' indicated by the musical accompaniment. Her confession propels him into a state of epistemological and erotic confusion, undermining his claims to truth and knowledge, which are staked out throughout the scene. Bill treats Alice as a patient, suggesting that her aggression is symptomatic of her having taken pot and dismissing her discomfiting amusement at his expense as a 'laughing fit'. His assertion that his female patients do not entertain sexual fantasies about him because 'Women don't – they basically just don't think like that' is then angrily paraphrased by Alice in a parody of Darwinism: men are sexual while women desire security and commitment. Bill replies to her exaggerated gloss saying quite seriously: 'A little oversimplified, Alice, but yes something like that.' His status as a doctor is thus used to give him the right to make dogmatic assertions about the non-existent nature of female sexuality, a common opinion in the nineteenth century that sounds somewhat incongruous in the setting of modern-day New York.[27]

However, Bill's assertions are occasionally presented as overemphatic and therefore unconvincing. Alice's suggestion that he might not be the consummate professional meets with instant denial: 'Sex is the last thing on my mind when I'm with a patient.' His posture while he makes this statement – sitting hunched over, his arms in front of him with his fists clenched – clearly suggests quite the reverse. He can therefore be seen to epitomise the state encapsulated by the title, his eyes wide open to view and classify the symptoms of others but shut to the erotic dimension of his own behaviour.[28] While the scene suggests that his dogmatic assertions arise through denial, he provokes Alice by using his professional position to sustain his self-appointed role of the voice of truth. She takes issue with his pronouncements on female sexuality, replying: 'If you men only knew.' As the conversation becomes more personal, his certain knowledge that she would never be unfaithful elicits the angry response: 'You're very, very sure of yourself, aren't you?' The certainty that has characterised all of Bill's convictions culminates in one short, disastrous assertion: 'I'm sure of you.'

Alice's confession can thus be seen as the means by which she removes herself from the realm of the indexed, catalogued and quantified, to the unknown. She does so by mobilising a trope of femininity as duplicity and the visual presentation of her confession makes it impossible to tell whether this is a story that is deliberately designed to discon-cert her husband, shocking him out of his complacent certainties, or a confession of a 'true' event. The frontal medium shots of Alice as she tells the story position her between the two red curtains at the window, giving her performance a theatrical quality. Import-antly, she is presented in this way when she 'confesses' to thinking about the naval officer while having sex with Bill; and the staging is entirely appropriate for her role of woman as duplicity, playing a part even as she 'gives herself'. The film cuts to medium close-ups

Alice positioned between the curtains while she tells her story. Still from *Eyes Wide Shut*

of her face in profile, which lessen the visibility of the curtains, as she leans towards Bill at key moments in the story. This form of shot is used when she explains that she thought of the officer while discussing their plans for the future and for their child, Helena. The impact of the story is evident in the counter-shots of Bill's reaction, shown largely in medium close-ups, which display his shocked and bewildered expression.

In using the trope of woman as dissimulatress to combat a patriarchal system of knowledge and truth, Alice can be seen to take up the role of the seductress. She opens up a space in which her self-doubts are no longer subordinated to her husband's complacent certainties, creating a play of appearances through her storytelling that can be read as a key moment of defiance. The emphasis on ambiguity and uncertainty is sustained throughout her story. Her 'confession' of feelings of sexual desire for another man, which has permeated the whole of her domestic life, is accompanied by a confirmation of the depth of her feelings for Bill: 'At the same time you were dearer to me than ever, and – and at that moment my love for you was both tender and sad.' The expression of simultaneous and conflicting emotions is typical of dream logic.[29] Freud's classic examples of such logic are: 'dreams of the death of persons of whom the dreamer is fond', which are said to express the infantile wish that the person, particularly siblings or parents, would die; while the emotions caused by the dream attest to the strength of the bond with the 'dead' person.[30]

However, Alice's play of appearances and corresponding complexity of emotion are short-circuited by Bill's literal response to her 'confession'. He leaves to attend to a recently bereaved patient, immediately indulging in a fantasy scenario in which Alice embarks on an affair with the naval officer, while he sits in the cab on the way there. His response consolidates the trajectory suggested by the music: 'Baby do bad, bad thing', thus repositioning the dissimulatress's play of veils as a moment of revelation in which his wife's 'true' sexual longings form the body beyond the veil. His epistemological and erotic confusion takes the familiar form of surface versus depth – is Alice the perfect wife and mother that she appears to be? The unconsummated erotic adventures on which he embarks in revenge can also be seen as another means of finding an answer: a search for the key feature that would differentiate Alice from the other women who are readily available to him and thus unworthy of his affections.

Schnitzler's novel makes clear the link between the revelation of Albertine's sexual fantasies and her subsequent reconstruction as the same as all other women. Embarking on his evening rounds in the hospital, Fridolin encounters a young girl with suspected bronchitis who smiles at him:

> She was the one who during a recent examination had taken the opportunity to press her breast so intimately against his cheek. Fridolin returned her gaze ungraciously and turned away with a frown. They're all the same, he thought bitterly, and Albertine no different from the rest – in fact she's the worst of them all. We'll have to part.[31]

The key difference between the book and the film is that this particular 'insight' – '[t]hey're all the same' – is presented as a fleeting moment of anxiety for Fridolin, whereas the film continually asserts this message through the visual presentation of the female characters. Their systematic de-individualisation is particularly evident in the orgy sequence.

The film's presentation of the orgy differs from the book in a variety of ways. The book emphasises the Christian iconography of the masquerade in that the men are dressed as monks and the women as nuns, while Fridolin as an initiate is appropriately attired as a pilgrim.[32] The film offers two links to Christianity: the figure who presides over the proceedings is dressed in red robes that resemble a cardinal's, and the rituals he performs involve the use of incense. However, reviewers commented on the inter-textual references to horror films: 'the mask-and-robe orgy, with its ponderous Gothic touches and echoes of *Histoire d'O*, feels like a stolid throwback to the more innocent times of Hammer horror or Roger Corman's Poe movies.'[33] The use of different varieties of mask also increases the range of cultural references: from Greek tragedy,[34] recalled by the satyr mask visible in the final scenario of sexual coupling that Bill views; to Punch and Judy, presented by the overtly phallic, hooked nose of the cloaked figure that leads Bill's redeemer away. The film is also far more explicit than the book, in which Fridolin merely glimpses a frenzied dance in an adjacent room that he never enters.[35]

Importantly, the women at the orgy in the film are all the same physical type, ecto-morphs with long legs and small breasts. This is in marked contrast to the book in which Fridolin is said to enjoy the variety of bodies on display.

> Fridolin's eyes roved hungrily from sensuous to slender figures, and from budding figures to figures in glorious full bloom; and the fact that each of these naked beauties still remained a mystery, and that from behind the masks large eyes as unfathomable as riddles sparkled at him, transformed his indescribably strong urge to watch into an almost intolerable torment of desire.[36]

The long shot in which the women dispense with their cloaks makes use of a circling Steadicam in which the figures are viewed from behind, the height of the camera show-ing them from knee to shoulder, cutting off their heads as it passes. The uniformity of physical type coupled with their regulation wear of black thongs, black shoes and chok-ers visible in the mid-ground of the shot, emphasises their interchangeability. In addition, the choice of physical type means that the women resemble Alice, thus visually sug-gesting that '[t]hey're all the same.'[37] Gross comments that the anonymous woman who rescues Bill is 'yet another substitute for Alice',[38] and she is also a con/fusion of two other female figures: Domino and Mandy.[39] This ambiguity is maintained in Bill's final encounter with Ziegler who answers the question: 'Do you know who she was?' with the assertion: 'She was a hooker that's what she was.' Ziegler agrees that the woman was Mandy while turning his back on Bill, a posture that does not serve to confirm his statement. In presenting the prostitutes as Alice's surrogates, the film asserts the links between all the women, rendering them intersubstitutional through their sexuality.

The link between Alice, Mandy and Domino means that Bill's search for the truth of what happened to his rescuer parallels his search for the truth of his wife. The female figures are ambiguous in that they are presented within both halves of the virgin/whore dichotomy: Alice is mother and adulteress; the rescuer is redeemer and prostitute. The presentation of the rescuer augments this ambiguity in that she is both powerful and powerless. She appears to save Bill from an extremely unpleasant situation: unmasked and vulnerable, he has been told that the assembly will strip him naked.[40] The cut to the low-angle long shot of the woman on the balcony and sudden zoom-in on her as she says: 'Stop', halting the proceedings, suggest her power over the assembly. However, the final medium long shot of her being led away by a black, cloaked figure, suggests the reverse because the low angle emphasises his height in relation to her. Moreover, his mask has an obscenely phallic nose, indicating that she is in danger of sexual violence. Ziegler inadvertently consolidates this visual cue in a later scene when he tries to reassure Bill of her safety: 'Nothing happened to her after you left that party that hadn't happened to her before. She had her brains fucked out.'

Bill's search for truth involves the resolution of ambiguity by emphasising one half of the virgin/whore dichotomy. He needs to view Mandy's death as the ultimate sacrifice on his behalf because it consolidates her status as pure redeemer. His thoughts about Alice follow a more familiar psychoanalytic trajectory in that the 'revelation' of her adulterous longings undermines her maternal purity. This is particularly obvious in a short scene back at his home after he has received the second warning to stop his investigations. He finds his wife seated at the dining room table with their daughter whom she is helping with her maths homework. Bill leaves them briefly to go to the kitchen and as he walks back the film cuts to a point-of-view shot of Alice and Helena at the table as the camera zooms in. There is a cut back to a medium shot of Bill and the zoom is repeated, as if indicating his contemplation of the view they presented, in conjunction with a reprise of Alice's description of her dream in voice-over form. The film cuts to another point-of-view shot, a medium close-up of Alice whose appearance – a pink shirt unbuttoned at the collar, her hair put up in haphazard fashion, glasses and natural make-up – consolidates the impression of maternality and authenticity. Her tearful voice-over narration of the dream continues with: 'And then I – I was fucking other men.' The disjunction between the image and the voice-over reaches its zenith at this point in that the line is delivered as Alice becomes aware of Bill's gaze, looking up and smiling back at him, thus presenting him with an ideal image of wifely affection.

The radical disjunction between the reprise of Alice's voice and her current image of ideal mother and wife positions her spoken revelations as the truth. The doubt cast over the veracity of this particular image is replicated in Roald Rynning's article in *Film Review*, which reproduces her smiling acknowledgment of her husband's gaze with the caption 'looking sweet in *Eyes Wide Shut* – but a secret is hidden behind the smile....'[41] This positioning of her 'confession' as a revelation of secret desires that undermine the image follows a psychoanalytic logic in which the civilised surface covers over erotic depths. The caption also encapsulates the logic of Bill's search. His certainties shaken by ambiguity, he begins a quest, penetrating the veil to find the hidden truth beneath.

The logic of the quest is finally undercut during Bill's last exchange with Ziegler, a scene that was written for the film. In this conversation, Ziegler reasserts the link between the female characters, re/working the sense in which they are all the same, by constructing Bill's rescuer as a dissimulatress. Ziegler's suggestion that the orgy was a 'charade' gains plausibility from the highly staged and subdued presentation of the 'sculptural entanglements' that form the basis of its voyeuristic pleasures.[42] However, it is impossible to tell whether Bill's rescuer genuinely saved him or merely pretended to do so in order to dissuade him from telling others what he had seen. Bill attempts to escape the logic of appearances by asserting the supremacy of death: 'What kind of fucking charade ends in death?' However, Ziegler undercuts this by suggesting that Bill is drawing illegitimate connections between random events. It is noteworthy that this construction of woman's play of appearances as a series of utterly disconnected surfaces enables Ziegler, and the other punters, to deny any responsibility for Mandy's death, thus ensuring that his self-serving explanation also appears implausible. Importantly, the proliferation of inconsistent roles that accrue to Mandy – redeemer, whore and junky – cluster around the vanishing point of her death, which sustains the impossibility of ever finding the 'truth'.

Alice as the ideal image of wifely affection. Still from *Eyes Wide Shut*

Ziegler's mobilisation of the trope of the dissimulatress thus conforms to chiasmic logic. Mandy symbolises the absence of truth, in accordance with the structure of denegation, while her multiple and inconsistent roles are symptomatic of metonymic proliferation. Mandy as dissimulatress is used to sustain the structures of patriarchal power, her self-abnegating use of speed and heroin ultimately ensuring that she cannot be pitted against the system. This last version of the dissimulatress differs considerably from Alice's radical use of the trope to unsettle the discourses of patriarchal 'truth'. Her capacity to turn the figure of the dissimulatress to her own ends means that she momentarily takes up the role of seductress. Alice's brief play of appearances during her storytelling thus resembles Gilda's final number: both female characters succeed in turning a man-made image into a space of play and defiance.

3 Playing with Appearances in *Moulin Rouge*

Moulin Rouge differs from the other films discussed in this chapter in its overt and celebratory use of intertextuality and theatricality, which was noted by virtually all its reviewers. Graham Fuller describes it as a 'self-consciously delirious immersion in artifice for artifice's sake' linking it to the 'passionate illusionism' of Michael Powell and Vincente Minnelli, among others.[43] Other critics have stressed the post-modern nature of Luhrmann's film, reading it as an exemplary instance of Baudrillard's hyperreal: 'a condition in which reality collapses to re-emerge as image, illusion or simulation'.[44] A detailed discussion of whether the film is post-modern or not is outside the scope of this book. However, Baudrillardian post-modernism repeatedly presents the pervasive structure of the hyperreal in nihilistic terms in that it is said to undermine reality, truth, knowledge, politics and subjectivity.[45] This sense of simulation as a kind of anarchic emptiness is not really part of *Moulin Rouge*. The film differs from Baudrillardian post-modernism by presenting artifice as a means of heightening emotion, a conjunction of theatricality and intensity that is more akin to camp.[46]

Moulin Rouge has been seen as the last in Luhrmann's trilogy of 'red curtain' films: 'films defined by a milieu allowing for heightened theatricality or artifice ... [and] by a simple narrative structure clearly derived from myth'.[47] The central myth from which *Moulin Rouge* derives is that of Orpheus. However, Luhrmann's glosses of the story as one of 'ideal love'[48] or simply '[a] relationship [that] cannot be ... and if you look back instead of moving on, it will destroy you',[49] show the very general nature of his interpretation. Fuller offers a more detailed analysis of Christian's descent into the underworld.

> He goes there to retrieve Satine, his Eurydice, who, as a courtesan, is spiritually dead. ... But in his moment of triumph, he breaches the conditions of their escape by looking back – he tells the Duke that Satine doesn't love him, consigning her to death once more.[50]

This version of Christian's quest, in which his love brings Eurydice back to life, overlooks a central aspect of the Western take-up of the myth in which Orpheus is fused with the figure of the poet as genius. Eurydice can only function as a muse because she is already dead – she is the price that Orpheus must be prepared to pay in order to become a great poet. In the same way, Christian can only begin to write his work on the Moulin Rouge after Satine has died.

Satine's links to death are reinforced by references to another series of myths, featuring the figure of the dying courtesan, which originate in the nineteenth century. These begin with Alexander Dumas' Marguerite in *La Dame aux Camélias*, who is renamed Violetta in Verdi's reworking of the story, the opera *La Traviata*. Dumas' novel formed the basis of several films, including the MGM production of *Camille*, starring Greta Garbo in the title role.[51] Importantly, each set of myths provides a different way of constructing the narrative trajectory of the film. Viewed through Orpheus, the high point of *Moulin Rouge* becomes Christian's rescue of Satine. He offers her a pure love, which provides the means by which she is spiritually reborn.[52] Tracing the myth of Marguerite/Violetta/Camille results in a rather different story in that the romance between Christian and Satine becomes a prelude to a key moment of renunciation, in which the female protagonist is persuaded to give up her lover for his own good. It is the act of renunciation that reconstructs the courtesan as a figure of nobility and generosity, thus constituting the means by which she redeems herself.[53]

My reading of the film will focus on the presentation of Satine, tracing how far her role of courtesan conforms to the seductress's play of appearances. I will follow the trajectories provided by both myths, noting the ways in which they intersect towards the end of the film. Satine's incipient death, her new-found love for Christian and her final act of renunciation all affect the play of appearances. I will argue that the presentation of Satine's love and her renunciation of Christian links both events to her death. This will also involve tracing the ways in which the film reasserts the dialectic of surface/depth, ultimately containing Satine within a harsh moral framework.

Satine is first presented during the opening sequence of the film, which is set in the present, showing Christian's devastation after her death. The shot is in black and white, indicating her reconstruction as a ghostly memory. The medium close-up of Satine wearing a top hat angled down over her face with a long cigarette holder in her gloved right hand, clearly references Dietrich. The stark side-lighting, more reminiscent of film noir than Sternberg's careful use of top lighting, causes the shadow of Satine's hand to fall across her face, hiding her expression and presenting her as enigmatic. The style of the image evokes memories of female screen icons, recalling the carefully choreographed portrait shots released by the studios during the 1930s and 40s.

The film makes use of saturated colour, reminiscent of Technicolor, once the flashback structure starts, telling the story in the present tense as though for the first time.[54] The initial memory bears a great resemblance to the close-ups of Satine as she performs her first number: 'Diamonds Are a Girl's Best Friend'. The first close-up shows the angled top hat and the use of colour draws attention to her makeup: white pan foundation, false eyelashes with dark liner emphasising the top line and red lipstick, creating the look of the 30s' vamp. Later shots show her costume, a sequined, silver corset in the style of a tailcoat. The black edging at the top of the bodice falls in two 'v' shapes, creating the impression of a bow, while the back of the costume is a series of silver strips that fall to create the effect of tails. The whole outfit clearly references Dietrich's famous appearance in tails in *Morocco* and owes something to the sequined lapels of the white tuxedo worn in *Blonde Venus*. The way in which Satine delivers the first line of the song: 'The French are glad to die for love', snapping out the last two words and thereby suggesting their foolishness, also consolidates the comparison.

The dense layering of intertextual references that informs the first number clearly presents Satine as a seductress in that she is a collage of illusions. The saturated reds presented throughout the number act as a reminder of the staging of Marilyn Monroe's version in which her bubblegum-pink strapless dress is presented against a bright red background.[55] Satine's costume change into a pale pink corset, which draws attention to her bust and pudenda with strategically placed sequined hearts, offers an instant vulgarisation of the song, thus paralleling Jane Russell's send-up of the number in *Gentlemen Prefer Blondes*. In that film, Dorothy's spirited performance of 'Diamonds' causes an entire courtroom to come to a halt. Her costume, a sequin-studded corset

Satine's corset/tailcoat – a homage to Dietrich. Still from *Moulin Rouge*

with silver trim over the bust and hips, is used to great effect when she shimmies in front of a *gendarme*, and the vulgar nature of her movements is humorously highlighted by the clanking cowbell accompaniment. Satine's costume has an additional train of pink feathers and the tactile surfaces of the sequins, fringing and feathers emphasise her version of the shimmy, which is performed to persuade Christian to dance with her.

The number also shows that Satine constructs herself as a play of appearances in her brief conversation with Zidler during the costume change. Their exchange takes the form of a rapid transition between shot and counter-shot, providing four medium close-ups of Satine in which she goes through a series of seductive roles. The first occurs as she asks Zidler the Duke's type; the shot shows her in Dietrich mode, her hair swept back from her face, as she reaches to remove her top hat. The second is a clear contrast: her loosened hair falls in soft waves about her face as she looks over her shoulder, which is trimmed with pink feathers, striking a coy pose and asking: 'Wilting flower?' in a high-pitched voice. In the third, she takes up the role of 'frightened bunny', her mouth opening wide as if to scream in fear. In the fourth, her hair falls over her face, making her red-lip-sticked snarl the central feature as she utters the final option: 'smouldering temptress' in low-pitched tones. The last is rapturously received by Zidler as the Duke's preference.

Satine's seamless transition between roles is then suspended in a moment of authenticity, as Zidler talks of their plans for a 'real show' and a 'real theatre'. The film cuts to Satine as she says that she'll be a 'real actress', providing a close-up of her expression as she sighs and looks down briefly. Her musical cue then interrupts and she instantly adopts a smile, leaping to her feet. The over-brightness of her show-smile authenticates her previous expression. This, coupled with the change to a closer shot, a standard indication of authenticity, emphasises that the moment offers a glimpse of her true motives and ambitions. It is here that Satine most resembles the figure of the seductress in that her roles are to be used to fund her ambition to become an actress. The play of appearances can thus be seen to fund a further play of appearances, a nice version of the Nietzschean/Baudrillardian twist in which the false becomes the site of truth.

Satine's fall from the swing at the end of the number mobilises a different series of references. Her consumptive symptoms clearly present her as the successor to Marguerite, Violetta and Camille. The moment at which she is carried out, her head and arms dangling down, creating an extreme spinal curve, constructs her as the nymph with the broken back.[56] Later, as she lies supine on her bed, the redness of her hair contrasting vividly with the extreme pallor of her skin, her pose and colouring recall the representation of women in pre-Raphaelite paintings.[57] The play of illusions that intersect in the figure of Satine is not halted in this presentation of her impending death. She maintains a frenetic farcical play of roles throughout rehearsals until her romance with Christian is discovered by Zidler. He argues that the affair will jeopardise the future of the Moulin Rouge: she has been exchanged for the deeds to the theatre and the Duke wishes to claim his property.

Satine's eventual visit to the tower for an intimate dinner with the Duke is a key scene because it shows the failure of her play of appearances and the way in which her role of seductress is ultimately contained by the twin forces of love and death. The scene begins with a reference to Dietrich's role of Shanghai Lily and I will go on to discuss the considerable differences between the two female protagonists. The film provides a long shot of Satine as she makes her entrance between two deep blue velvet curtains, halting in front of them within a pool of light created by the spotlight placed high above her head. She tilts her head up towards the light source, which etches out the scrolling on the black lace veil that covers her face and draws attention to the whiteness of her skin beside the black satin of her asymmetrical off-the-shoulder gown. The film returns to the long shot as she raises her veil. This is immediately followed by a close-up of her face, which is presented as yet another veil through the revelation of her pan makeup and red lipstick. The top-lighting also picks out the curve of her artificial lashes, casting shadows onto her face and giving her the distinctive heavy-lidded look so characteristic of Dietrich.

The shots from *Moulin Rouge* resemble a star moment that occurs towards the end of *Shanghai Express*. Dietrich/Lily has reprised her profane act and returns to her cabin on the train after an argument with Doc. She closes the door behind her, switching off the light. She tilts her face up towards the remaining light source, a single top-light that emphasises the sockets of her eyes and hollows out her cheekbones, giving her face an etched, skeletal quality. The film provides two medium close-ups in succession: in the first, she gazes upwards, enclosed in her own thoughts; in the second, she lowers her gaze, the shadows cast by her artificial eyelashes creating her languorous, heavy-lidded look. This lighting set-up is very distinctive in that Sternberg developed it specifically for Dietrich. While Kidman's face does not have the same high cheekbones and therefore cannot appear similarly hollowed out, the resemblance between their postures – the tilt up towards the light, and the resulting presentation of the eyes – is striking.[58] While the images from *Shanghai Express* construct Dietrich as both distant and sexual, suggesting a control of her allure that is maintained until the end, the images from *Moulin Rouge* preface Satine's loss of control over the Duke.

The two forces that threaten Satine's play of appearances are presented through the use of cross-cutting throughout the scene in the tower. The film cuts between a tango version of 'Roxanne', presented as the archetypal narrative of a man who falls in love with a prostitute, Christian's singing to Satine, and her dinner with the Duke. The formulaic dance presents the courtesan's inevitable spiral of destruction, and the gradual crescendo to its inexorable tragic conclusion represents the force of death. Christian's song for Satine assures her of his continued love and the cross-cutting to the tower suggests that she is under siege from both forces. Within the context of the tower, Christian's love becomes a threat because it halts the play of appearances that is necessary to appease the Duke. Satine's distant and imperious act begins to fail as the Duke presents her with a diamond necklace. She views herself in the mirror as he fastens it, the doubling of her faces clearly indicative of her roles for two lovers, and the mirror image is used when she asks the Duke about the ending of the play, thus referencing its author, Christian. The Duke then moves into the mirror space saying: 'Let Zidler keep his fairy-tale ending' and Satine looks down, away from him, visibly reassured, her façade cracking.

The final crumbling of Satine's mask is played out when she sees Christian from the tower window as the Duke begins to caress her and is subsequently unable to 'pretend any more' and return his embraces. Her refusal meets with a violent response. The Duke attempts to choke her with the diamonds by inserting his hand between the necklace and her neck. Satine's entrapment within a violent situation is further signalled when she is stripped of her dress. This is paralleled by the tango in which the dancer, Lily, is presented within a closed circle of men, being thrown from one to another. The cross-cutting presents the two female figures as mirror images. Satine turns her face away to the right as if to block out the prospect of her inevitable rape, and the film immediately cuts to the dance where Lily's neck is apparently broken by the singer and lolls towards the left. The strong parallel drawn between Satine and Lily, the courtesan who reforms and the prostitute who continues to ply her trade, suggests that both will meet the same tragic fate. Satine's rescue by Chocolat is thus only a momentary suspension of the process. Satine cannot be seen to be redeemed by love – the visual assertion of her inevitable fate attests that she is still subject to punishment. In this way, her death becomes an inexorable process, a punishment that takes a grotesquely appropriate form in that, as a figure of corruption, she is herself being corroded from the inside.[59]

The crumbling of Satine's mask reinstalls the binary of surface/depth. This is reinforced by the scene in which Zidler persuades her to save Christian's life by convincing him that she has ceased to love him. He exhorts her to act: 'Use your talent to save him.' The following number, 'The Show Must Go On', consolidates the distinction between outside and inside, surface and depth. Satine's contribution to the song are the lines: 'Inside my heart is breaking/My make-up may be flaking/But my smile stays on' as she views her multiple images in a triptych mirror. Her costume includes a black hat with a veil, which she lowers in a brief pause between the second and third lines, thus indicating that it functions as a mode of concealment, hiding the depths of her love for Christian. Her gradual take-up of the role of the heartless courtesan is apparent when she enters onto the stage between two red velvet curtains, frontally lit by the spotlight, which highlights her face as she struggles for composure.

The presentation of Satine's preparation for the role also constructs it as a supreme act of self-sacrifice. The triptych form of the mirror suggests the redemptive nature of her act, constructing her image as a religious icon. The *mise en scène* conjoins the self-sacrifice of Marguerite/Violetta/Camille with the second death of Eurydice. As Satine walks off the stage into the heart of light presented by the frontal spot, she becomes a dark silhouette. She resembles the shadow-figure of Eurydice, which Orpheus glimpses before she is taken from him to the depths of the underworld once again. This sense of Satine's act of self-sacrifice as a form of death is maintained in the following scene with Christian. Her composure nearly breaking, she turns away from him and there is a cut to an extreme close-up of her anguished face, presenting her eyes and mouth as she seems to sob, struggling for breath. This linking of her anguish to her consumptive symptoms emphasises that Satine, like Eurydice, dies twice: metaphorically through self-sacrifice and literally from consumption at the end of the film. However, the key difference between the two female characters is that Eurydice's death is not her choice. Indeed, it is impossible to know what she thinks of Orpheus's turning back because she never functions as the narrator of her own story. In contrast, Satine chooses her own death because protecting Christian is an act of supreme self-sacrifice in which she voluntarily gives up her own desires, ambitions and dreams.

The use of intertextual references to Dietrich is also continued in the scene with Christian. Satine's final mask, raising her eyebrow at Christian's distraught response briefly borrows Dietrich's characteristic mockery and insouciance. However, all the references ultimately emphasise the great differences between the figures of Shanghai Lily and Satine. The former mobilises an image of indecency to open up a space in which she is able to critique Doc's values and to create her own perspective, setting out her terms for their future together. Lily is thus able to challenge bourgeois morality, positioning herself outside its dictates by taking up the role of goddess. In contrast, Satine's decision to choose the Duke and give up Christian is an act of self-sacrifice that requires a total renunciation of her own perspective. This is presented as a form of death and clearly constitutes a moment of complete denegation. In taking up the role of the worst woman, the courtesan who chooses money over love, for the best reasons, Satine reverses her position within the moral order, transforming herself from whore to saint. However, the transformation positions her firmly within a harsh system of values that she cannot challenge or change. Her act of self-sacrifice marks her disintegration as seductress: her play of appearances is contained by the re-emergence of binary logic and the underlying structure of denegation.

I have chosen to end with *Moulin Rouge* because the Dietrich references highlight the differences between this film and *Shanghai Express*. Importantly, the figure of the seductress is not constructed in the same way across the three films discussed in the final chapter. Gilda and Alice succeed in mobilising the play of appearances as a space of defiance (albeit briefly in Alice's case). Satine does present illusion as a site of authenticity but this is not sustained across the film. All three films also differ from those of the Dietrich/Sternberg cycle in offering an overarching narrative trajectory that is bound to the male protagonist, seen in Johnny's voice-over, Bill's search for truth, and Christian's version of Orpheus's quest. It is perhaps not surprising that within this context the play of appearances offered by Gilda and Alice takes the form of defiant deconstructions of patriarchal conceptions of female sexuality, rather than a sustained presentation of their own perspectives. This suggests that Shanghai Lily's Nietzschean presentation of the seductress who creates her own perspective may well be one of the most positive inflections of the figure.

This tracing of the ways in which the figure of the seductress is repeatedly remade and reviewed through the key images that instantiate her is intended to exemplify the kind of provisional, perspectival theorising that I have advocated throughout this book. The theoretical concept is provisional and precarious because it arises out of specific configurations of philosophical and filmic images. Importantly, using the figure of the seductress as a lens enables us to view films differently. The seductress thus recalls Baubô in that she effects a shift of perspective that enables the spectator to see another story, one that is constructed through the play of appearances, drawing together the details of costume, décor, makeup, lighting, songs, dance and laughter. In turn, the films also rework key philosophical concepts. They thus provide a means of rethinking woman's role as the icon of beauty, art and truth, allowing the charting of positive representations and reconstructions of femininity. This is of vital importance at the present moment because it provides a means of challenging the valorisation of masculinity which underpins the current ascendance of the ostensibly feminist prototype of the female action hero.

In thinking through what it means to theorise, I have been concerned to challenge the pugilistic models promulgated by Carroll *et al*. Being provoked to thought is not the same as being offered the means to think through a particular issue. The encounter between Baubô and Demeter sets up a model of thinking as a development or shift of perspective that is facilitated by the proffering and acceptance of a gift. This interlinking of thought and generosity generates an awareness of the debts we owe to those whose work enables the formation of our own, as well as a sense of being part of a continuing debate. The methodology that I have developed for linking philosophical and filmic images would not exist without the work of Le Doeuff and Irigaray, among many others, and I hope that it will be taken up and changed in the future. The recognition of the conceptual potential of filmic images sets up the possibility of a diverse series of productive encounters between philosophy, film theory and film texts, sustaining one of many possible futures for film theory.

Notes

1. B. Nichols, 'Film Theory and the Revolt against Master Narratives', in C. Gledhill and L. Williams (eds), *Reinventing Film Studies* (London: Arnold, 2000), p. 45.
2. M-A. Doane, *Femmes Fatales: Feminism, Film Theory, Psychoanalysis* (London and New York: Routledge, 1991), p. 49.
3. C. Zucker, *The Idea of the Image: Josef von Sternberg's Dietrich Films* (London and Toronto, Associated University Presses, 1988), pp. 109, 114–15.

4. *Gilda* (C. Vidor, Columbia, 1946).

5. *Eyes Wide Shut* (S. Kubrick, Warner Bros, 1999); *Moulin Rouge* (B. Luhrmann, Twentieth Century-Fox, 2001).

6. R. Dyer, 'Resistance through Charisma: Rita Hayworth and *Gilda*', in E. A. Kaplan (ed.), *Women in Film Noir* (London: BFI, 1998), p. 120.

7. Aspects of Hayworth's star persona conflict significantly with the narrative logic in an earlier film, *Cover Girl*, which was also scripted by Virginia van Upp and directed by Charles Vidor. In this film, her fame gained through posing for magazine covers is presented as an illegitimate form of success because it is said not to be the result of hard work. This line of narrative clearly conflicts with Hayworth's status as a pin-up. See *Cover Girl* (C. Vidor, Columbia, 1944).

8. A. Martin, '"Gilda Didn't Do Any of Those Things You've Been Losing Sleep over!": The Central Women of 40s Films Noirs', in E. A. Kaplan (ed.), *Women in Film Noir* (London: BFI, 1998), p. 215.

9. This use of the medium close-up is repeated when Gilda first meets Gabe Evans. She looks over his shoulder, suddenly changing her mind about accepting his invitation for a drink, which is explained when the film cuts to a point-of-view shot of Johnny entering the club.

10. Dyer, 'Resistance through Charisma', p. 119.

11. Ibid.

12. For Kofman's definition of Nietzsche's concept of degeneracy, see S. Kofman, 'Baubô: Theological Perversion and Fetishism', in M. A. Gillespie and T. B. Strong (eds), *Nietzsche's New Seas: Explorations in Philosophy, Aesthetics and Politics* (Chicago, IL and London: University of Chicago Press, 1988), p. 180.

13. Dyer provides a very convincing reading of the ways in which the film implies a homosexual relationship between Johnny and Ballin. R. Dyer, 'Queer Noir', in R. Dyer (ed.), *The Culture of Queers* (London: Routledge, 2002), pp. 107–9.

14. This clearly differs from Derrida's construction in which it is the illegitimacy of *woman* controlling the game of desire that results in its destructiveness.

15. J. Place, 'Women in Film Noir', in E. A. Kaplan (ed.), *Women in Film Noir*, rev. edn (London: BFI, 1998), p. 63.

16. Dyer, 'Resistance through Charisma', pp. 120–1.

17. Ibid.

18. Ibid., p. 121. Dyer argues that Hayworth's association with movement enables her to evade objectification.

19. Ibid., p. 119.

20. See for example Martin, '"Gilda Didn't Do Any Of Those Things You've Been Losing Sleep over!"', pp. 215, 218.

21. A. Schnitzler, *Dream Story*, J. M. Q. Davies (trans.) (London: Penguin, 1999).

22. F. Raphael, 'Introduction', *Dream Story*, J. M. Q. Davies (trans.) (London: Penguin, 1999), p. xii.

23. L. Gross, 'Too Late the Hero', *Sight and Sound* vol. 9 no. 9, September 1999, p. 22.

24. S. Kubrick, *Eyes Wide Shut*, DVD, Warner Home Video (UK) Ltd, 2000.

25. F. Nietzsche, *The Gay Science*, W. Kaufmann (trans.) (New York: Vintage Books, 1974), p. 317.

26. W. Kaufmann, 'Translator's Notes', *The Gay Science*, p. 317, fn. 94.

27. This cannot be blamed on the source material. The literary source provides a brief gloss of Fridolin and Albertine's exchanges: '[i]nnocent yet ominous questions and vague ambiguous answers passed to and fro between them;' before going into direct speech as *each* embarks on a confession of their desires for another person. Schnitzler, *Dream Story*, pp. 5–8.

28. Barbara Creed offers a similar reading of Bill: 'Cruise ... plays a character in *Eyes Wide Shut* who lives on the surface of things, who is in desperate need of a bad dream, a nightmare – an Unconscious, perhaps – to wake him up to the possibilities of the real world.' B. Creed, 'The Cyberstar: Digital Pleasures and the End of the Unconscious', *Screen* vol. 41 no. 1, Spring 2000, p. 82.

29. Gross also traces examples of dream logic within the film, arguing that Bill's narrative trajectory begins as an examination dream and later becomes an anxiety dream. Gross, 'Too Late the Hero', pp. 20–1.

30. S. Freud, *The Interpretation of Dreams*, J. Strachey (ed. and trans.) (London: Penguin, 1991). The quotation is a heading on p. 347, from which I have removed the capitals. The discussion of this type of dream occurs on pp. 347–74.

31. Schnitzler, *Dream Story*, pp. 74–5.

32. Ibid., pp. 44–5.

33. C. Whitehouse, 'Eyes without a Face', *Sight and Sound* vol. 9 no. 9, September 1999, p. 39.

34. Gross, 'Too Late the Hero', p. 22.

35. Schnitzler, *Dream Story*, p. 48.

36. Ibid., p. 46.

37. Ibid., p. 75.

38. Gross, 'Too Late the Hero', p. 22.

39. The link between the young prostitute Fridolin picks up and the woman who redeems him is also suggested in the book in that Mizzi's red lips resemble his redeemer's 'blood-red mouth'. Schnitzler, *Dream Story*, pp. 24–5, 45.

40 Fridolin's mask is not removed in the book. Ibid., p. 52.

41. R. Rynning, '18 Months Hard Labour', *Film Review*, October 1999, pp. 56–7.

42. Whitehouse, 'Eyes without a Face', p. 39.

43. G. Fuller, 'Strictly Red', *Sight and Sound* vol. 11 no. 6, June 2001, pp. 15–16.

44. R. Turk, 'Children of the Digital Revolution', *Metro* nos 129–30, Spring 2001, p. 8.

45. For a further discussion of Baudrillard's nihilistic definition of the post-modern see C. Constable, 'Postmodernism and Film', in S. Connor (ed.), *The Cambridge Companion to Postmodernism* (Cambridge: Cambridge University Press, 2004), pp. 43–7, 49–50.

46. Dyer discusses the conjunction of 'qualities that are elsewhere felt as antithetical: theatricality and authenticity' and 'intensity and irony' as key aspects of a gay sensibility in his chapter on Judy Garland in R. Dyer, *Heavenly Bodies: Film Stars and Society* (London: BFI and Macmillan, 1987), pp. 154–5.

47. G. Andrew, 'Raise the Red Curtain', *National Film Theatre Programme*, September 2001, p. 28.

48. B. Luhrmann, 'Interview with Nicole Kidman', *Interview*, May 2001, p. 108.

49. B. Luhrmann quoted in Fuller, 'Strictly Red', p. 16.

50. Fuller, 'Strictly Red', p. 16.

51. *Camille* (G. Cukor, MGM, 1936).

52. A reading offered by Nicole Kidman and Baz Luhrmann in Luhrmann, 'Interview with Nicole Kidman', p. 108.

53. In Verdi's opera, *La Traviata*, Alfredo's father persuades Violetta to give him up by telling her of the husband he has found for his daughter who is entirely socially acceptable and for whom she will be a perfect wife. Catherine Clément provides this commentary of Violetta's moment of renunciation: 'She will never enter the family. And it is at this moment that she gives up; her melody becomes sublime, now she surpasses herself. If she can no longer be the whore, and cannot be the wife, she can still take on the role of nun.' C. Clément, *Opera or the Undoing of Women*, B. Wing (trans.) (London: Virago, 1989), p. 63.

54. For a more detailed account of the use of colour grades in the film see Turk, 'Children of the Digital Revolution', pp. 12–13.

55. *Gentlemen Prefer Blondes* (H. Hawks, TCF, 1953).

56. B. Dijkstra, *Idols of Perversity: Fantasies of Feminine Evil in Fin-de-Siècle Culture* (New York and Oxford: Oxford University Press, 1986), pp. 97–108.

57. Ibid., pp. 42–3.

58. I therefore disagree with Fuller who argues that Satine resembles Hayworth/Gilda in this scene. Fuller, 'Strictly Red', p. 14.

59. Catherine Clément discusses the symbolism of the courtesan's corrupting body in *Opera or the Undoing of Women*, p. 62.

Bibliography

Published written material

Andrew, G., 'Raise the Red Curtain', *National Film Theatre Programme*, September 2001, pp. 28–30.

Battersby, C., 'Stages on Kant's Way: Aesthetics, Morality and the Gendered Sublime', in P. Brand and C. Korsmeyer (eds), *Feminism and Tradition in Aesthetics* (University Park: Pennsylvania State University Press, 1995), pp. 88–114.

Baudrillard, J., *Simulations*, P. Foss, P. Patton and P. Beitchman (trans.) (New York: Semiotext(e), 1983).

Baudrillard, J., *Seduction*, B. Singer (trans.) (London: Macmillan, 1990).

Bolt, B., 'Shedding Light for the Matter', *Hypatia Special Issue: Going Australian: Reconfiguring Feminism and Philosophy* vol. 15 no. 2, Spring 2000, pp. 202–16.

Bordwell, D., *Making Meaning: Inference and Rhetoric in the Interpretation of Cinema* (Cambridge, MA and London: Harvard University Press, 1989).

Bordwell, D. and Carroll, N. (eds), *Post-Theory: Reconstructing Film Studies* (Madison and London: University of Wisconsin Press, 1996).

Bordwell, D., 'Contemporary Film Studies and the Vicissitudes of Grand Theory', in D. Bordwell and N. Carroll (eds), *Post-Theory: Reconstructing Film Studies* (Madison and London: University of Wisconsin Press, 1996), pp. 3–36.

Braidotti, R., *Patterns of Dissonance*, E. Guild (trans.) (Oxford: Blackwell and Polity Press, 1991).

Branston, G., 'Why Theory?', in C. Gledhill and L. Williams (eds), *Reinventing Film Studies* (London: Arnold, 2000), pp. 18–33.

Burke, E., *A Philosophical Enquiry into the Origin of our Ideas of the Sublime and the Beautiful*, J. Boulton (ed.) (Oxford: Oxford University Press, 1990).

Butler, A., 'Feminist Theory and Women's Films at the Turn of the Century', *Screen* vol. 41 no. 1, Spring 2000, pp. 73–9.

Carroll, N., 'Prospects for Film Theory: A Personal Assessment', in D. Bordwell and N. Carroll (eds), *Post-Theory: Reconstructing Film Studies* (Madison and London: University of Wisconsin Press, 1996), pp. 37–68.

Citron, M. *et al.*, 'Woman and Film: A Discussion of Feminist Aesthetics', *New German Critique*, 1978.

Clément, C., *Opera or the Undoing of Women*, B. Wing (trans.) (London: Virago, 1989).

Constable, C., 'Postmodernism and Film', in S. Connor (ed.), *The Cambridge Companion to Postmodernism* (Cambridge: Cambridge University Press, 2004), pp. 43–61.

Creed, B., *The Monstrous Feminine: Film, Feminism, Psychoanalysis* (London and New York: Routledge, 1993).

Creed, B., 'The Cyberstar: Digital Pleasures and the End of the Unconscious', *Screen* vol. 41 no. 1, Spring 2000, pp. 79–86.

Deleuze, G., 'Coldness and Cruelty', in *Masochism*, J. McNeil (trans.) (New York: Zone Books, 1991), pp. 9–137.

Derrida, J., *Spurs*, B. Harlow (trans.), S. Agosti (intro.) (Chicago, IL and London: University of Chicago Press, 1978).

Dijkstra, B., *Idols of Perversity: Fantasies of Feminine Evil in Fin-de-Siècle Culture* (New York and Oxford: Oxford University Press, 1986), pp. 119–59.

Doane, M-A., *Femmes Fatales: Feminism, Film Theory, Psychoanalysis* (London and New York: Routledge, 1991).

Dyer, R., *Heavenly Bodies: Film Stars and Society* (London: BFI and Macmillan, 1987).

Dyer, R., *White* (London: Routledge, 1997).

Dyer, R., 'Resistance through Charisma: Rita Hayworth and *Gilda*', in E. A. Kaplan (ed.), *Women in Film Noir* (London: BFI, 1998), pp. 115–22.

Dyer, R., 'Queer Noir', in *The Culture of Queers* (London: Routledge, 2002), pp. 90–115.

Freud, S., 'On Narcissism', *The Standard Edition of the Complete Works of Freud*, vol. 14 (London: Hogarth Press, 1957), pp. 69–102.

Freud, S., 'Beyond the Pleasure Principle', in *On Metapsychology and the Theory of Psychoanalysis. The Penguin Freud Library*, vol. 11 (London: Penguin, 1991), pp. 283–7.

Freud, S., *The Interpretation of Dreams*, J. Strachey (ed. and trans.) (London: Penguin, 1991).

Fuller, G., 'Strictly Red', *Sight and Sound* vol. 11 no. 6, June 2001, pp. 14–17.

Green, O. O., 'Six Films of Joseph von Sternberg', *Movie* vol. 13, Summer 1965, pp. 26–31.

Gross, L., 'Too Late the Hero', *Sight and Sound* vol. 9 no. 9, September 1999, pp. 20–3.

Irigaray, L., *Speculum of the Other Woman*, G. C. Gill (trans.) (Ithaca, NY: Cornell University Press, 1985).

Irigaray, L., 'The Power of Discourse and the Subordination of the Feminine', in *This Sex is Not One*, C. Porter and C. Burke (trans.) (Ithaca, NY: Cornell University Press, 1985).

Irigaray, L., *Marine Lover of Friedrich Nietzsche*, G. C. Gill (trans.) (New York: Columbia University Press, 1991).

Irigaray, L., 'The Poverty of Psychoanalysis', in M. Whitford (ed.), *The Irigaray Reader,* D. Macey and M. Whitford (trans.) (Oxford: Blackwell, 1991), pp. 79–103.

Jacobowitz, F., 'Power and the Masquerade: *The Devil Is a Woman*', *CineAction!*, no. 8 Spring 1987, pp. 33–41.

Jacobs, L., *The Wages of Sin: Censorship and the Fallen Woman Film 1928–42* (Madison: University of Wisconsin Press, 1991).

Kant, I., *The Critique of Judgement*, W. Pluhar (trans.) (Indianapolis, IN and Cambridge: Hackett Publishing Company, 1987).

Kaufmann, W., *Nietzsche: Philosopher, Psychologist, Anti-Christ* (Princeton, NJ: Princeton University Press, 1968).

Kofman, S., *The Enigma of Woman*, C. Porter (trans.) (Ithaca, NY: Cornell University Press, 1985).

Kofman, S., 'Baubô: Theological Perversion and Fetishism', in M. A. Gillespie and T. B. Strong (eds), *Nietzsche's New Seas: Explorations in Philosophy, Aesthetics and Politics* (Chicago, IL and London: University of Chicago Press, 1988), pp. 175–202.

Kubie, L., 'The Drive to Become Both Sexes', in H. J. Schlesinger (ed.), *Symbols and Neurosis: Selected Papers of L. S. Kubie* (New York: International Universities Press, 1978), pp. 190–215.

Kuhn, A. (ed.), 'Millenial Editorial', *Screen* vol. 41 no. 1, Spring, 2000.

Lacan, J., 'God and the *Jouissance* of the Woman', 'A Love Letter', in J. Mitchell and J. Rose (eds), *Feminine Sexuality: Jacques Lacan and the École Freudienne*, J. Rose (trans.) (London: Macmillan, 1982), pp. 137–61.

Le Doeuff, M., *The Philosophical Imaginary*, C. Gordon (trans.) (London: Athlone Press, 1989).

Luhrmann, B., 'Interview with Nicole Kidman', *Interview*, May 2001, pp. 102–11.

Marlow, C., *Dr Faustus*, Michael Mangan (ed.) (London: Penguin, 1987).

Martin, A., '"Gilda Didn't Do Any of Those Things You've Been Losing Sleep over!": The Central Women of 40s Films Noirs', in E. A. Kaplan (ed.), *Women in Film Noir* (London: BFI, 1998), pp. 202–28.

Mérimée, P., *Carmen* (Paris: Bordas, 1966).

Metz, C., *Psychoanalysis and Cinema: An Imaginary Signifier*, C. Britton, A. Williams, B. Brewster and A. Guzzetti (trans.) (London: Macmillan, 1982).

Mulvey, L., 'Visual Pleasure and Narrative Cinema', in *Visual and Other Pleasures* (London: Macmillan, 1989), pp. 14–26.

Nichols, B., 'Film Theory and the Revolt against Master Narratives', in C. Gledhill and L. Williams (eds), *Reinventing Film Studies* (London: Arnold, 2000), pp. 34–52.

Nichols, B., *Representing Reality: Issues and Concepts in Documentary* (Bloomington: Indiana University Press, 1991).

Nietzsche, F., *The Birth of Tragedy*, W. Kaufmann (trans.) (New York: Vintage Books, 1967).

Nietzsche, F., *The Will to Power*, W. Kaufmann (ed. and trans.) (New York: Vintage Books, 1968).

Nietzsche, F., *Thus Spake Zarathustra*, in *The Portable Nietzsche*, W. Kaufmann (ed. and trans.) (London: Chatto and Windus, 1971), pp. 103–439.

Nietzsche, F., *The Twilight of the Idols*, in *The Portable Nietzsche*, W. Kaufmann (ed. and trans.) (London: Chatto and Windus, 1971), pp. 463–656.

Nietzsche, F., *Fragments Posthumes, Werke: Kritische Gesamtausgabe*, G. Colli and M. Montinari (eds) (Berlin: de Gruyter, 1972), vol. 9, pp. 79–97.

Nietzsche, F., *The Gay Science*, W. Kaufmann (trans.) (New York: Vintage Books, 1974).

Nietzsche, F., 'On Truth and Lies in a Non-moral Sense', in *Philosophy and Truth: Selections from Nietzsche's Notebooks of the Early 1870s*, D. Breazeale (trans.) (Atlantic Highlands, NJ and London: Humanities Press International, 1979), pp. 79–97.

Oliver, K., *Womanising Nietzsche: Philosophy's Relation to the Feminine* (New York: London: Routledge, 1995).

Oms, M., 'Joseph von Sternberg', in P. Baxter (ed.), *Sternberg* (London: BFI, 1980), pp. 59–80.

Ovid, *Metamorphoses*, F. J. Miller (trans.), G. P. Goold (ed.); 2nd edn, 2 vols (London: Heinemann, 1984).

Perkins, T., 'Who (and What) Is It For?', in C. Gledhill and L. Williams (eds), *Reinventing Film Studies* (London: Arnold, 2000), pp. 76–95.

Place, J., 'Women in Film Noir' in E. A. Kaplan (ed.), *Women in Film Noir*; rev. edn (London: BFI, 1998), pp. 47–68.

Plato, *The Republic*, D. Lee (trans.) (London: Penguin, 1987).

Raphael, F., 'Introduction' to A. Schnitzler, *Dream Story*, J. M. Q. Davies (trans.) (London: Penguin, 1999).

Riva, M., *Marlene Dietrich* (London: Coronet Books, 1994).

Rynning, R., '18 Months Hard Labour', *Film Review*, October 1999, pp. 54–9.

Sacher-Masoch, L. von, *Venus in Furs*, in *Masochism*, J. McNeil (trans.) (New York: Zone Books, 1991), pp. 136–271.

Sarris, A., *The Films of Josef von Sternberg* (New York: Museum of Modern Art, 1966).

Schnitzler, A., *Dream Story*, J. M. Q. Davies (trans.) (London: Penguin, 1999).

Segal, N., *Narcissus and Echo: Women in the French Récit* (Manchester: Manchester University Press, 1988).

Silk, M. S. and Stern, J. P., *Nietzsche on Tragedy* (Cambridge: Cambridge University Press, 1981).

Silverman, K., *The Acoustic Mirror: The Female Voice in Psychoanalysis and Cinema* (Bloomington: Indiana University Press, 1988).

Studlar, G., *In the Realm of Pleasure: Von Sternberg, Dietrich and the Masochistic Aesthetic* (Urbana and Chicago: University of Illinois Press, 1988).

Tripp, E., *Dictionary of Classical Mythology* (London and Glasgow: Collins, 1970).

Turk, R., 'Children of the Digital Revolution', *Metro* nos 129–30, Spring 2001, pp. 6–15.

Vernant, J-P., *Mortals and Immortals*, F. I. Zeitlin (ed. and trans.) (Princeton, NJ: Princeton University Press, 1992).

Whitehouse, C., 'Eyes without a Face', *Sight and Sound* vol. 9, no. 9, September 1999, pp. 38–9.

Whitford, M., 'Rereading Irigaray', in T. Brennan (ed.), *Between Feminism and Psychoanalysis* (London: Routledge, 1989), pp. 106–26.

Wilson, G., *Narration in Light: Studies in Cinematic Point of View* (Baltimore, MD and London: Johns Hopkins University Press, 1986).

Winkler, J. J., *The Constraints of Desire: An Anthology of Sex and Gender in Ancient Greece* (London: Routledge, 1990).

Wood, R., 'Venus de Marlene', *Film Comment* vol. 14, March/April 1978, pp. 58–63.

Žižek, S., *The Fright of Real Tears: Krzysztof Kieślowski between Theory and Post-Theory* (London: BFI, 2001).

Zucker, C., 'Some Observations on von Sternberg and Dietrich', *The Cinema Journal* vol. 19 no. 2, Spring 1980, pp. 17–24.

Zucker, C., *The Idea of the Image: Josef von Sternberg's Dietrich Films* (London and Toronto, Associated University Presses, 1988).

Zucker, C., 'I Am Dietrich and Dietrich Is Me: An Investigation of Performance Style in *Morocco* and *Shanghai Express*', in C. Zucker (ed.), *Making Visible the Invisible: An Anthology of Original Essays on Film Acting* (Metuchen, NJ and London: Scarecrow Press, 1990), pp. 255–94.

Films

Blonde Venus. Dir. Josef von Sternberg. Paramount, 1932.

Camille. Dir. George Cukor. MGM, 1936.

Cover Girl. Dir. Charles Vidor. Columbia, 1944.

The Devil Is a Woman. Dir. Josef von Sternberg. Paramount, 1935.

Eyes Wide Shut. Dir. Stanley Kubrick. Warner Bros, 1999.

Gentlemen Prefer Blondes. Dir. Howard Hawks. TCF, 1953.

Gilda, Dir. Charles Vidor. Columbia, 1946.

Moulin Rouge. Dir. Baz Luhrmann. Twentieth Century-Fox, 2001.

The Scarlet Empress. Dir. Josef von Sternberg. Paramount, 1934.

Shanghai Express. Dir. Josef von Sternberg. Paramount, 1931.

Index

Page numbers in **bold** indicate detailed analysis; those in *italic* denote illustrations; *n* = endnote.

List of Illustrations

Whilst considerable effort has been made to correctly identify the copyright holders, this has not been possible in all cases. We apologise for any apparent negligence and any omissions or corrections brought to our attention will be remedied in any future editions.

The Scarlet Empress, Paramount Productions; *The Devil Is a Woman*, Paramount Productions; *Shanghai Express*, Paramount Publix Corporation; *Gilda*, Columbia Pictures Corporation; *Eyes Wide Shut*, © Warner Bros.; *Moulin Rouge*, © Twentieth Century Fox Film Corporation.